The Harvard Business School Guide to Careers in Management Consulting 2001 Edition

Edited by
Lily Wong

Harvard Business School
Class of 2001

IN ASSOCIATION WITH THE HARVARD BUSINESS SCHOOL MANAGEMENT CONSULTING CLUB

ISBN 1-57851-323-5
ISSN 0741-3092

Contents

Preface   *v*

Acknowledgments   *v*

**Is Management Consulting the Right   *1*
Career—For You?**

James Waldroop
Associate Director, Career Development Programs
Harvard Business School

Tim Butler
Director, Career Development Programs
Harvard Business School

The Management Consulting Industry   *5*

David J. Collis
Visiting Associate Professor, Yale School of
Management

**50 Largest Management Consulting   *8*
Firms**

**The Management Consulting Industry: *9*
A Top Management Consultant's
Perspective**

Allan Kennedy
Managing Director, Roland Berger & Partner Limited

Consulting Versus Investment Banking   *11*

Peter Labon
Class of 1993, Harvard Business School

**On the Career Choice Between   *13*
Management Consulting and Operating
Management**

Clayton M. Christensen
Professor, Technology and Operations Management and
General Management, Harvard Business School

**Interview: A Perspective on E-   *15*
Commerce Consulting**

Jonathan D. Kissane
Manager, The Boston Consulting Group, San Francisco
Office

E-Commerce Consulting Roundtable   *17*

Sameer Aurora
Director, Business Strategy Practice, ZEFER

Oliver Bardon
Project Leader, The Boston Consulting Group

Lawler Kang
Managing Director, Boston Operations, Scient
Corporation

Being a Summer Associate   *20*

Catherine H. Bohutinsky
Class of 1995, Harvard Business School

Reflections on First-Year Recruiting   *22*

Phil Collins
Class of 1993, Harvard Business School

About This Project   *25*

Profiled Companies

Abt Associates Inc.	26
Alliance Consulting Group, Inc.	30
American Management Systems, Inc.	33
Arthur D. Little, Inc.	36
A.T. Kearney, Inc.	40
Bain & Company, Inc.	43
Booz•Allen & Hamilton	46
The Boston Consulting Group, Inc.	49
Braun Consulting, Business Strategy Group	51
The Cambridge Group	56
Cambridge Strategic Management Group (CSMG)	59
CFI Group, Inc.	62
Charles River Associates Incorporated	64
Cornerstone Research	66
Corporate Directions, Inc.	69
CSC Consulting	71
CSC Healthcare Payor/Provider Consulting	76
Dean & Company	79
Deloitte Consulting	82
Delta Consulting Group	87
Diamond Technology Partners Incorporated	90
Digitas LLC	93
Edgar, Dunn & Company	96
Ernst & Young LLP	98
The Farrell Group	103
First Annapolis Consulting, Inc.	106
First Manhattan Consulting Group	109
Gemini Consulting	113
Greenwich Associates	115
Hamilton•HMC	118
Hay Group, Inc.	122
Health Advances, Inc.	124
I•F Consulting, Inc.	127
Integral, Inc.	130
John Barry & Associates	132
KPMG, LLP Consulting Practice	134
Kurt Salmon Associates	137
L.E.K. Consulting LLC	141
Marakon Associates	145
Mars & Co	149
McKinsey & Company, Inc.	151
Mercer Management Consulting, Inc.	152
Monitor Group	156
Navigant Consulting/Strategic Decisions Group	159
Nextera Enterprises, Inc.	163
Oliver, Wyman & Company, LLC	166
The Parthenon Group	169
PHB Hagler Bailly, Inc.	172
Pittiglio Rabin Todd & McGrath	175
PricewaterhouseCoopers Management Consulting Services	180
Quantum Associates, Inc.	183
Roland Berger & Partners	186
San Francisco Consulting Group	188
Scient Corporation	191
Sibson & Company	194
Swander Pace & Company	198
Towers Perrin	201
Value Partners	206
ZEFER	209
ZS Associates	211

Management Consulting Career Resources

215

Mallory Stark
Career Resources Librarian
Baker Library, Harvard Business School

Mailing List

220

Preface

This is the twelfth edition of *The Harvard Business School Guide to Careers in Management Consulting* produced by the Harvard Business School Management Consulting Club and Harvard Business School Publishing. The guide provides information on the careers available to MBA students interested in management consulting. The commentaries provided by professors, students, and consultants will give MBA students a broad perspective of the management consulting industry. In addition, the company profiles will be a useful reference before and during the interviewing process.

This guide provides a comprehensive look at the management consulting career as well as advice on the job search itself. As an introduction, Drs. James Waldroop and Timothy Butler offer insights on career self-assessment for those considering a career in management consulting. Professor David Collis presents an overview of the industry and related trends. These articles are supplemented by Consultants News' ranking of consulting firms based on key metrics, including revenues and number of professional staff. Next, a consultant with almost 25 years of experience gives his perspective on the industry. In the following section, Professor Clayton Christensen provides insight on the career choice between management consulting and operating management. In the next two articles, e-commerce consulting practitioners offer their insights on this fast-growing field. Several Harvard Business School students then relate their summer and full-time experiences and describe their job search process. The remainder of the guide consists of individual company profiles as submitted by each firm.

Readers will find this career guide useful in all stages of the recruitment process. The guide will provide a broad introduction to the management consulting field and help in determining a fit with the consulting career at the initial stages. Using the company profiles as a reference guide, students can contact the appropriate firms and obtain additional information. Lastly, during the interview process, this guide can be a great source of information for understanding the recruiting process and obtaining some basic facts. It is hoped that this guide will be a valuable resource for MBA students considering a management consulting career.

Acknowledgments

Many individuals spend considerable time and effort each year to publish the *Career Guide*. We would like to take this opportunity to thank the following individuals who made this guide possible:

Claudia Bruce of HBS Publishing deserves the majority of the credit for this year's publication. Her expertise, organization, and patience were crucial to successful completion. To Claudia, we are very grateful.

We are also grateful to Kennedy Information for their continued support of the guide, as well as to the contributing authors of the personal commentaries.

Finally, we extend our sincere thanks to the recruiters and staff at the consulting firms who contributed to the profile articles. As a result of their support, we are able to provide the reader with an accurate and current reference guide.

Is Management Consulting the Right Career—For You?

Drs. James Waldroop and Timothy Butler

Drs. Waldroop and Butler are directors of career development programs at the Harvard Business School and principals and co-founders of Waldroop Butler Associates, a consulting firm in Brookline, Massachusetts that specializes in career development assessment and counseling and executive coaching. They are the developers of CareerLeader™, *an Internet-based, interactive career assessment program (www.careerdiscovery.com/hbsp), and the authors of* Discovering Your Career in Business *(Addison-Wesley, 1997),* "The Executive as Coach" *(the* Harvard Business Review, *November/December 1996) and* "Finding the Job You Should Want" *(Fortune, March 2, 1998).*

If you're considering working in management consulting, you're probably just starting out in your career: you're either about to graduate from college or business school, or are within a year or two of either milestone. This is an ideal time to take a step back to look at yourself before heading down one career path or another. Everyone agrees thoughtful career self-assessment is a terrific idea—and then 90% don't carry through with it. Some people "drift" into a good career, but that's a *very* high-risk approach to life. Careful self-assessment and strategic career planning can save you a lot of grief down the road. This applies especially to those thinking about management consulting, which is often painted as a "failsafe" move that can only be a benefit—an attractive idea, but, unfortunately, false.

Good self-assessment can be carried out in a number of ways; at a minimum it should include a careful and subtle assessment of your "deep personality structure" interests, your work reward values, your business career-relevant abilities, and other aspects of your personality. Our approach includes conducting an in-depth interview and examination of a client's life history, employing sophisticated, objective, psychological assessment instruments, and soliciting letters from six to ten people who know the client well. You could do much of this on your own. What is important is not *how* you do it but *that* you do it. Taking the time now will put you way ahead.

We've worked with hundreds of MBA students and recent graduates during the collective thirty years we've been at the Harvard Business School. For some of them, going into management consulting was precisely the right thing to do. For others it made absolutely no sense at all. Let's talk about who falls into which group, and hope you will be one of those who go into consulting for good reasons—or who steer away from it, again for good reasons.

Three things are important to understand. First, management consulting, whether for a few years or for a lifetime, can be a lot of fun: great challenges, bright colleagues, a fast pace, and lots of variety. Second, management consulting is really three careers rolled into one—the consultant, the engagement manager, and the partner—with each stage involving very different activities. As a result, the opportunity to realize different interests, the rewards, and the key competencies necessary for success change with each stage. And third, most people who go into management consulting do so as a strategic "stopover" career move, either between undergraduate and business school or between business school and their "real job." We'll get to those folks in a moment, but let's begin by discussing the people who actually make their careers in the field of management consulting.

Consulting as a Business Career

We've had extensive experience working with future, current, and former management consultants. We've also had the opportunity to collect data on a large number of consulting professionals. The career assessment model utilized in *CareerLeader,* our business career self-assessment program, is the product of this research and experience; it's what we'll be using to describe the career of the management consultant, the typical interests of consultants, the rewards most plentifully available in a management consulting career, and the abilities most necessary for success in this career.

CareerLeader is based on a 12-year research study examining the match between people's personality structures and the work they find meaningful and in which they are successful. It comprises three career self-assessment inventories—the *Business Career Interest Inventory*™, the *Management and Professional Reward Profile*™, and the *Management and Professional Abilities Profile*™ (see page 4)—that measure people's interests, reward values, and abilities. The structures on which each of these instruments is based serve as a guide for this discussion.

Consultants' Interests. Our research into the interests and core activities of business professionals revealed eight sets of activities that comprise, in varying mixtures, almost all work done in business settings. The *Business Career Interest Inventory* was then designed to measure people's interests in those "business core functions." In looking at management consulting *professionals* (those with more than five years' experience, happy with their careers, and likely to continue in this career path), a distinct pattern emerged. These individuals had a very strong interest in *Theory Development and Conceptual Thinking*, much stronger than that among business professionals in general. In fact, their interest in *Theory Development and Conceptual Thinking* was stronger than in any other function (with *Enterprise Control* and *Influence Through Language and Ideas* the next strongest). In a sense, people who make their careers in management consulting almost look more like business academics than "business people."

This interest pattern is quite distinct from that of most other business professions. It is also markedly different, by the way, from the interest pattern of consultants with five or fewer years experience, most of whom will not remain in management consulting for the rest of their careers. For a look at the interest patterns of these two groups, go to our Web site and click on the Career Interest Patterns link in the Reader's Page section of the home page.

Consultants' Rewards. *CareerLeader*'s value assessment instrument, the *Management and Professional Reward Profile,* measures the value you place on thirteen different rewards most commonly available in business settings (such as *Financial Gain, Autonomy,* and *Variety*). The rewards you are most likely to get through working in management consulting, and those most commonly prized by the consultants with whom we have worked, include *Variety* and *Intellectual Challenge*, with *Prestige* and *Affiliation* also found in abundance in this career. On the other hand, two rewards, *Autonomy* and *Lifestyle,* are in decidedly short supply, especially in the early stages of a management consulting career.

If you want a lot of *Autonomy* and highly value other, non-work-related, elements of your *Lifestyle,* you are likely to find consulting a bad fit over the long term. Alternately, if you do *not* enjoy *Intellectual Challenge, Variety*, and *Affiliation,* you may at the very least feel that a lot of what you are doing is unrewarding—and feel rather different from many of your colleagues. The *absence* of high value on these rewards is not as significant as the *presence* of high value on the rewards of *Autonomy* and *Intellectual Challenge,* which is a definite warning sign.

Consultants' Abilities. *CareerLeader*'s abilities assessment instrument, the *Management and Professional Abilities Profile,* measures people's business-related abilities in three different areas—*Problem Solving, Taking Initiative,* and *Interpersonal Effectiveness*—with different specific abilities measured in each of these groups. Not surprisingly, the abilities crucial to success as an early-stage consultant are quite different from those of a director (with the role of project manager calling for abilities spanning both of the other roles). This is part of what makes having a successful career in management consulting so challenging: the qualities that make someone a terrific consultant do not automatically mean that the person will be very successful in managing client engagements; and the excellent engagement manager might not possess the abilities necessary to be a successful partner. Think of the caterpillar's metamorphosis into a chrysalis, then into a butterfly—all the same animal, but each stage very different.

Focusing on the partnership phase, the abilities in the *Interpersonal Effectiveness* area, such as *Sociability* (the ability to form relationships is crucial for developing and managing client relationships), *Confidence,* and *Communication* are most critical for success, with others—*Creativity, Quick Thinking, Power Orientation, Multi-focus,* which is the ability to juggle many responsibilities, and *Leveraging* time effectively—also being important. Contrast this with the first phase of the career—working as a consultant—when *Critical Thinking* and *Quantitative Analysis* are of greatest importance. We sometimes tell people they would make wonderful partners in consulting firms, if only they could jump over the steps leading up to that point! Unfortunately, we have yet to see a job description for a director-level position that says no experience is necessary.

Consulting as a Strategic Career Step

Now we turn to the question we have heard hundreds of times over the years at HBS: "I know I don't want to make a career of consulting, but I've been doing X, and I want to end up doing Y. Does spending a few years in consulting make sense? Will it prepare me well/will I learn useful skills/will I acquire useful knowledge—or will it position me well for what I ultimately want to do?"

As a step between undergraduate and a graduate MBA program, management consulting has a great deal to offer. You learn a lot about analyzing different business situations, hone your analytical skills, and learn to present your ideas clearly and convincingly—all skills that will hold you in good stead in the business school classroom. Of course, what you don't learn is management skills, and you don't acquire a depth of knowledge about any business function, such as finance. But that presents little if any disadvantage. So there's a lot of upside and very little, if any, downside to spending two or three years in consulting in between your BA and MBA programs. Of course, if you already know that you want to go into a particular field—especially one that is fairly specialized, such as investment banking or real estate development—you should feel free to pursue those areas straight away. But if you're not clear about your direction, and know that an MBA is in your future, spending those interim years working in management consulting can be a great learning experience.

As a strategic step *post*-MBA, however, doing a two- to four-year stint in management consulting needs more careful consideration. Many MBA students choose to go into management consulting simply to defer their ultimate career decision, or to avoid closing down any options. The usual rationale for the former group is that they haven't settled on an industry in which they want to work, and will be exposed to a wide range of industry experiences during their consulting tenure, which will help them choose a "home." This may or may not be true depending on the firm and the particular office in which you work, but it is a rather expensive—in terms of your time—way to explore the business landscape. Spending time reading about different career possibilities and talking to fellow students, alumni/ae, and business professionals in various careers of interest is likely to give you a better sense of your interests than spending two years working on a handful of consulting assignments.

The *real* rub for many students is that of closing options. Life up until graduate school has, for many people, been about increasing opportunities—and now you have to make a choice that is going to close some doors. Consulting firms present themselves as sort of a "duty-free zone," where you're able to preserve all your options. But of course, by going *anywhere* you are closing options, regardless of what anyone tells you. Two or three years later, potential employers will evaluate you as a (soon to be) former consultant, not as a new MBA who's been in a state of suspended animation for those years. Some will not be interested in you, either because of your price tag or because they want someone who already has experience in a given function. Closing down options, while a definite and somewhat scary shift, is what you *should* be doing. Sooner or later you have to make a choice, and de-

termine a focus. A career strategy with no focus is like a business strategy with no focus—it's an oxymoron.

Some consulting organizations tout the opportunities their alumni/ae have to move directly into management positions of great responsibility. Certainly that happens—for some few people. But in our experience, most consultants leave for strategic planning/business development or other analytical positions—the positions where they have demonstrated capability and for which their high salaries are justified. Those who are hired into direct management positions most often have had substantial experience in a given industry or function before starting their MBA programs. Of course, there are exceptions, just as there are successful entrepreneurs who started their ventures immediately after leaving consulting—or business school, for that matter. But those are "long-odds" bets. One to four years as a consultant teaches you very little about being a manager, and even less about being an entrepreneur. One savvy entrepreneurial financier puts it bluntly: "I wouldn't invest in a new MBA or ex-consultant's business venture if it were the last investment opportunity on earth. It's not a matter of *if* they fail, but *when* they fail."

So as a strategic move, this step is by no means a "no-brainer." It may make sense for the person with no previous business experience—say, a former military officer or non-profit professional—or for the person who will be locating in an economic center with a relatively small number of members of the "power elite" and for whom a job in a top consulting firm will provide an entree into that circle. But if it's simply a decision that enables you to delay choosing a real career direction, think again—it's far better to bite the bullet and make that choice *now*.

In sum, if you're considering management consulting as a life career, look at your interests, what work rewards you most highly value, and what your strongest abilities are—then match those against the profile of the career consultant. If you're thinking about it as a brief way station, it may make a lot of sense and be a great help to you. It may be a net neutral. Or it may actually slow down your career progress. So think just as carefully about a move into management consulting as you would about any other career step or path.

There is no such thing as a free lunch or a free career move.

Business Career Interest Inventory Scales and Descriptions

Application of Technology: Taking an engineering-like approach to business problems, and using technology to solve them (e.g., production and operations process analysis; business process redesign; production planning)

Quantitative Analysis: Problem solving that relies on mathematical and financial analysis (e.g., determining the most advantageous debt/equity structure for a business; analyzing market research)

Theory Development and Conceptual Thinking: Taking a broadly conceptual, quasi-academic approach to business problems (e.g., developing a new general economic theory or model of market behavior)

Creative Production: Highly creative activities (e.g., the generation of new business ideas; the development of new marketing concepts)

Counseling and Mentoring: Developing personal relationships in the work setting and helping others in their careers (e.g., coaching, training, and mentoring)

Managing People and Relationships: Accomplishing business goals through working directly with people (e.g., as a manager, team leader, director, or supervisor)

Enterprise Control: Having ultimate strategy-setting and decision-making authority, and resource control for an operation (e.g., as a division manager, president, CEO, partner in a professional services firm, or entrepreneur)

Influence Through Language and Ideas: Exercising influence through the skillful use of persuasion (e.g., negotiating, deal-making, sales, and relationship development)

Management and Professional Abilities Profile Scales and Descriptions

Problem Solving

Critical Thinking: Able to think critically (define a problem and determine the information needed to solve it; understand unspoken assumptions; form and test hypotheses; and judge the validity of conclusions).

Quantitative Analysis: Skillful in using quantitative analysis to understand business issues.

Creativity: Able to think creatively, generating new ideas and approaches to issues, and recognizing new opportunities.

Quick Thinking: Have a quick intellect—I pick up new information and ideas easily and can "think on my feet."

Taking Initiative

Dominance: Ambitious, forceful, competitive, comfortable with using power and taking risks.

Action-orientation: Action-oriented—I am someone who makes decisions and then makes sure they are implemented.

Multi-focus: Able to juggle many ideas, responsibilities, and projects at once.

Leveraging: Able to leverage my time well (e.g., set priorities and keep to them, delegate when appropriate).

Interpersonal Effectiveness

Confidence: Able to feel and project self-confidence—I can be persuasive even in uncertain and difficult situations.

Leading/Managing: Able to lead, motivate, and directly manage other people effectively.

Sociability: Socially venturesome and self-assured—I form and maintain relationships easily.

Teamwork: A team player, cooperative, work well as part of a group.

Communication: Able to listen well—Write and speak to individuals and groups in a clear and effective manner.

Management and Professional Reward Profile Scales and Descriptions

Financial Gain: The position provides excellent opportunity for exceptional financial reward.

Power and Influence: The position offers the opportunity to exercise power and influence (to be an influential decision maker).

Variety: The position offers a great deal of variety in the nature of the work performed.

Lifestyle: The position allows ample time to pursue other important aspects of my lifestyle (family, leisure activities, etc.).

Autonomy: The position offers considerable autonomy and independence.

Intellectual Challenge: The position offers consistent intellectual challenge.

Altruism: The position offers the satisfaction of regularly helping others with their individual or business concerns.

Security: The position offers a great deal of security in terms of predictable salary, benefits, and future employment.

Prestige: The position is with an organization that commands a great deal of prestige in its field.

Affiliation: The position offers a setting with enjoyable colleagues with whom I feel a sense of belonging.

Positioning: The position offers experience and access to people and opportunities that will position me well for my next career move.

Managing People: The position offers the opportunity to manage and direct other people.

Recognition: The position is in an environment where individual accomplishments are recognized with praise from peers and superiors.

The Management Consulting Industry

David J. Collis

David J. Collis is a visiting associate professor at Yale School of Management. Professor Collis has extensive experience with consulting firms.

Approximately 500,000 people worldwide work full-time in the management consulting industry, generating about $100 billion in annual revenues.[1] Just over half of these consultants come from the United States; another quarter come from Europe. While management consulting fluctuates with the business cycle, the industry has nevertheless grown more than four times as fast as GNP over the past decade. Such a large, dynamic industry is by no means homogeneous, however. This article describes how the management consulting industry can be segmented and identifies some important trends in the industry, with attendant implications for those intending to pursue a career in management consulting.

Segmentation

The first, and probably most significant, way to segment the consulting industry is to compare large and small firms. Most consulting firms are small, often one-person operations: half of all consulting firms generate less than $500,000 in annual billings, and one-third employ fewer than four people. If the typical consulting firm is small, however, the typical consultant works for a large firm: the 50 largest consulting firms in the United States account for approximately three-quarters of domestic revenue, and an estimated three-quarters of all consultants work in firms employing more than 100 professionals. This skewed size distribution reflects the low barriers to entry to this industry. Anyone can hang out a shingle bearing the title "Consultant" and many former executives do just that. Corporate policies of early retirement, downsizing, and outsourcing have created both the supply and the demand for independent consultants, and many of these small shops exist, often serving a single client. Whether these firms are attractive starting points for new consultants is debatable, since they lack both the breadth of clients and depth of support of the big firms. However, veteran consultants often end their careers in their own consulting firms.

A second, and often overlooked, distinction in consulting is between in-house and external consultants. While the industry definition, strictly speaking, covers only outside consultants, many large corporations have their own internal consulting arms, usually affiliated with a planning department. For those who are not convinced that consulting is a lifetime career but who want a variety of experiences and exposure to senior management problems at an early stage in their careers, albeit in a more limited number of settings—there are five times as many external consultants as internal consultants[2]—internal consulting can be an attractive option. Internal consultants perform essentially the same functions as external consultants, while enjoying a more direct career path into line management. Contrary to the prevailing belief, only a very few consultants make a direct transfer to a top executive position in a client organization—and only then after many years in the consulting firm. Transfers at junior levels are more common, but most of the 20% annual rate of turnover among consultants is not due to consultants' being hired by clients.

The third important basis for segmentation in the consulting industry is degree of specialization. While all firms provide a variety of services, most consulting firms generate the majority of their revenue from one type of work. The two main dimensions of specialization are function—for example, logistics, organization design, management information systems (MIS), or management education—and customer group or industry—for example, health care, financial services, or government.

Of these specializations, the largest is MIS consulting, which is, for the most part, the domain of the accounting firms: five of the ten largest consulting firms in the world are the consulting arms of the big five accounting firms. In the United States alone, these firms generate over $9 billion in billings annually. The third largest specialization is compensation and benefits consulting. Four of the top 20 U.S. consulting firms fall into this category, with annual billings exceeding $1.5 billion. In second place as a specialization is management/strategy consulting. This area includes the generalist management consultants, such as McKinsey, Booz•Allen, and their newer first cousins, the strategy consultants, such as BCG and Bain. Although these firms are ostensibly full-line consultants, clients often find their cost structure uneconomic for consulting on functional activities such as logistics. Instead, the generalist consultants concentrate on higher value-added consulting for senior management. The other functional or industry specialists in consulting tend to be small, reflecting their origins as one-person shops run by an executive with a particular skill or industry knowledge. Understanding how each consulting firm specializes, and ensuring that it matches your interests, is a vital first step in considering which firms to approach for a position.

The consulting industry no longer draws a distinction between formulation and implementation. All firms in all categories of consulting recognize that their role must involve effective change in the client organization, and differences among them are now of degree, not of substance. Some specialists in "change management" exist, but even they would like to be involved in developing the direction of change. Similarly, although some firms may be known for a particular technique tool, such as a BCG and the experience curve in the 1970s, or Marakon and value-based management more recently, these reputations are usually more a reflection of marketing programs than of a fundamentally different approach to consulting. When the publicity for a firm surrounds a particular solution to a general problem, like time-based competition for strategy, it is usually not representative of a profound difference in the type of work the firm undertakes.

A last distinction among consulting firms is their degree of globalization. Most firms now have offices or affiliations outside their home country, but the extent of nondomestic business varies substantially. Among the world's top 20 consultants, for example, one firm, Hewitt Associates, does only 5% of its work outside the United States, compared with McKinsey's 60% and the U.K. firm PA's 95%. However, even those firms with extensive overseas networks tend to have independent offices, so they can be responsive to local needs. This implies that working for an international consulting will not necessarily allow you to work overseas. You usually have to ask explicitly for an overseas assignment and often have to recruit with the overseas office in addition to the domestic office.

Trends

Management consulting will continue to grow, more cyclically than in the past, but still faster than GNP. The rationale for hiring consultants—to access the specific expertise needed to quickly solve a current problem—will remain and will, if anything, cover more tasks in the future as firms reconsider the costs of all their internal functions. In fact, predicting which corporate activities will be outsourced could give you a head start in identifying the next growth specialty in consulting.

The industry will also continue to move to an hourglass shape: increasingly, there is a bimodal distribution of firms into the large (annual billings in excess of $100 million) and small (less than $5 million in annual billings). This structure results both from the ease of entry for newcomers and from competitive advantages of larger firms—reputation, diversified client base, and broader geographic base. While a few firms are able to break through the mid-size plateau to become recognized large players—or are acquired by other firms looking for broader scope—many bump along unsteadily at $10 million to $20 million in billings before falling back as their initial momentum subsides. For the potential consultant, this suggests that the key question to be answered before committing to the attractions of fast promotion at a newer rapidly growing consulting firms is, " Does it have the capability to break through to the first tier?" This question is particularly important if you anticipate a lifetime career in consulting: More than half of the consulting firms currently operating did not exist 15 years ago, and only 1% of consulting firms are more than 50 years old.

Other industry trends are the acquisitions by outsiders of consulting firms and the move toward broad-scope consulting firms, providing a variety of consulting specialties. At least half of the top 20 firms have made recent acquisitions—three of which propelled the acquiring parties into the top 20—and there have been more than 50 substantial acquisitions in the last decade. The rationale for these acquisitions lies in the economies of scope that a broad-line competitor can exploit, particularly in marketing. It has been estimated that only a third of a consultant's business comes from repeat clients, while new business, increasingly, is won in competitive bids against comparable consulting firms. As a result, about 20% of a consulting firm's costs lie in acquiring clients. If an accounting firm can leverage its audit relationship into MIS consulting or if a strategy consulting report can recommend hiring the sister benefits consulting firm for the follow-on organization study, this expense can be substantially reduced.

Unfortunately, the success of broad-scope consulting firms and of outside ownership remains doubtful. Saatchi & Saatchi is the most obvious example of failure of an outsider to build a broad-scope consulting business, but even those companies like Mercer, which are still operating successfully, have yet to demonstrate the value of broad scope. Citibank tried and exited consulting, and the accounting firms are still struggling to establish a relationship with their consulting arms that peaceably compensates consultants more than auditors; maintains a wall between consulting and auditing; and yet leverages the audit relationship into consulting work. Indeed, three of them, Arthur Andersen, PriceWaterhouseCoopers, and Ernst and Young, appear to have given up the struggle.

The issue really relates to the clients' decision-making process. The purchaser of the audit—the CFO or controller—is, for example, usually not the purchaser of strategy consulting. Nor is the ease of buying a range of consulting services from a single source of much value to a client when compared to the ability to choose the best specialist for a given type of work. As a result, most of the broad-scope firms are essentially umbrella holding companies for a set of independent specialists having little interaction with one another. One reason is the difficulty inherent in merging cultures. There have been, for example, few acquisitions of one strategy consulting firm by another, partly because the problems resulting from merging cultures cause the firms' major asset—people—to leave. In considering a career in consulting, I therefore suggest that the ultimate ownership of the firm you might work for is not of great importance. Although it is true that these acquisitions are occurring, their impact on your daily activities, particularly in the junior positions, will be relatively limited. Working at Mitchell Madison (now owned by USWeb/CKS), for example, would not be dissimilar to working at Monitor, or at Vertex when it was independent.

There is, however, one industry trend that *will* affect you: globalization. To serve the increasing global needs of clients effectively, any large consulting firm today needs a global network of offices. This network can be created by establishing alliances with overseas affiliates but is now more often achieved by setting up foreign offices. This is an expensive process that has been one reason why medium-sized consulting firms have willingly sold to outsiders prepared to make the necessary investments. While most foreign offices are currently operated with a great deal of autonomy, to match the globalization of clients, consulting firms are likely to further integrate their worldwide operations.

As consulting firms increase their geographic scope, global competition is also likely to increase. Today, U.S. firms dominate the U.S. market, European firms the European market, and Asia is undeveloped both as a market and as a source of consultants. Twenty years from now there will be far more interaction among geographic markets and, I suspect, a larger Asian presence. As future management consultants, you must be prepared to learn a foreign language and to travel overseas, both to serve your clients effectively and to learn from best practice in other countries. Although this prescription is true for all executives, it is doubly true for management consultants, who must be leaders in the development of skills if they are to continue to provide value to clients.

The final trend with implications for management consultants is the continuing pressure that increased rivalry places on consulting firms to truly provide value to clients. In practical terms, this means that consultants will have to be less formulaic than in the past. The rapid diffusion of information and techniques within the industry prevents anyone from monopolizing a concept for any length of time and means that clients are often familiar with the new frameworks themselves. The value provided by consulting firms will have to come from their ability to apply concepts and to customize them for particular client needs, not simply from their possession of a particular technology.

To meet these sorts of demands, it is likely that the employee profile of consulting firms will alter somewhat. No longer will a 24-year-old MBA be able to add value simply by applying a concept the client has not seen before. Instead, consulting firms will work more closely with client management in defining and analyzing problems and in formulating and implementing solutions. This will require a more experienced consultant, more capable of understanding the manager's role, and more versed in people skills than the functional expert of the past. These senior consultants will be supported by junior "para-consultants" who can perform the mechanistic, repetitive tasks more cost-effectively. Thus, the pyramid structure inside consulting firms will change—on average in the large firms today, one partner supports 11 consultants—as the number of very senior and very junior employees swells.

Finally, the good news is that to truly meet client demands for value for money, consulting will have to become an even more exciting, challenging, and, ultimately, rewarding career than ever before.

---

1. Data estimates are from Kennedy Information Research Group.
2. *Journal of Management Consulting* 3 (Summer 1984).

50 LARGEST MANAGEMENT CONSULTING FIRMS

Rank	Firm name	Fiscal Year End	1998 Global Consulting Revenues ($M)	Global Consulting 1-Year Growth	1998 Global Consultants	1998 U.S. Consulting Revenues ($M)	1998 U.S. Consultants
1	Andersen Consulting	12/31/98	$7,129	25%	53,416	$3,578	24,546
2	PricewaterhouseCoopers	6/30/98	$6,000	40%	40,800	$2,700	17,470
3	Ernst & Young	9/30/98	$3,870	35%	16,450	$2,400	7,800
4	Deloitte Consulting	8/30/98	$3,240	40%	19,560	$1,480	6,000
5	CSC	4/2/99	$3,000	17%	20,000	$1,900	13,000
6	KPMG	6/30/98	$3,000	30%	14,094	$1,516	5,661
7	McKinsey & Company	12/31/98	$2,500	14%	5,184	$1,023	2,074
8	Cap Gemini Group	12/31/98	$2,261	37%	NA	$272	NA
9	Mercer Consulting Group	12/31/98	$1,543	15%	11,304	$926	5,518
10	Arthur Andersen	8/31/98	$1,368	44%	9,196	$691	4,420
11	A.T. Kearney	12/31/98	$1,234	17%	2,880	$664	1,086
12	Towers Perrin	12/31/98	$1,230	12%	8,155	$909	5,697
13	Booz•Allen & Hamilton	3/31/99	$1,204	12%	6,540	$900	5,591
14	IBM Consulting	12/31/98	$990	13%	5,060	$570	641
15	American Management Systems	12/31/98	$913	24%	7,398	$733	6,443
16	Keane	12/31/98	$872	55%	10,829	$802	10,217
17	Hewitt Associates	10/1/98	$858	21%	9,700	$808	NA
18	Sema Group	12/31/98	$836	23%	NA	$9	NA
19	Logica	6/30/98	$790	39%	6,383	$79	NA
20	Boston Consulting Group	12/31/98	$730	11%	1,940	$215	512
21	Watson Wyatt Worldwide	6/30/98	$720	7%	3,730	$442	2,310
22	DMR Consulting Group	12/31/98	$666	22%	9,500	$313	NA
23	CMG	12/31/98	$636	54%	6,005	$0	NA
24	Aon Consulting	12/31/98	$615	11%	4,100	$387	2,250
25	Cambridge Technology Partners	12/31/98	$612	40%	4,500	$422	NA
26	Arthur D. Little	12/31/98	$608	3%	2,141	$226	986
27	Bain & Company	12/31/98	$564	18%	1,650	$255	750
28	debis Systemhaus	12/31/98	$468	19%	13,300	$0	NA
29	PA Consulting Group	12/31/98	$440	20%	1,741	$25	55
30	Woodrow Milliman	12/31/98	$433	10%	1,625	$230	563
31	Origin	NA	$400	5%	3,200	$44	NA
32	Telcordia Technologies (formerly Bellcore)	1/31/99	$366	8%	1,400	$305	1,140
33	Buck Consultants	12/31/98	$332	10%	2,909	$256	1,810
34	Metzler Group	12/31/98	$330	150%	1,600	$320	1,500
35	Roland Berger & Partner	12/31/98	$320	12%	957	$0	0
36	Technology Solutions Company	12/31/98	$318	41%	1,460	$287	1,242
37	Whittman-Hart	12/31/98	$308	69%	2,950	$293	2,803
38	CTG	12/31/98	$304	15%	6,000	$267	4,855
39	CBSI	12/31/98	$301	44%	4,062	$289	NA
40	Renaissance Worldwide	12/26/98	$287	31%	1,500	$260	NA
41	Hay Group	9/30/98	$281	10%	1,011	$108	327
42	Mitchell Madison Group	12/31/98	$257	29%	714	$169	468
43	Perot Systems	12/31/98	$249	27%	NA	$160	NA
44	INS	12/31/98	$238	73%	1,758	$220	NA
45	McGladrey & Pullen	7/31/98	$226	29%	1,367	$93	562
46	CIBER	6/30/98	$226	41%	1,645	$226	1,645
47	Monitor Company	12/31/98	$225	15%	850	$100	NA
48	First Consulting Group	12/31/98	$196	43%	1,267	$187	1,267
49	Horwath International	12/31/98	$194	15%	2,085	$117	876
50	Hagler Bailly	12/31/98	$178	109%	489	$107	490

Notes: NA = not available.
  a. We suspect the consulting revenues reported include a significant amount of outsourcing activity.
  b. Number of consultants includes all staff, not just billable professionals.
  c. Includes revenues from Sedgwick acquisition since date of acquisition only (9/98).

The Management Consulting Industry: A Top Management Consultant's Perspective

Allan Kennedy

Allan Kennedy is the Managing Director of Roland Berger & Partner Limited, the London office of Europe's largest indigenous top management consulting firm. Previously he has served as Managing Director of Mercer Management Consulting Limited and Managing Partner of McKinsey & Company's Boston office. In addition to his long career as a consultant, he has done a considerable amount of writing on management topics; most notably, he was a coauthor with Terry Deal of the best-selling book Corporate Cultures.

I have been a management consultant for almost 25 years. During those years, I have been privileged to work with clients in upward of 20 industries. I have also had the opportunity to visit virtually every major country in the world—some of them many times. And most important, I have met many wonderful people, watched some of the world's best managers in action, and formed (mainly with clients) many lasting friendships. I have also witnessed the profession of consulting change dramatically since I joined it. But, as you can tell from my current occupation, I still love the profession and think it is one of the finest professions for some individuals to pursue.

In what follows, I will share with you some of my cumulative experience along several lines: (1) why clients hire consultants, (2) how consultants deliver value to clients, (3) the importance of having the highest professional and ethical standards as a consultant, and, finally, (4) who should think about becoming a consultant.

Why Clients Hire Consultants

Simply put, clients hire consultants to get something done they cannot get done within their own organization. Thus, consultants are neither a luxury that clients can choose to hire or not, nor are they ever considered an integral part of any client's organization—even clients with a history of relatively heavy reliance on consultants. These simple points should be profoundly understood by any person who wishes to be an effective consultant—they are there to make something beneficial happen (and their ultimate reputation results from achieving this objective with regularity), and they are never insiders—no matter how close they become to individuals at the client.

At a more subtle level, let me tabulate some of the specific reasons clients hire consultants:

1. To solve an unusual problem they believe they have inadequate expertise themselves to solve.
2. To get an objective view of some issue about which there is controversy within the organization.
3. To help drive a change (in attitude, behavior, strategy) throughout the organization when they perceive a lack of internal leadership to accomplish this objective.
4. To "variablize" their staffing. Despite the high fees consultants charge, it is often more economic for a client to hire a consultant on an in-and-out basis to address an issue than it is for the client to build up an in-house staff to accomplish the same objective.
5. To keep in touch with the state-of-the-art thinking about a particular aspect of management. While millions of managers around the world innovate regularly, consulting firms are, in effect, the hotbed of R&D on management topics. Many managers recognize this and use consultants periodically to keep themselves abreast of best current practice in a given area.

There are other reasons, I am sure, why clients hire consultants; these are the main ones I have encountered in my career.

How Consultants Deliver Value

Consultants deliver value, first and foremost, by successfully getting done the job they are engaged to do. You are not with the client to impress them or to sell more consulting work. These outcomes are simply a by-product of doing your main job well.

In addition to this basic premise, consultants add value to clients—depending often on the individual and his or her proclivities—by:

- Being totally objective. (Never get involved in a client's internal politics.)

- Knowing your subject matter well. (Good consultants stay abreast of the state-of-the-art in their chosen area.)

- Wherever possible, knowing in depth the industry in which your client works (even if this involves some unpaid investment on your part).

- Wherever possible, bringing lateral or creative thinking to the subject you are asked to address. (Never be content to accept the "canned" answer to a problem.)

- Providing confidential counsel to senior client executives whose companies you get to know well (but never crossing the line of evaluating their people for them because you will never have sufficient exposure or perspective to do it well).

The Importance of High Professional Standards

Consultants exist to serve the needs of their clients—not vice versa. Never forget this: The client's interest must always come first.

Always remember to remain objective—no matter how close you get to a client. The best consultant is one who has a robust portfolio of clients; the differing needs of each client almost force you to keep a true sense of objectivity.

Always search for facts to underpin your hunches (in formal circles, these are called hypotheses) about the solution to your client's problem. You will be surprised how often facts will alter your views; you will be gratified by how much your client appreciates the hard work you put in to get the facts right—and it is hard work.

And, finally, always be honest with your clients even if being honest means telling them something they don't want to know. You will find clients respect you more (and rehire you more often) if they know they can trust you to pull no punches in what you tell them. This does not mean to be impolite or rude—just clear and honest.

Who Should Become a Consultant

In my view, too many people who attend business school get enamored of the supposed glamour of consulting and make this their primary career goal upon graduation. What folly!

Consulting is a serious profession that requires a set of distinct characteristics to be successful. Some of the more important of these characteristics are the following:

- Numeracy. All good consultants do a lot of quantitative analyses.

- Good writing skills. Your output as a consultant is a report or presentation. You must be skilled at preparing such documents.

- Conceptual ability. Consultants bounce around from problem to problem; you will not succeed as a consultant unless you have the conceptual ability to live such a pogo-stick life.

- Ability and willingness to focus on details. Truth is almost always found in the detail; you must revel in sorting through it to be successful.

- Ability to work hard. The average consultant works 60 hours per week; unless you actually enjoy this, forget this career.

- Service orientation. Consultants serve clients; they never command them. Unless you are comfortable with this role for the long term, forget consulting as a career.

Finally, the most important characteristic of a true consultant is intellectual curiosity about just about everything. Unless knowing more about virtually everything around you fascinates you, seek some other avenue to achieve your goals.

If you do meet these criteria, however, try consulting. It is a wonderful profession to pursue.

Consulting Versus Investment Banking

Peter Labon
Class of 1993, Harvard Business School

For those who have worked in one of these two industries, the other is often intriguing. Others who come to HBS with experience in neither often wonder what they're all about. Once the first recruiting weekend rolls around, students who interview with both consulting and banking firms get a clearer understanding of why it's called "Hell weekend." Anything you can do to narrow down your interests ahead of time will save you a lot of grief and should be easy to do given how many students and professors are knowledgeable about the two industries.

For the purpose of this discussion, management consulting will refer mainly to the large strategic consulting firms, and investment banking will include corporate finance, mergers and acquisitions, project finance, and real estate, while excluding sales and trading. It is difficult to compare consulting and banking without making broad generalizations, the first of which is that both are advisory businesses, provide a challenging career, and look for similar qualities in their candidates. In order to decide between the two, it is more useful to look at the differences that center around the scope of the job, nature of the work, lifestyle, and remuneration.

Scope of the Job

Both consultants and bankers are advisors to corporations. The difference lies in the scope of the advice: As a group, bankers are finance specialists, and consultants are business generalists.

Bankers focus on finance issues exclusively, such as management of debt and equity underwritings, advice on M&A transactions, financing of real estate, corporate or public projects, and other complex financial problems. The advice bankers provide requires them to be comfortable with and interested in the areas of finance, accounting, tax, law, and negotiation. The exact mix of skills required depends on the specific area within an investment bank. For example, in M&A you will need to understand business valuation methodologies, deal financing, pooling of interest and purchase accounting, various tax treatments available for business combinations, issues of corporate governance related to making and responding to merger offers, and how to negotiate the most favorable deal for your client.

Consultants usually start as generalists and spend their time on whatever are the most important issues facing their clients, such as marketing, sales force effectiveness, or manufacturing. Consulting requires a broad set of skills that can be applied to any project. Functional and industry-specific knowledge is based on work experience prior to consulting and the succession of projects in consulting. You will tend to start new projects without any prior experience and proceed to become an expert, rather than enter situations you have already seen many times before.

Professionals in both industries often start out as generalists but can specialize by industry or function. As a consultant you can be a telecommunications expert or a marketing specialist. As a banker you can also be a telecommunications expert or focus on M&A assignments.

Given that bankers and consultants deal with a different set of issues, they also tend to interact with different sets of people within client organizations. Bankers typically work with top executive and finance managers. Consultants work with managers in all functions and at all levels of the organization. Dealing with a larger group of people who differ widely in terms of education and experience requires a broader set of interpersonal skills.

Nature of the Job

Consulting assignments tend to have a longer time frame than banking transactions; therefore, as an associate, you may work on two to four assignments per year, whereas as a banker, you may work on ten times as many transactions. If you like to take ownership of a problem and work on it steadily for a few months until you understand the issues in depth, come up with a solution, and develop an implementation plan, while ensuring that the client buys in to your ideas, consulting might be for you. On the other hand, if you like working in a faster-paced environment on multiple simultaneous short projects, you may prefer banking.

Both consulting and banking involve selling advisory services. First, you have to sell potential clients on the idea of hiring you, and then you have to sell your ideas so that the client will implement them. Banking tends to be more relationship- and sales-oriented given that you work on significantly more projects than in consulting, and someone has to sell them to clients. Depending on which product (banking or consulting services) you are more comfortable selling and how much selling you want to do, you might prefer one career over the other. Although you might not be directly responsible for sales pitches for a number of years, you will definitely be involved in putting them together from the start of your career.

Lifestyle

How would you like to live in New York, London, or Tokyo? As a banker it is important that you like one of these three cities because that is where you will find the majority of jobs. As a consultant you have more latitude in finding an office in a location of your liking, although that doesn't guarantee you will be spending a lot of time in that city if all your clients are elsewhere and a hectic travel schedule keeps you away from home for much of the week.

You will work hard in both industries; however, the shorter-term nature of assignments in banking will probably result in longer and more unpredictable hours, especially at the beginning of your career. As you become more senior, the two probably equalize since then you will be responding to client demands. The higher investment of time in the early years as a banker, and higher remuneration in later years, seems to lead to people who enter the business with a longer-term horizon as compared to consultants, who often expect to quit consulting and start a new venture after a couple of years. If lifestyle is a very important consideration for you, carefully examine differences across firms in both industries and between offices in the same firm, because the variance in norms is wide.

Remuneration

Both industries are famous for leading MBA remuneration relative to other career choices. Compensation is driven by the economics of the two businesses, which are quite different. Consultants bill by the hour, and senior people make money by charging more for associates than they pay them. Ensuring a high percentage of billable hours determines how much money comes into the firm. There is clearly a natural limit on revenues based on how many hours a consultant can stay awake during the year and how many consultants are working for you. In banking, fees are more often based on a percentage of the transaction value without a direct relationship to how long it took to put the deal together. Revenues in banking are responsive to the state of the capital markets; thus, bonus compensation fluctuates significantly, especially within any given product group. For example, when M&A was booming, everybody was making piles of money, but the boom ended and people were laid off or switched into other areas. These differences in economics lead to bankers generally earning more over the long term than consultants. Given today's state of the MBA recruiting market, consultants will receive higher signing bonuses and starting salaries but lower annual bonuses. This difference in cash flows in the early years has a significant influence on how you will want to structure the servicing of your MBA debt.

And If You Still Can't Decide . . .

If you would like to work on both finance issues and general management issues, don't mind working really hard, and want to make a lot of money, you might consider a buyout firm. This career alternative will allow you to find a company to buy, execute the transaction, arrange the various levels of financing, help management develop and execute a strategy, and later bring the company public.

Good luck.

On the Career Choice Between Management Consulting and Operating Management

Clayton M. Christensen
Professor, Technology and Operations Management and General Management, Harvard Business School

As a Harvard MBA student in 1978, I had an enjoyable and challenging summer job with one of the major strategy consulting firms and then accepted a full-time offer with another of the major strategy consultancies, where I spent the subsequent five years in a stimulating, immensely enjoyable career. In 1984 I turned in an entirely different direction and founded, with three MIT professors, a venture capital-backed company to make products with advanced ceramic materials such as silicon nitride and aluminum oxide, using a process my partners had conceived. My partners and the engineering team they recruited were the technical brains of the company, and I was the president. We are fortunate that the company has been relatively successful. In 1989 I left our company and returned to HBS to complete my doctorate and fulfill a lifelong ambition to teach, and was able to join the Technology and Operations Management faculty in 1992. Because I am familiar with the HBS environment and was fortunate to have had rewarding experiences in management consulting and operating management, the editors of this book asked me to summarize my perspectives on these two very different careers.

I had never thought of management consulting until I came to HBS (the first time) and faced the stark expense of supporting my young family in Boston while financing my education. Although I confess that my initial attraction to the profession was financial, I quickly found the work and my colleagues to be interesting beyond my expectations. It would be fair to say that there is no other profession where one gets such a succession of intriguing, complex managerial and competitive problems to analyze and solve. My clients included manufacturers of electric wall sockets, toilet paper, consumer power tools, chain saws, electric motors, and automobiles—all normal, "boring" products we encounter every day. But this was why consulting was so fun. All these products, which I had looked at but thought little about for so long, came alive for me as I worked for their manufacturers. Fifteen years after the project, I never plug an electric drill into a wall socket without thinking about how wiring devices and power tools are designed, manufactured, distributed, and sold. Ordinary things became fascinating to me as I learned the detail behind them through my consulting

engagements. And I was able to understand them in the rich, conceptual context we have developed and employed within our firm. I joined the firm thinking I'd stay for two years and then leave for a real job. I stayed for five and would have stayed much longer, had I not had the chance to help start a new company.

The work of management consulting is, at its essence, data collection and analysis. If the information needed to make good decisions existed and were arranged in a way that yielded clear answers, managers would have little need for consultants. Consultants add value by collecting information that is hard to get—often by pulling it out of people's heads—and then by analyzing it in a way that defines attractive ways to solve managerial and competitive problems. Harvard's case study system is great preparation for consulting because what we are best at teaching here is how to analyze managerial and competitive problems. In general, my observation is that many students who enjoy and do well at the sorts of analytical work they see in the MBA program can enjoy and do well at management consulting. Some consulting firms compete in the recruiting battles by claiming that they work with clients to implement the recommendations that result from their work in data collection and analysis. But what they mean by implementation is the formulation of more detailed sets of recommendations and action plans. Such recommendations, whether at a detailed or general level, are the end of the consultant's work and the start of the work of the operating manager.

My greatest fear in leaving consulting for operating management was that my pace of learning would decline. I found, in fact, that this was not an issue. Figuring out what jobs needed to be done; how to pick the right people for the jobs that needed to be done; motivating our people to be innovative and thorough; organizing the efforts of scores of talented people so that everyone's autonomous efforts meshed smoothly into substantial group achievements; convincing investors that our company had potential; learning about our customers' problems and then convincing them that we could develop products to solve their problems—the intellectual challenge embodied in each of these tasks was for me at least as great as anything I had seen in consulting. Learning to succeed at these tasks of operating management was something I had not learned well at HBS or in management consulting. The analysis of managerial problems and the formulation of plans of action are things we teach well at HBS and practice well in consulting firms. But the process of management is a very different job from data gathering and analysis. I had to learn the process of management on the job. I had not learned it well in school or in consulting, and I'm not sure the most valuable skills of operating management can be learned in an abstract, analytical environment.

One of the greatest ex ante attractions of operating management was the potential satisfaction I might feel from building tangible things such as products, organizations, and shareholder value. Although these building activities certainly proved to be an immense source of satisfaction in my work as an operating manager, I do not feel that the satisfaction an operating manager gets from building and delivering tangible products and services is inherently different in magnitude from the satisfaction a consultant gets from scoping out and charting a solution path to a tough competitive problem. Both types of products and services are challenging to build and can add great value to those who buy them.

To me, the unique reward of operating management was the chance it gave me to affect the lives of the people who worked with me in what I hope was a profound and positive way. As an operating manager, you exert substantial influence over your employees' total life experience—they work with you or for you eight to 12 hours per day. What your employees learn, what they achieve, what talents they cultivate, and the satisfaction they get from peer associations all profoundly affect their happiness and self-esteem. The opportunity I had as an operating manager to affect these things directly, and help the people I worked with build happy and fulfilling lives, was the greatest reward in my career as an operating manager.

Interview: A Perspective on E-Commerce Consulting

Jonathan D. Kissane
Manager, The Boston Consulting Group, San Francisco Office

What value do consultants provide e-commerce businesses?

BCG's consulting practice focuses on three areas of value creation. First, consultants create new e-commerce businesses. BCG does not generally share its casework publicly, but in one example—a project code-named T2—consultants worked with clients to shape and build a new online business, which addresses opportunities in the travel industry. Without BCG's input and energy, this business would not have been launched.

Second, consultants bring well-established strategy techniques to newly established online firms that are beginning to realize that strategy remains important to success. While early-movers in the e-commerce arena enjoyed relatively easy success in comparison to later entrants, all companies do have to become profitable in their lines of business. Some of these successful, early e-commerce players have turned to BCG to help continue their success, since our consultants know how to identify and execute against valuable markets, customer segments, and business models. The new economy is still subject to fundamental economic rules, which are only now appearing in new complex technology-based flavors.

Third, BCG consultants continue to work with traditional firms that must execute their prior businesses more effectively in the Internet-enabled business world. Executives from long-established firms still rely on BCG to find opportunities in the e-commerce and traditional lines of business.

What is the scope and nature of work performed?

BCG casework focuses on each of the three areas of e-commerce value creation mentioned above. In addition, we continue to supply top-level strategic advice to executives in matters not directly related to e-commerce. The main differences between these two areas of work are that e-commerce cases tend to move more quickly, they require case team members to understand both the importance of technology and the underlying businesses, and

they offer consultants more obvious opportunities to make a significant impact on new businesses.

Projects vary significantly. Examples from my career at BCG include: defining and determining the value of a new market opportunity; establishing strategic partnerships on behalf of clients; hiring, and even managing, permanent and temporary resources for building a new business; creating and testing a proposed product or service offering with potential customers; assessing an acquisition opportunity; streamlining a purchasing process to take advantage of new technologies; and orchestrating the operational merger of two firms.

How is being a consultant in this industry different from other industries?

Working for BCG is clearly different from working in other lines of consulting. Many consider BCG the grandfather of strategy consulting, and we are gaining acceptance as the premier e-commerce strategy firm. Together, these aspects of our reputation grant us access to the top executives in both traditional and newly emerging industries. They trust us to understand their businesses, to understand the important role that e-commerce should play in their industries, and to help them achieve success. We are earnest about creating new businesses, growing old businesses, and enabling our clients to capitalize on their strengths. Together, our experience and momentum enable our exciting work to make significant changes to the competitive landscape.

Relative to other firms, including start-ups and other industries, we provide our consultants with a potent mixture of early responsibility and learning, coupled with a successful track record based on years of experience with sound business practices. Those who join BCG can expect to learn from individual experiences and to enjoy capitalizing on powerful and proven techniques.

What is most satisfying about working in this industry?

I have found that BCG offers an incredibly diverse set of opportunities to its consultants. They enjoy the chance to improve their personal skills, dive into many types of businesses, and make a significant impact on their clients' firms. Each consultant builds abilities that will serve long, successful careers in many possible fields.

BCG invests heavily in its staff, building exceptional personal skills. Each of our consultants has an opportunity to learn firsthand about technology and its impact on modern business practices, how to manage client and case teams, how to conduct business across international boundaries, how to shape executive thinking, and how to grow into more difficult and challenging responsibilities.

BCG's mix of work is unrivaled in exposing consultants to numerous companies, industries, and business models. Consultants have the chance to absorb and deploy an entire toolkit of business techniques that others might not see in decades of more-narrowly-focused work.

BCG does not write reports that sit on the shelves of its clients. We work in teams with our clients to change the way they conduct their business. In the end, the measure of satisfaction in our work comes from the degree of impact we have upon our clients and their success. Consultants learn by doing, just as much as they learn by thinking.

Can you describe some projects you have been involved with?

One of my most significant projects at BCG was advising the executive team of an Internet site that provided consumers with information to choose the best products for their homes. I worked with the initial case team and clients to flesh out the business concept and test it with consumers. I was involved during the new company's initial phase, when the start-up grew from a handful to over a couple of dozen employees. During this time, I was able to contribute to a number of strategic and operational decisions, and learn from the day-to-day decisions being made.

In addition to advising numerous clients on e-commerce matters, my other case work clusters around high-tech, but includes clients in the following industries: terrestrial and satellite-based telecommunications, networking hardware, pharmaceuticals, healthcare, consumer goods, and insurance.

What makes BCG a leader in this area?

BCG remains a leader in the field of business because it continues to capitalize on its strengths and to pave new paths through innovative initiatives. In e-commerce, BCG has three major distinguishing efforts under way. First, we have a partnership with Shop.org that permits us to work with thousands of Internet retailers to understand and shape their evolving business practices. BCG has compiled the best source of information on Internet commerce, which it holds confidentially and summarizes in reports made available to its partners. With superior information, BCG and its clients make better decisions.

Second, BCG is building a venture-styled practice in order to foster even more new enterprises. We have recently announced our partnership with iFormation, a joint venture among BCG, Goldman Sachs, and General Atlantic Partners.

Third, BCG is growing its WebLab initiative, which enables clients and case teams to explore new businesses rapidly, through accelerated Internet development. This is valuable for defining new Internet businesses, testing them with customers, generating funding, and moving into operation.

BCG will continue to explore innovative opportunities to generate significant value for its clients and its consultants.

E-Commerce Consulting Roundtable

Sameer Aurora
Columbia School of Business, Class of 1993
Director, Business Strategy Practice, ZEFER

Oliver Bardon
Ph.D., Physics, Massachusetts Institute of Technology
Project Leader, Boston Consulting Group

Lawler Kang
Wharton, Class of 1996
Managing Director, Boston Operations, Scient Corporation

Describe your background and explain why you chose a career in e-commerce consulting?

Lawler Kang: My relevant experiences include starting a dot-com in B-School and working for a venture catalyst firm that helped take small Net companies to market. I chose this field because I believe that we are at the epicenter of the greatest change in how business is conducted since the Industrial Revolution. At no time since have we had the ability to fundamentally re-sculpt the way people and companies communicate and transact their affairs on a global basis. Working for a leader in this field is a lot of fun!

Oliver Bardon: My background is in physics research. I obtained a Ph.D. in experimental particle physics from MIT and continued as a postdoc for a few years in the same field, at MIT and Fermi National Accelerator Lab. From there I came to BCG about three years ago.

My career change was motivated by a desire to shift from long-term basic research to more applied work, with much more immediate, tangible impact. I chose a career in strategy consulting largely because of the variety and continuous change in the challenges that we help our clients face as their business environments evolve. Over the past few years, electronic commerce has become a driver of this evolution and therefore an increasingly important element of our clients' strategies and my own work.

Sameer Aurora: My background is an eclectic combination of classic business strategy and experience in start-ups. After graduating with an MBA from Columbia Business School, I worked as a management consultant at Booz•Allen & Hamilton. More recently, I worked at the MTV Networks division of Viacom helping to launch new channels in Asia. In my present role at ZEFER Boston, I lead the business strategy practice and have grown the group sevenfold in the last nine months.

I chose e-commerce consulting at ZEFER for a host of interrelated reasons. First, this was an opportunity for me to work at the ground floor of a fast-growing Internet consulting firm committed to working with clients to help reshape their industries. Second, this opportunity allowed me to fuse my business strategy background and consulting skills with my keen interest in working at a start-up. Third, being focused on the fast-growing and dynamic internet space has enabled me to contribute to the restructuring of industries and markets by the most disruptive technology of our times. Finally, I chose an Internet consulting firm that not only prescribes strategy, but actually implements businesses for clients and evolves them over time.

Describe your firm and your e-commerce consulting practice, including the type of clients you serve and typical projects you accept. How does your firm distinguish itself in the marketplace? Does your firm take equity in the e-businesses that you advise?

Sameer Aurora: ZEFER, incubated at Harvard Business School, is a fast-growing Internet strategy consulting firm that builds businesses online for clients. We offer full-service capabilities to our clients, including Business Strategy, Experience Design, Technology Strategy and Implementation, and Program Management. Our client portfolio is a blend of Fortune 2000 companies seeking to leverage the Internet to transform their businesses, and dot-com startups attacking traditional industry structures.

Typical projects tend to be full life-cycle: we start by partnering with the client to develop compelling business strategies that include a portfolio of Internet options. Preserving strategic options value is particularly important in today's rapidly changing business environment. Once the strategic assessment phase is complete, we architect or blueprint specific Internet initiatives selected for implementation. The blueprints include site information architecture, validated business models, features and functionality requirements, and viable technical platforms. In the next phase, we build and launch the online initiative. After launch, we iteratively evolve the underlying strategy, features, and functionality of the online business.

ZEFER is competitively differentiated through a combination of key attributes: we are truly strategy-led, we implement and evolve Internet initiatives for clients, and we work in an interdisciplinary environment across business, design, and technology. Competitor segments include the classic strategy consulting firms, systems integrators, the Big Five accounting/consulting firms, interactive agencies, and other pure-play Internet consulting firms.

After careful evaluation, we sometimes take equity and incubate start-ups that are particularly compelling and are category or constituency killers.

Lawler Kang: Scient was born and bred to do one thing: build dominating e-businesses from the ground up. Currently 30% of our revenues come from start-ups, with the remainder generated by Global Fortune 2000 corporations. We have developed a three-stage approach that we use in all engagements: conceive, architect, and engineer. Being a NASDAQ listing, we do not work for equity in lieu of fees; however, Scient Capital, a wholly owned subsidiary of Scient, does make investments in our clients.

Oliver Bardon: BCG is a general strategy consulting firm. We've distinguished ourselves by combining deep insight into our clients' business environments with innovative approaches to the evolution of their strategies as these environments change. Electronic commerce is an increasingly important driver of such change. As such, it is an important element of every BCG consultant's knowledge base. While we do have an e-commerce group that leads projects such as our research collaboration with shop.org, all consultants have the opportunity to do e-commerce projects and are expected to become fluent in e-commerce work.

In e-commerce, just as in other areas, we distinguish ourselves by bringing a broad strategy perspective to all projects. Our understanding of the "traditional" issues that all companies continue to face, even as they go online, has proven valuable in building robust, complete strategies around e-commerce ideas.

Our e-commerce clients are primarily incumbents, with some venture capitalists and completely new ventures as well. Our role usually focuses on assessing and developing e-business opportunities, and taking them into the first stages of implementation. In some cases, BCG personnel will effectively run the new business while preparing for a transition to a new permanent staff. We do take equity in e-businesses when the situation makes sense both for our clients and for BCG.

What have been your greatest challenges and rewards in e-commerce consulting? What advice can you offer students considering a career in this field?

Oliver Bardon: I've faced some of the same challenges as e-commerce entrepreneurs—to convince others of the value and viability of new business ideas, and to get organizations to move very quickly to develop these ideas. These challenges have had a different flavor because my clients have usually been incumbents looking to move into e-commerce. New ideas have had to compete with existing ways of doing business, often threatened with competition and cannibalization by the new e-commerce channel. The organizations needing to move quickly have sometimes been established ones with existing practices and inertia that the brand-new entrepreneurial organizations may not have to deal with.

The greatest rewards have been overcoming these particular challenges. In e-commerce timeframes, I've seen projects into implementation, knowing that a new business has been embraced. I've helped to enable and witnessed the transformation of individuals and organizations who initially doubted their ability to move at Internet speed.

To a new student considering this field, I'd reiterate that e-commerce is one element of overall strategy—an important one, but only one. I find this true both for incumbents and for e-commerce start-ups. My most important role has often been to integrate e-commerce with other more traditional strategic considerations—for example, factors such as traditional channels, organization, and product development. I'd advise looking for a role that allows you to learn and to practice a broad strategic view, while still potentially focusing on e-commerce.

Sameer Aurora: One of our greatest challenges has been managing our explosive growth. In the last 12 months, we've grown from 45 to 650 people. Our tremendous expansion has coincided with the need to maintain the original culture and shared values that underpin who we are as a company. Since our culture evolves with every new employee, we have paid particular attention to recruiting people whose values are consistent with our culture. We have also put in place programs and processes to build a firm based on shared practices and principles consistent with our vision.

I would say to students considering a career in Internet consulting that it takes greater courage to help reshape industries and up-end traditional structures than it does to work at a more conventional firm maintaining the status quo. Figure out what you are passionate about and follow your dream. The big, traditional consulting firms and investment banks will always be around—you can always go the safe route. In the mean time, look around you, this is a unique moment in our history—new ways of thinking and doing are reshaping the world. And make sure you get pre-IPO equity options!

Lawler Kang: I have had only one challenge: finding and hiring legendary colleagues. My two major rewards have been: impacting and redefining business on a global scale, and being able to relish in the cultural bliss of Scient. I would advise a thorough exploration of the firms with which you are interested in working (prior to interviewing) and ensuring that your people skills match or exceed your quantitative masteries.

Being a Summer Associate

Catherine H. Bohutinsky
Class of 1995, Harvard Business School

During the summer of 1994, I spent 10 weeks working as a summer associate in a medium-sized strategy consulting firm. Prior to entering Harvard Business School, I worked for a large technology-based consulting firm, as well as for myself as an independent operations research consultant to a Fortune 500 company. Hence, my experience to date had been in technology consulting as opposed to strategy consulting. I felt that the experience with this firm would give me a good idea as to whether to pursue strategy consulting as a career option. The article that follows will discuss the general characteristics of a good summer associate experience and will provide insights into what you should expect to achieve as a summer associate.

Characteristics of a Good Summer Experience

Before beginning your summer experience, it is important to think about what you want to accomplish with your summer. Remember that the firm hired you because it saw the potential for you to make an attractive addition to the team. Think about why you picked this company, what skills you would like to develop, and whether a full-time offer is your ultimate goal.

It is likely that the staffing officer will ask you what type of assignment you would like to work on over the summer. In terms of utilizing your past experience, it may make sense either to pick an industry that you are comfortable with or an industry that will utilize skills learned in your previous work experience. However, you may want to choose an industry unrelated to your past experience with the purpose of broadening your scope.

There are horror stories of consultants working 100 hours per week and never having a life outside of work. Most firms have improved on their ability to let you manage your time, but consulting remains a demanding career choice. It will make sense for you to be on a project that is the best representation of the type of work, as well as the length of hours, that you could expect as a full-time employee. If travel is a large part of the "typical" assignment at the firm, it may make sense for you to try a job that involves travel in order for you to simulate the full-time experience.

Much of consulting work involves working in a team setting. Hence, it is extremely important that you get to know the people and the culture of the firm. Take advantage of social events that will allow you to get to know others in the firm. If you don't like the people, you will most likely not enjoy working there full time.

Among the experiences that you should look for in a summer position, client interaction is key. The best consultants have excellent client interaction skills. Take as many opportunities as you can to carry the relationship with the client further. Let your manager know if you don't feel that you are getting enough client interaction. It is also important that you participate in concept development and analysis. Much of the work done by consulting firms involves client interviews, data analysis, and concept synthesis. Be involved and take the initiative in providing value to your team.

It is important to get a good feel for the type of work performed by the firm. Take advantage of opportunities to attend presentations on client work outside of your assignments. Talk to other first year full-time consultants about the type of work they are performing. Are they getting significant client contact? Do they feel that they are broadening their skills and being continuously challenged? Are they able to control which assignments they are staffed on? These are all questions that will help you to make the best decision for the long term.

What You Want to Achieve by the End of the Summer

By the end of the summer, you should have improved your problem solving skills and deepened your knowledge of a specific industry or industries. You should have a fairly good picture of the people and culture of your firm and a good idea of what it would be like to work in consulting full time. You should feel fairly comfortable in the work environment and feel that you added value to your team. In addition, you should have made some good contacts in the industry.

At the end of the summer, you may receive an offer for a full-time job from the firm, and you should have a fairly good idea of whether you will accept or reject it. Again, assess your fit with the people at the office, the type of work the firm performs, and the type of clients the firm works for. If you are satisfied with your assessment, you are halfway home.

The next step is to decide whether you find consulting fulfilling as a full-time experience. Consulting pays well and is challenging and interesting. It is also generally considered to be a more demanding career choice than most others. It is important that you assess the trade-offs involved in making consulting your career choice.

If you feel that this is not the lifestyle you would like to lead, then the summer experience has helped you to narrow your job focus for the second year. If you decide that consulting is a good career choice for you, then the experience may prove to be the first step toward a fulfilling career in consulting. Either way, you will be better off having learned something about yourself through the experience as a summer associate.

Reflections on First-Year Recruiting

Phil Collins
Class of 1993, Harvard Business School

If investment banking was the career of choice in the 1980s, one could argue that management consulting has replaced it as the most sought-after business profession in the 1990s. As a result, obtaining summer positions in the consulting industry has become increasingly competitive.

Why Consulting?

Perhaps the first and most important step in first-year recruiting is deciding what type of summer position is right for you, based on your interests and long-term career plans. Your time and energy will be limited, and effective recruiting will by necessity require significant focus. Don't let the herd set your priorities. Make sure you understand and can explain clearly why you are interested in consulting for the summer. Otherwise, you may end up with a great summer position for all the wrong reasons— a choice you may regret in the long run as you begin planning for your full-time career.

Once you decide to pursue a job in the consulting field, your focus will shift to the most critical step: getting an offer. As competitiveness for summer positions in consulting has intensified, it has become increasingly important for prospective candidates to expend considerable effort in preparing for the recruiting process in order to ensure that their skills are appropriately highlighted and communicated.

Knowing the Firms

One of the most difficult aspects of preparing for a consulting job search is that there are many types of consulting firms, each with its own selection criteria. An effective job search will require you to assemble a considerable amount of information about each of the firms, which will be useful in two ways: This information will assist you in determining which firms you would be interested in working for, and it will be crucial in preparing for interviews.

Preparing materials and attending recruiting briefings and career fairs will be helpful, but also take advantage of any opportunity to learn about the firms from the consultants themselves, who will give you a detailed and realistic understanding of the firms' focuses and values. Another valuable resource not to be overlooked is your classmates who worked at particular firms before business school or who went through summer consulting programs with firms.

Generally, firms differ along a few important dimensions, and it is important to understand how each firm differentiates itself. Consider the following issues:

- Type of work. Does the firm specialize along functional, industry, or geographic lines? Are new consultants encouraged to be specialists or generalists? At what level of the client's organization does the firm work? Does it have a very strong practice in certain specialties, or does it attempt to be strong across a number of areas? What kinds of problems has the firm worked on before, and do these engagements sound interesting?

- Focus on implementation. After developing a set of recommendations, does the firm actively participate in implementation?

- Practice development. Does the firm have a strong commitment to developing competencies in its practice and to disseminating its expertise throughout the firm?

- Focus on professional development. What kinds of resources does the firm bring to bear on problems? What is the role of a new consultant on a project? What kind of training programs does the firm have, and how does it support the professional development of its consultants?

Getting an Offer

Once you have a good understanding of the various consulting firms, you should be able to identify those in which you have a sincere interest and will be ready to begin pursuing a summer position in earnest. Here are some tips:

1. Understand what consulting firms are looking for. While understanding the characteristics of each firm will be helpful, most firms are looking for the same kind of people: smart, creative problem solvers whose

interpersonal skills will allow them to work well in a team environment. Given the nature of the work, consulting firms are also looking for people who are energetic and have an appetite for new challenges, traits often demonstrated by a record of past achievement. Given that most students at top business schools possess all of these requirements to some degree, successful candidates must communicate their unique strengths clearly and convincingly.

2. Understand clearly why you want a job in consulting. There are no experience prerequisites for getting a summer job in consulting, other than knowing why you want it and being able to communicate clearly your conviction. Consulting firms hire people from a wide variety of backgrounds, but a major career change may require some explanation.

3. Frame your skills and experience in terms of how you can add value to the firm and its clients. Provide concrete examples from your previous experience demonstrating that you have been a creative problem solver, that you are successful working in teams, and that you have leadership abilities.

4. Identify your weaknesses. Look carefully at your résumé and identify your weak spots. What are the one or two questions that you hope they will not ask? They will, so prepare clear and convincing answers.

5. Be yourself and be honest. While it is important to be at your best in framing and communicating your skills, it is also important to be honest and to be yourself. Getting a job at a firm full of people with whom you may not get along or where you would not enjoy the type of work is not in the best interest of either you or the firm. A couple of bad interview experiences with a particular firm should indicate that this is not a place where you would be happy spending your summer— let alone your career. Be grateful that you figured this out early, and move on with enthusiasm to the next interview.

6. Save the best interview for last. There is a learning curve in this process, so schedule your interviews accordingly. Experience will allow you to become more relaxed, confident, and convincing.

7. Ask insightful questions. Firms will inevitably ask you at the end of the interview if you have any questions. You should have some. Good questions are firm, specific, and thoughtful. They should be designed to demonstrate a strong understanding of the firm and to help you gain further insight into whether the firm is a top choice for you.

Preparing for the Case Interview

Nothing causes more anxiety in first-year students trying to land a summer job in consulting than the prospect of interview cases. For most firms, interviews and cases make or break a candidacy. They are clearly a crucial element in evaluating prospective employees and not nearly as frightening as one might expect. A good case interview is no more than a discussion about an interesting and challenging business problem, and it provides an opportunity to showcase your knowledge and skills. Viewed in this way, the case interview can become considerably less daunting.

Firms use cases to evaluate your analytic abilities and problem-solving skills. Keep in mind that they are not looking for a "correct" answer but instead are trying to understand how you think and how you approach problems. This is an important distinction with implications for how you should respond to case situations. Keep the following points in mind:

1. Stay calm. Listen carefully and take time to think clearly about the problem before formulating a response. This is especially important because it is difficult to recover from a hasty start.

2. Take notes. The last thing you should have to worry about is remembering case facts and numbers, so feel free to take notes during the case portion of the interview. This often helps you to concentrate on the problem-solving aspect of the case.

3. Ask questions. The questions you ask are often as important as your answers in helping the interviewer understand how you think and what issues you believe are important for further clarification and consideration. If you make assumptions, state them clearly.

4. Identify the most important issues in the case up front. Try to determine what is critical, as opposed to what is merely interesting, and develop hypotheses to explain what is driving the important issues. If you are on the wrong track, the interviewer will often interrupt you and provide additional data.

5. Develop a framework for approaching the problem. Break the problem down into its constituent parts, and approach them in a logical way rather than generating random thoughts. Give the interviewer a road map of where you are going to take the discussion. The framework is a key to understanding how you think and approach problems and illustrates your ability to approach problems in a systematic way.

6. Be flexible. Adapt your analysis to the problem, and develop a framework that is appropriate. Don't try to force every problem to conform to a generic, prefabricated, and inflexible analytical framework. Each problem is unique and will require a unique approach.

7. Think causally and logically. What are the underlying causes of the case situation, and what impact have they had? Develop a clear and logical chain of reasoning, and understand the linkages among key elements of the problem.

8. Drive to action. Given an understanding of the key issues, causes, and linkages, what opportunities does the client have to take actions that will improve its performance?

Keep in mind that each firm approaches cases in a different way. Some cases are long and complex, encompassing a number of issues and presenting a lot of data; others may be much shorter or less quantitative. You may be handed pages of data and asked for your impressions, or a situation may be described to you in a qualitative way. Some firms may ask you to analyze an industry you have worked in, while other firms will deliberately ask you about industries with which you are unfamiliar. Some cases might require microeconomic analysis, while others may rely on knowledge of first-year marketing. Most often, the cases will require integration of knowledge of a number of subjects and functional areas.

The bottom line is that case interviews have been designed so that you cannot study for them, so don't bother. Review the major frameworks developed in first-year courses, brush up on your microeconomics, and then concentrate on ways of strengthening and demonstrating your problem-solving skills. One good way to do this is to practice a few mock cases with another student.

A consulting job search will require a great deal of time and effort; it can also be a challenging, rewarding, and even fun experience. You will meet a wide variety of intelligent and interesting people, you will be challenged to think on your feet as you work through complex business problems, and you will gain a broader understanding of the different firms and of consulting as a career.

About This Project

During the spring of 2000, consulting firms that are usually interested in recruiting MBA students were contacted and asked to respond to the questionnaire below. The companies' responses, which appear in the following section, are printed, for the most part, as received.

Company Description

Describe your firm by type of consulting work performed and by types of clients served. What changes are planned in the next few years in terms of services, clients, or locations of offices?

Describe your organizational structure. Is the firm geographically structured or based around practices? If you have practices, please list them.

Who are your competitors, and how does your approach to consulting differ from theirs?

Summarize your growth in terms of revenues (both domestic and international) and professional staff over the past year; over the past five years.

Approximately how many professionals do you have at each level, i.e., how wide is your pyramid?

Consultant's Job Description

Describe the career path and corresponding responsibilities for an MBA at your firm.

As an MBA advances through the firm, how much is he or she required to specialize by level?

How big is a typical case team? How many cases does a consultant work on simultaneously?

Discuss the lifestyle aspects of a career with your firm; i.e., average hours per week, amount of travel, flexibility to change offices.

What is your firm's turnover rate for professionals? What careers do your ex-consultants typically pursue after leaving?

The Recruiting Process

Describe your recruiting process and the criteria by which you select candidates.

From which schools do you actively recruit? Do you consider applicants from other schools?

How many full-time consultants do you expect to hire in the coming year?

How many summer interns do you expect to hire? If you have a formal summer program, please describe it. Please be sure to indicate whether the program is in place for all offices or just some.

Human Resources Practices

Describe your firm's performance appraisal system for consultants. Are there explicit criteria against which an MBA is evaluated before being promoted? How many times a year is there a performance appraisal and hence an opportunity for promotion? Is there an upward evaluation process too?

What benefits does your company provide for maternity, paternity, or adoption leave?

Please describe any initial training programs or ongoing professional development programs for young professionals.

Describe your firm's outplacement services.

Does your firm provide for on-site day care? If not, do you provide compensation for day care? Is flextime possible?

Abt Associates Inc.

55 Wheeler Street
Cambridge, MA 02138-1168
(617) 492-7100
Fax: (617) 492-5219

MBA Recruiting Contact(s):
Michael Henderson, Human Resources
(617) 349-2402

Locations of Offices:
Cambridge, Lexington, MA; Bethesda, MD;
Washington, D.C.; Chicago, IL; Cairo; Johannesburg.
Overseas project offices as required (currently in Santo
Domingo, Dominican Republic; San Salvador, El
Salvador; Tegucigalpa, Honduras; Lima, Peru; Addis
Ababa, Ethiopia; Kigali, Rwanda; Dakar, Senegal;
Bamako, Mali; Lusaka, Zambia; Amman, Jordan;
Almaty, Kazakhstan; Jalal-Abad, Kyrgyzstan; Bishkek,
Kyrgyzstan; Tashkent, Uzbekistan; and Palikir,
Federated States of Micronesia).

Total Number of Professionals (U.S. and worldwide):
800

Ownership Structure of Firm:
Employee-owned corporation

Company Description

*Describe your firm by type of consulting work performed
and by types of clients served. What changes are planned
in the next few years in terms of services, clients, or locations of offices?*

Abt Associates Inc. is a broad-based consulting and research firm serving clients in business, industry, and government. We provide research-based consulting, that is,
advice and problem solving based on innovative and rigorous analysis of the client's problems. The company's
clients are firms and trade associations in the financial
services, health care, high-technology, telecommunications, pharmaceutical, and automotive industries. We also
provide our services to virtually every U.S. government
agency and numerous multinational agencies. We provide to these clients strategic planning, service quality
measurement and management, management consulting,
human resources, market research, new product development, program evaluation, policy analysis, technical assistance, and program operation services.

In the next few years, we plan to continue to grow globally in the areas of our substantive strengths. We are currently very strong in the United States and the developing
world; over the next few years, we will continue moving
more strongly into the newly developed world, the newly
democratized countries of Central and Eastern Europe,
and the European nations.

*Describe your organizational structure. Is the firm geo-
graphically structured or based around practices? If you
have practices, please list them.*

Founded in 1965, Abt Associates is an employee-owned
corporation. Our organizational structure revolves around
areas, practice-based units that focus on substantive market and technical domains. As new markets are targeted
and developed, new areas may come into being. Currently, our areas are:

Health Care Consulting
Financial Services
Information Technology and Telecommunications
Biostatistics and Epidemiology
Clinical Operations
Pharmacoeconomics
Survey Research
Health Services Research and Evaluation
Clinical Research and Epidemiology
International Development
International Health
Environmental Research
Technology Analytics
Law and Public Policy
Housing and Community Revitalization
Education and Child Development

*Who are your competitors, and how does your approach
to consulting differ from theirs?*

Abt Associates is so diversified and competes in such a
broad range of fields and sectors that our competitors depend on the field in question. In general, our competitors
are large management consulting, accounting, market research, and public policy research firms.

Abt Associates' research-based consulting approach
means that we do not bring off-the-shelf methodologies,
concepts, solutions, or world views to address our clients'
problems. Instead, we work with our clients collaboratively on defining their real needs and then developing
the approach that best attacks the problems. We then provide consulting on the implementation and monitoring of
our recommendations. We are as likely to help our clients
recast the questions proposed to us and then deal with
them as we are to address the questions originally posed.

We are known for our innovative design of research-based solutions and the depth of our analytic capabilities. In the area of service quality measurement and management, for example, Abt Associates has developed an innovative events-based approach to measuring customer satisfaction accurately and meaningfully. This approach also helps us determine how increasing customer satisfaction is related to increasing revenues.

Summarize your growth in terms of revenues (both domestic and international) and professional staff over the past year; over the past five years.

Abt Associates has been on a steady growth track over the past five years. Our revenues grew more than 20% over the last fiscal year. Staff size increased more than 12% to 1,000. Our growth has been such that we recently promoted from within five staff to vice president, in addition to effecting numerous promotions of staff below this management level.

Approximately how many professionals do you have at each level, i.e., how wide is your pyramid?

Approximately 40% of our professional staff are at the junior level, 30% at the intermediate level, and 30% at the senior level.

Consultant's Job Description

Describe the career path and corresponding responsibilities for an MBA at your firm.

Because of our diversity, Abt Associates recruits and hires staff with a wide variety of educational backgrounds, degrees, and experience. The career path at Abt Associates consists of the following levels:

    Research Assistant
    Junior Analyst
    Market Analyst
    Senior Market Analyst
    Associate
    Senior Associate
    Vice President

MBAs hired at Abt Associates are likely to come in at any level between market analyst and senior associate, depending on the extent and nature of their experience, and they advance to higher levels consistent with their capability, drive, and talent. At higher career levels, staff take on increasingly higher levels of sales and marketing responsibility, have greater case management responsibilities, and assume greater levels of client contact. Ulti-

mately, a staff member may be put in charge of an entire practice area.

Staff who work in areas of the company that are predominantly public policy oriented follow a similar career path, with different level designations. There is considerable flexibility for staff movement from our private sector practices to the public policy practices, and vice versa.

As an MBA advances through the firm, how much is he or she required to specialize by level?

As a staff member grows within the company, he or she may begin to specialize in either a content arena (e.g., delivery of banking services) or a technical arena (e.g., product positioning strategy). As a staff member becomes more specialized with career advancement, he or she may also become more diversified in the topics to which that specialization is applied. A specialist in the delivery of banking services may be called upon to apply his or her expertise to the delivery of telecommunication services, for example, or a specialist in customer satisfaction measurement may be called upon to apply this expertise in health care, financial, or information technology contexts.

How big is a typical case team? How many cases does a consultant work on simultaneously?

Case teams can range in size from one to twenty staff members and in duration from one week to several years. Members of case teams can come from virtually any area of the company; they are selected on the basis of their capabilities and interest. Case teams may be augmented by the services of various support functions, such as survey implementation support provided by our Survey Research area. Case teams have both considerable authority and direct responsibility for carrying out their assignments. A consultant may work on one to four cases or projects simultaneously, depending on the size of the assignment, its duration, and the skills called for.

Discuss the lifestyle aspects of a career with your firm; i.e., average hours per week, amount of travel, flexibility to change offices.

Hours can be long and travel extensive but probably less so at Abt Associates than at other professional firms. We supply an atmosphere of fascinating work, congenial colleagues, unusual responsibility and independence, and technical and managerial support as a context for our work. The shared excitement with what we do and shared participation in doing it have made Abt Associates a remarkable place in which to work.

Staff may relocate to other offices of the company with their area manager's approval. No staff are moved to other offices involuntarily.

What is your firm's turnover rate for professionals? What careers do your ex-consultants pursue after leaving?

The average tenure of staff at Abt Associates is about five years; this has been increasing gradually over time. Turnover is relatively low for senior staff. Because of the good opportunities for growth within the firm, talented staff members who enjoy working at Abt Associates have the opportunity to grow with us. Most consultants who leave do so voluntarily for attractive opportunities in other organizations. Our alumni have pursued careers in industry, other consulting organizations, academia, and government. Several ultimately have returned to work with us after their other work experiences. We actively stay in touch with our alumni through an annual newsletter and other means.

The Recruiting Process

Describe your recruiting process and the criteria by which you select candidates.

Abt Associates casts a wide net in its recruitment process. We recruit professional staff through universities, professional associations, contacts in business and industry, and recruitment firms. Candidates are rigorously evaluated, first by review of their credentials, references, and work product samples and then through face-to-face interviews with the appropriate senior practice staff.

We evaluate candidates on their growth potential, type of expertise and extent of knowledge of the field, analytic and problem-solving capabilities, and writing and presentation skills. Depending on the position, candidates must also have proved ability to apply certain research methods or at least to understand them.

From which schools do you actively recruit? Do you consider applicants from other schools?

Because Abt Associates looks for a wide variety of talent and experience, we do not confine our recruiting to any particular schools. Our staff come from leading educational institutions throughout the world.

Abt Associates' continued growth augurs well for continued recruiting for talented staff. Although we have no specific numerical targets, it is likely that we will be recruiting over the next year 40–60 full-time professional staff members having a variety of experience levels, educational backgrounds, and degrees.

Human Resources Practices

Describe your firm's performance appraisal system for consultants. Are there explicit criteria against which an MBA is evaluated before being promoted? How many times a year is there a performance appraisal and hence an opportunity for promotion? Is there an upward evaluation process too?

All new employees are evaluated after their first three months with the company. Abt Associates has an annual performance evaluation cycle for all other employees, in which the employee's primary supervisor provides written performance evaluation data, which are discussed in a performance evaluation conference with the employee. If appropriate, input is also sought from secondary supervisors of the employee. Employee performance for the year is evaluated against goals set by the employee and employee's supervisor the year before.

Although promotions are often tied to the annual performance appraisal cycle, they are not limited to that one time each year and may occur at any time the employee's performance warrants it.

The company has a long-standing practice of requesting anonymous upward assessments at the same time the downward assessment process is done. Employees fill out forms appraising their supervisors, which are collected, aggregated, and presented without identifying information on them to each supervisor. These upward appraisals are used as part of the process of evaluating supervisors.

What benefits does your company provide for maternity, paternity, or adoption leave?

For over two decades, the company has provided for maternity, paternity, and adoption leave. Our policy in each of these categories is competitive with those of other similar companies.

Please describe any initial training programs or ongoing professional development programs for professionals.

New staff professionals are assigned a "buddy" from the current staff to help the new employee navigate his or her way through the company, answer questions, provide advice, and share experiences with the new employee. The company offers extensive software training on site for all software packages currently used at Abt Associates. The company offers tuition reimbursement up to a specified limit and for a limited number of employees, for work-related courses successfully passed by employees. Finally, the company generally pays for employees' attendance at conferences at which they are making presentations.

Describe your firm's outplacement services.

On a limited case-by-case basis, the company may provide the services of an outplacement firm to (primarily senior) staff leaving our employ.

Does your firm provide for on-site day care? If not, do you provide compensation for day care? Is flextime possible?

For over two decades, Abt Associates has had an on-site day care center at its Cambridge office. Although this center is an independent entity, it gives admission preference to the children of Abt Associates employees.

The company has a formal telecommuting policy. Arrangements for flexible work schedules can be worked out at the discretion of the employee's area or department manager.

Alliance Consulting Group, Inc.

745 Boylston Street
Boston, MA 02116
(617) 424-1111
Fax: (617) 424-1112
Web site: www.alliancecg.com

MBA Recruiting Contact(s):
Michelle Benoit, Director of Human Resources

Locations of Offices:
Boston, MA; San Jose, CA

Total Number of Professionals (U.S. and worldwide):
About 45

Company Description

Describe your firm by type of consulting work performed and by types of clients served. What changes are planned in the next few years in terms of services, clients, or locations of offices?

Alliance Consulting Group, Inc. is a strategy consulting firm with offices in Boston, Massachusetts and San Jose, California. Founded in 1986, Alliance is committed to helping business leaders take charge of their organizations and achieve sustainable performance improvements. Building upon a traditional strategy foundation, Alliance has moved aggressively into the Internet arena and is taking the lead in helping companies develop and implement e-business strategies in both the business-to-business and business-to-consumer spaces. Alliance has also developed an early lead in working with the technology infrastructure providers who are powering the Internet revolution.

Alliance is organized around three business lines:

- Profiting from E-Business: Design and implement successful e-business strategies in both the business-to-business and business-to-consumer arenas, bringing together technology and strategy know-how.

- Mastering Strategic Transitions: Guide business leaders through periods of change caused by new leadership, changing market conditions, shifting technology

and competition, translating vision into actionable strategy.

- Launching New Ventures: Work with start-ups and their investors to rapidly turn new business concepts into successful ventures supported by a successful and sustainable business model.

Alliance works with Fortune 500 companies from a wide range of industries, with a particularly strong presence in telecommunications, financial services, consumer products and high-technology. We also work with many entrepreneurial, Internet-related start up companies, in some cases accepting equity from those firms in lieu of fees.

Who are your competitors, and how does your approach to consulting differ from theirs?

Alliance competes with other top-tier strategy and management consulting firms. As our e-business practice grows, we are also facing new competition and partnering opportunities from specialty IT strategy and implementation firms. We identify two major sources of competitive advantage.

The Collaborative Approach

Alliance has pioneered a collaborative approach to strategy development that consistently delivers exceptional value to our clients. At the beginning of a project, we form joint teams with the client, bringing our consultants in direct and consistent contact with key client stakeholders. Our consultants provide the conceptual frameworks and analytical rigor to facilitate the overall strategy effort, teaching the art of strategy while solving specific issues. Because of the close collaboration, clients gain the tools needed to continually evaluate their company's strategy and spread enthusiastic commitment to action throughout the organization. Change happens.

Tech-Savvy Business Sense

Due to our relatively small size, Alliance has been able to rapidly build a strong technology knowledge base and work with some of the early leaders in the Internet space. Our consultants are among the industry's most experienced in dealing with issues of e-business strategy, Internet infrastructure, and new Internet ventures. This tech-savvy mindset, coupled with Alliance's traditional strategy background produces a unique and particularly effective client experience and competitive advantage.

Summarize your growth in terms of revenues (both domestic and international) and professional staff over the past year; over the past five years.

Our company has grown steadily in the past, roughly 10% to 20% annually. As the demand for Internet-related strategy services increases, we expect firm growth to accelerate. Moving forward, Alliance plans to grow its client base and internal resources at an aggressive, but sustainable rate.

Internationally, we have developed stable relationships with other leading consulting firms, including C. Melcher and Partner, a large European-owned consulting firm, and CDI, a large Japanese-owned consulting firm. These relationships facilitate our work with multi-national clients and allow us to enjoy referrals, exchange ideas, and transfer staff to foreign offices.

Approximately how many professionals do you have at each level, i.e., how wide is your pyramid?

Alliance has five professional levels: vice-president, principal, manager, consultant, and associate consultant. Alliance's small size and narrow pyramid facilitate a mentoring environment and team-building among our employees. Alliance is a place where people learn from each other.

Business school graduates typically enter as consultants who, because of the nature of our approach, are expected to assume broad responsibility and independently manage client case teams from the start.

Consultant's Job Description

Describe the career path and corresponding responsibilities for an MBA at your firm.

Responsibilities include working closely with senior managers and project teams to achieve significant improvements in client company results. We achieve these goals through rigorous business analysis, creative problem solving, coaching of client personnel, and management of the change process. Consultants also actively participate in enhancing the growth and profitability of Alliance by assuming internal management responsibilities.

How big is a typical case team? How many cases does a consultant work on simultaneously?

A given client engagement can involve any number of Alliance professionals depending on the size and the scope of the project. Larger engagements will typically be divided into teams that have one or more consultants working with several client managers and operating staff. Associates and consultants typically work on one or two projects at a time, though they may also contribute to other projects requiring their skills and expertise.

Discuss the lifestyle aspects of a career with your firm; i.e., average hours per week, amount of travel, flexibility to change offices.

Working at Alliance appeals to a diverse group of people with a variety of professional and personal interests. The number of hours worked varies considerably over the course of a project. Travel involves an average of one to two nights a week away from home. As a firm, Alliance encourages its professionals to maintain a healthy balance between work and personal life. As individuals, we try to have fun while we work.

What is your firm's turnover rate for professionals? What careers do your ex-consultants typically pursue after leaving?

The firm's turnover rate is typical for consulting firms. Many of our alumni have pursued their own entrepreneurial ventures or careers in industry.

The Recruiting Process

Describe your recruiting process and the criteria by which you select candidates.

We look for self-starters who thrive in a team environment. They must have a serious work ethic and a good sense of humor. We value an outstanding academic record, strong quantitative and analytical abilities, communications skills, and demonstrated leadership qualities.

We rely on both self-initiated applications and on-campus recruiting. Interested and qualified applicants are encouraged to send a cover letter and resume to the recruiting coordinator.

How many full-time consultants do you expect to hire in the coming year?

The number of full-time consultants hired year-to-year varies. We expect to hire six to eight summer interns and seven to ten consultants based on our current growth plan.

Human Resources Practices

Describe your firm's performance appraisal system for consultants. Are there explicit criteria against which an MBA is evaluated before being promoted? How many times a year is there a performance appraisal and hence an opportunity for promotion? Is there an upward evaluation process too?

Performance evaluations take place every six months, as well as at the end of each project. Promotions are considered every six months. The evaluation is based on past performance and looks at a consultant's overall contribution to the firm's success. Most consultants are encouraged to stay with the firm.

Please describe any initial training programs or ongoing professional development programs for young professionals.

Initial training focuses on Alliance's approach to consulting practices and client relationships. Through mentoring relationships, new employees are introduced to the key tools and techniques used by our firm. Alliance encourages continuing education, and will subsidize relevant and qualified academic courses in which consultants choose to enroll.

American Management Systems, Inc.

4050 Legato Road
Fairfax, VA 22033
(703) 267-5000
Web site: amsinc.com
E-mail: ams_recruiting@amsinc.com

MBA Recruiting Contact(s):
Allan Jones, Manager, College Recruiting

Locations of Offices:
57 offices worldwide

1999 Revenues: $1.25 billion

Total Number of Professionals (U.S. and worldwide):
8,200

Company Description

Describe your firm by the type of consulting work performed and by the types of clients served. What changes are planned in the next few years in terms of services, clients, or location of offices?

Founded in 1970, AMS is a billion-dollar international business and information technology consulting firm. We have 10,000 innovators and thought leaders in 57 offices worldwide. They work side-by-side with clients in large commercial and government organizations to transform how they operate. Our work impacts the lives of thousands of people daily.

We provide a full range of consulting and systems development services—from strategic business and technology analysis, to business process renewal and change management, to the full implementation of solutions.

AMS helps clients achieve their goals by providing solutions based on a combination of business and technology consulting that is grounded in expertise in our clients' industries, a proven capability to apply the power of information technology, and dedication to meeting our commitments.

We specialize in work with financial institutions, telecommunications firms, insurance companies, state and local governments, educational institutions, federal government agencies, health care providers, and electric and gas utilities.

Our people work in creative partnerships with clients that frequently lead to long-term business relationships. In fact, approximately 85% of our work comes from organizations that were clients the previous year. This pattern has held true throughout our history.

Virtually all work at AMS is carried out by teams comprised of people with diverse experience and backgrounds. We hire talented people with skills along many dimensions: expertise in using the tools of management analysis, practical knowledge of the information technologies best suited to our clients' needs, and management skills to direct the efforts of project teams. Industry-specific and functional skills are equally valuable.

Demand remains particularly strong for AMS services, and we expect continued growth. We will accomplish this by building business on existing client relationships and with new clients in the markets we serve worldwide.

Ebusiness-related revenues represent 40% of our overall revenues. This is an increase of more than 100% over 1998. Once again, this proves that AMS is at the forefront of combining thought leadership and technological innovation.

Who are your competitors, and how does your approach to consulting differ from theirs?

Our competition varies by target market. In providing consulting services to banks, for example, the set of competitors is different from those we meet in our business for telecommunications firms or state and local governments. Across all markets, we compete with management consulting divisions of large firms.

Our approach, however, differs from these firms. We are organized into separate business units, each of which has full profit and loss responsibility for doing business with clients in a target market. This is a major difference that sets us apart from the "partnership" organization. The management team in each business unit is responsible for planning its business, developing marketing programs, selling, conducting research and development, providing product and customer support service, and, of course, consulting to clients. At the same time, they can draw on significant corporate resources to support their objectives.

This structure allows us to concentrate our in-depth experience to serve the industry-specific needs of our clients. We understand their industries, market conditions, business practices, and organizational environments. This, in turn, allows us to help clients select and deploy strategic technologies that take advantage of market opportunities as they emerge.

Summarize your growth in terms of revenues (both domestic and international) and professional staff.

It's pretty simple: we've grown every year since the company's inception. That's 30 years of consecutive growth, impressive any way you measure it. We currently are one of the 20 largest consulting firms worldwide. Our revenue increase also translates into an increase in professional staff. In 1999 alone, we successfully recruited and assimilated 2,100 people.

Revenues from international clients account for 20% of AMS's total revenues. In 1998, European revenues were $152.5 million. AMS now serves more than 50 clients in 12 countries from our 15 European office locations.

Consultant's Job Description

Describe the career path and corresponding responsibilities for an MBA at your firm.

An MBA's initial position at AMS depends on his or her work experience. A person with several years of relevant experience may begin by leading a team or helping us develop a new practice area. On the other hand, an individual with an MBA and no work experience typically starts as a consultant on a client project.

Career growth in terms of responsibilities and compensation will be determined by performance: becoming an expert in the application of systems technology in one of our target markets, demonstrating project management and consulting skills, helping win new business, and suggesting and being able to implement new products and services. How quickly an MBA advances into a leadership role depends on his or her own initiative.

How big is a typical case team? How many cases does a consultant work on simultaneously?

Some projects are staffed with a single person, and some may number 50 or more, including client staff and subcontractors. Projects with three to eight people are the norm. Typically a consultant works on one project at a time, and the duration is three to nine months. When a person demonstrates a particular expertise that is useful for many projects in a business unit, he or she may be in demand on two or three projects simultaneously.

Discuss the lifestyle aspects of a career with your firm; i.e., average hours per week, amount of travel, flexibility to change offices.

Work at AMS is both rewarding and intellectually demanding. An average workweek is 50 hours, and occasionally 60- to 70-hour weeks are necessary. Travel requirements are consistent with industry practice and vary by project assignment. Some of our operating groups, by virtue of their office locations, serve mainly in-town clients.

Regarding culture, we put a high premium on teamwork, cooperation, and open communications. We also make it clear that no member of the AMS team, however senior, is unapproachable. That makes for frequent and productive interactions at all levels.

Another important consideration: we have never adhered to a time-clock philosophy; staff members work hard but determine their most productive schedules.

AMS people are bright, creative, and self-motivated. We are committed to maintaining a quality work environment that is intellectually challenging with leading-edge work. We also provide opportunities for rapid advancement and personal development. Flexibility in balancing work/life issues also is an essential part of what defines us.

The Recruiting Process

Describe your recruiting process and the criteria by which you select candidates.

AMS actively recruits from MBA programs worldwide, but we focus our attention on our top 25 schools. We identify our candidates through our faculty contacts and résumé books. We also encourage MBAs who have found us through their research to contact us directly. Each MBA candidate is given careful consideration.

After initial screening to determine a match between a candidate's interests and our needs, the next step typically is an on-site visit to one of our major locations.

We hire candidates who possess skills from all points on the business and technology spectrum. We want people who have performed well in school, of course. But the candidates who really make an impact have solid consulting, interpersonal, problem-solving, and analytical skills.

We also look for candidates who come equipped with intellectual curiosity and a propensity to take on a significant role in a functional area. Perhaps just as important, these candidates must appreciate the value that information technology adds to each business scenario.

How many full-time consultants do you expect to hire in the coming year?

For the recruiting year 1999–2000, we expect to hire approximately 650 people from universities. Of that number, approximately 100 will be consultants hired directly from MBA programs.

How many summer interns do you expect to hire? If you have a formal summer program, please describe it. Please be sure to indicate whether the program is in place for all offices or just some.

In the past two summers, we hired more than 75 summer interns and more than 25% of those interns were MBAs. We anticipate an even larger program for the summer of 2000.

Our internship opportunities are designed to provide a meaningful experience for the student and reflect the roles and responsibilities of a full-time AMS consultant. Our goal is to provide a specific assignment for each intern that leverages his or her background and interests on a client project team.

Human Resources Practices

Please describe any initial training programs or ongoing professional development programs for professionals.

Training and career development has always been a critical part of who we are. Indeed, *Computerworld* recently ranked AMS in the top 10 of companies that fund training for its employees. We annually spend $45 million of our revenues on companywide employee training.

We recently unveiled AMS University, a program that takes into account geographic diversity, technology, and, above all, career development. It's a *virtual* university, representing learning and career development without boundaries. AMSU also provides the opportunity to gain insights from some of the best minds in business and information technology.

AMSU curricula includes topics needed to make our professionals successful in the work they do every day. A well-integrated array of classroom experiences, computer-based training, and distance learning comprise the learning vehicles. Courses cover a spectrum of skills: technical, functional, managerial, and interpersonal topics.

Arthur D. Little, Inc.

Acorn Park
Cambridge, MA 02140
(617) 498-5000
Fax: (617) 498-7140
Web site: www.arthurdlittle.com

MBA Recruiting Contact(s):
Tom DeMello

Locations of Offices:
52 offices in 31 countries

Total Number of Professionals (U.S. and worldwide):
3,463 professional staff worldwide

Company Description

Describe your firm by type of consulting work performed and by types of clients served. What changes are planned in the next few years in terms of services, clients, or locations of offices?

When Arthur D. Little started the company in 1886, he essentially invented management consulting. Dr. Little founded this business by applying analytical rigor to creative problem solving in the service of competitive strategy for clients.

For more than a century, Arthur D. Little has helped great global companies, governments and public agencies, and emerging ventures and their financial partners with their most pressing business challenges. From offices and laboratories in 31 countries on five continents, we help our clients by using innovation to create new value in new ways—new businesses, new methods, and new products and services. Large international companies (75% of the Fortune 100 and their global equivalents) call on Arthur D. Little for help when they want to create breakthrough outcomes in top-line growth, bottom-line results, and strategic speed and flexibility.

Describe your organizational structure. Is the firm geographically structured or based around practices? If you have practices, please list them.

We are organized into specific functional and industry practices—most global, some regional. Upon joining ADL, each consultant is aligned with both a functional and an industry practice. This provides our staff the opportunity to leverage their depth in an industry practice while working with many clients through their functional expertise. The majority of our clients operate in several industries, typically internationally, so our depth and breadth of experience is of great value to them.

Services Offered

Corporate Finance
Design & Development
Environment, Safety & Risk
Information Management
Marketing & Customer Management
Operations Management
Organization
Strategy
Technology & Innovation Management
Technology Creation & Exploitation

Industries Served

Automotive
Chemicals
Consumer Goods and Services
Energy
Financial Services
Health Care
Public Sector Services
Resources
TIME (Telecom, Information technology, Media, and
     Electronics)
Transportation
Utilities

Who are your competitors, and how does your approach to consulting differ from theirs?

Arthur D. Little competes with leading management consulting firms around the world. Our business objective is to use what we know about innovation to help clients achieve their objectives. We have a unique approach: combining experience in a range of industries with expertise in multiple functional areas to help our clients reach their goals. There is no other consulting firm that provides this range or combination of services.

Summarize your growth in terms of revenues (both domestic and international) and professional staff over the past year; over the past five years.

Last year, Arthur D. Little's revenues were $608 M. The greatest growth has taken place in Europe with a 17% in compounded annual growth over the past five years. In 1998, our staff grew to 3,463 employees worldwide.

Approximately how many professionals do you have at each level, i.e., how wide is your pyramid?

One of the unique benefits of working at Arthur D. Little is the high ratio of senior professionals to junior professionals. Because of our commitment to hiring experienced individuals, our pyramid structure is narrow. Our case teams are typically staffed with a ratio of one director to two managers and/or knowledge experts to three consultants. This means more delivered experience and knowledge for our clients and faster learning and critical responsibility for you. You will move up the experience curve quickly as you learn directly from senior ADL professionals as well as from our clients' senior staff. This leads to greater degrees of responsibility earlier in your consulting career.

Consultant's Job Description

Describe the career path and corresponding responsibilities for an MBA at your firm.

MBAs enter Arthur D. Little as consultants and are immediately exposed to a wide variety of case team activities. During their initial year with us, the MBA's problem-solving and technical competencies are intensely tested. We value the results of a creative thought process backed up with solid methodology. From the day you join us, you are involved in active casework, meeting with clients and staff members at all levels of the organization. As your career develops, you assume progressively more complex responsibilities for client interaction, case implementation, and project management. Arthur D. Little is a meritocracy and your progress along the career track is up to you. The first rung on the ladder is being selected to join us.

The next levels, manager and senior manager, are a career progression that involve leadership of the case team and fulfillment of client expectations for engagements. We allow consultants the flexibility of focusing on either the case/people management area or the industry/function area. Our managers have the opportunity and support to become the leading experts in their areas of expertise.

The next career development stage is that of associate director. Associate directors are responsible for new business development. Finally, our directors sell and manage our key accounts—those premier accounts that cross global, industry, and functional lines.

How big is a typical case team? How many cases does a consultant work on simultaneously?

The size of the case team varies with the scope and complexity of the engagement. A typical case usually involves from three to ten people. Consultants usually work on one or two cases at the same time.

Discuss the lifestyle aspects of a career with your firm; i.e., average hours per week, amount of travel, flexibility to change offices.

The professional demands on consultants at Arthur D. Little are high. In return for unparalleled learning, generous salaries, and handsome benefits, you are expected to work long hours and travel frequently. However, we deliver on our promise to help people maintain a balance in their lives. We recognize our staff members' responsibilities to their careers, families, communities, and personal well-being.

One reason we want to help you achieve a good balance between your personal and professional lives is that we hire people we plan to keep. To that end, we make every effort to support transfers from one ADL office to another both on a domestic as well as a global basis. We don't subscribe to the belief that turnover breeds success. Every new ADL consultant has the potential to become a director.

What is the firm's turnover rate for professionals? What careers do your ex-consultants typically pursue after leaving?

Turnover at Arthur D. Little has been lower than the industry standard. When consultants leave Arthur D. Little, for reasons other than retirement, they often move to senior leadership positions in the industries they know best. ADL alumni lead global enterprises.

The Recruiting Process

Describe your recruiting process and the criteria by which you select candidates.

Our recruitment process is rigorous. We look for people who are not only highly intelligent and resourceful, but forward-thinking, confident, and creative as well. Because we work so closely with our clients, ADL consultants must be effective at teaming and partnering. We believe that leadership ability is an essential element of this effective team behavior and screen for this as well. Our consultants are exceptional communicators with highly developed interpersonal skills—poise, tact, and organizational savvy. But all that is nothing without outstanding analytical skills, and experience and education to give structure and meaning to the analysis. In addition to several years of relevant industry experience, many of our younger staff members are coming to us with multiple graduate degrees: a joint M.D./MBA, for example, or graduate engineering degrees along with their business degree.

From which schools do you actively recruit? Do you consider applicants from other schools?

Arthur D. Little recruits entry-level MBAs from only the very top business schools in the United States and overseas. Our customers manage the leading companies around the world and expect only the best. We look for these candidates from a short list of the most selective graduate schools, not only of business, but science and technology, medicine, law, and public policy from around the world.

How many full-time consultants do you expect to hire in the coming year?

Over the past few years, Arthur D. Little has experienced tremendous growth in its worldwide consulting business. This growth is carefully planned so it is sustainable as we move forward. We anticipate hiring 70–80 MBAs and other postgraduates in 1999.

How many summer interns do you expect to hire? If you have a formal summer program, please describe it.

Arthur D. Little anticipates hiring between 25 and 30 summer interns in 1999 across our global offices. Our summer intern program is an exciting experience designed to interest first-year MBAs in consulting as a career. It also acts as a qualifying period for consultants, many of whom are invited to return to Arthur D. Little on a full-time basis. During the summer internship program, consultants are trained in Arthur D. Little methodologies, models, and approaches, which they apply immediately in their case assignments. Our interns enjoy high visibility with our clients as fully integrated members of our case teams.

Human Resources Practices

Describe your firm's performance appraisal system for consultants. Are there explicit criteria against which an MBA is evaluated before being promoted? How many times a year is there a performance appraisal and hence an opportunity for promotion? Is there an upward evaluation process as well?

Arthur D. Little's performance evaluation process places particular emphasis on staff development. Each staff member has a coach who provides timely and helpful feedback, and receives it in turn. Rapid skills-building is part of our methodology for developing staff and ensuring performance achievement. In addition, the criteria for moving through the consulting career stages have been clearly specified. Each career stage has criteria that are both qualitative and quantitative and are reviewed in the context of performance measurement and promotion. The consultants' progression through the career stages is influenced by their contribution to Arthur D. Little's accumulated knowledge base as well as superior casework.

Performance reviews take place at the end of each case, at mid-year, and finally at the formal end-of-year cycle.

What benefits does your company provide for maternity, paternity, or adoption leave?

Arthur D. Little has an exceptionally comprehensive and progressive benefits program for all its employees. Where possible based on local country legislation and customs, we provide all of these forms of leave.

Please describe any initial training programs or ongoing professional development programs for young professionals.

Arthur D. Little recognizes that intellectual capital is its primary resource, and therefore has a strong commitment to professional development. We hold formal courses in worldwide locations to address proprietary product knowledge, methodologies, and the full range of consulting skills. Moreover, we select and hire individuals who have the capability and desire to contribute to continuously renewing our greatest asset . . . the knowledge capital built by our staff.

There are currently training programs in place for each consulting career stage in addition to conferences, colloquia, and seminars for our consultants at various levels of their careers. We encourage industry training and participation in conferences, user groups, and professional associations. Our senior staff and other knowledge experts provide internal training sessions in locations worldwide.

Describe your firm's outplacement services.

When an employee and the firm mutually decide to part company, an individualized and generous plan is arranged to help the employee with the transition. This plan may involve an arrangement with an external, professional outplacement firm. In many cases, we have helped employees find challenging positions with our clients, perhaps to continue with a case or related project. We maintain an active "ADL Alumni" network.

Does your firm provide for on-site day care? If not, do you provide compensation for day care? Is flextime possible?

Although Arthur D. Little does not have an on-site day care facility, it does provide its employees with resources to select and help pay for day care services. Arthur D. Little provides a referral service that acts as a guide to day care professionals in the area. We also offer a pretax dependent care spending account. This account allows employees to set aside money on a pretax basis in order to defray the costs of day care. As appropriate, flextime arrangements can be made for staff who request it. Our focus is on the quality of work that is produced, not the time of day in which it is produced.

A.T. Kearney, Inc.

222 West Adams Street
Chicago, IL 60606
(312) 223-6030
Web site: www.atkearney.com

MBA Recruiting Contact(s):
Campus Recruiting
222 W. Adams Street
Chicago, IL 60606
(312) 223-6030
E-mail: campusrecruiting@atkearney.com

Locations of Offices:
60 offices in 30 countries

Total Number of Professionals (U.S. and worldwide):
About 2,200; employees, about 3,600

Company Description

Describe your firm by type of consulting work performed and by types of clients served. What changes are planned in the next few years in terms of services, clients, or locations of offices?

A.T. Kearney, Inc., the management consulting subsidiary of EDS, is a global management consulting firm with worldwide headquarters in Chicago. A.T. Kearney has about 3,600 consulting and administrative employees in 30 countries throughout the Americas, Europe, and Asia and continues its global expansion. Potential future sites include Chile, India, South Africa, and Turkey.

As one of a small number of global, multidisciplined, high-value-added general management consulting firms, we offer clients a unique continuum of management consulting services. From strategic insights to organization and operations, culminating in implementation with information technology expertise, we have solid experience and expertise in all major industries and practice areas. In concert with EDS, a leader in the global information industry, we have intensified our ability to link business solutions with the sophisticated use of information services and technology.

Our consulting skills encompass:

- Benchmarking and Best Practices Analysis
- Business and Marketing Strategy
- Business Transformation/Business Process Redesign
- Economics
- Environment, Health, and Safety
- Executive Search
- Global Business Policy
- Logistics
- Manufacturing
- Marketing and Sales
- Restructuring and Privatization
- Strategic Information Technology
- Strategic Sourcing
- Supply Chain Management

Although we work in virtually every industry, we have special depth and expertise in the following sectors:

- Aerospace and Defense
- Automotive
- Chemicals
- Communications and Electronics
- Consumer Products
- Financial Institutions
- Health Care and Pharmaceuticals
- Oil and Gas
- Public Sector
- Retail
- Transportation
- Utilities

Who are your competitors, and how does your approach to consulting differ from theirs?

More than 80% of our engagements in 1996 were for clients we have previously served. A.T. Kearney competes with other large general management consulting firms, with consulting groups within the large accounting firms, and with specialized consulting firms that offer services in one of our practice areas.

We work closely with the client, integrating members of the client's staff into the project team. As a result, we seek individuals who can communicate effectively with all levels of a client organization, from the CEO to the supervisory level.

Another characteristic that distinguishes A.T. Kearney's approach is our strong emphasis on helping our clients gain the most powerful contributions from every part of their business. We focus on outcomes—what a client gains by working with A.T. Kearney. Clients know us, trust us, and love working with us because we are achieving, resourceful, and perceptive people.

Consultant's Job Description

Describe the career path and corresponding responsibilities for an MBA at your firm.

The A.T. Kearney organization basically has four levels: Associate, Manager, Principal, and Vice President. Associates participate in all the activities of an engagement, including data gathering, developing conclusions and recommendations, working with clients, preparing reports, and making client presentations. Normally a new Associate works on one assignment at a time. A typical engagement involves a team of three to five people, including a project manager, and may last three to four months. All members of a project team receive performance evaluations at the end of an engagement. Managers perform consulting tasks and may be responsible for directing the activities of client engagements. Principals consult, manage projects, and are responsible for business development. Vice Presidents perform all of these tasks and are responsible for the overall quality of consulting work performed on an assignment and for maintaining ongoing relationships with clients.

All new employees are assigned to the general practice or to an industry functional practice. Promotions are made on the basis of performance on client engagements, relationships with client personnel, and business development. We have formal procedures to evaluate performance, discuss personal development, and act on promotions regularly.

Discuss the lifestyle aspects of a career with your firm; i.e., average hours per week, amount of travel, flexibility to change offices.

The decision to enter management consulting is a lifestyle as well as a professional career decision. The amount of travel required will vary depending on assignment and the consultant's office location. Significant travel and extended work hours are part of a consultant's career, but so are the challenges of working with colleagues and clients of varied backgrounds and interests and the rewards of personal and professional growth.

What is your firm's turnover rate for professionals? What careers do your ex-consultants typically pursue after leaving?

Our turnover is, on average, about 13%—below that of other general management consulting firms. Consultants

who leave A.T. Kearney pursue a variety of different jobs, including industry and entrepreneurial endeavors.

The Recruiting Process

Describe your recruiting process and the criteria by which you select candidates.

A.T. Kearney maintains an ongoing recruiting effort to expand and upgrade its staff continually. We seek individuals with significant industry experience (minimum of three years full-time). Prior consulting experience is not required but is an asset to candidates.

In general, the ideal A.T. Kearney candidate has an excellent educational background and meaningful work experience, along with maturity, flexibility, and outstanding communication skills. Our compensation levels and promotion potential are competitive with those of other firms.

From which schools do you actively recruit? Do you consider applicants from other schools?

We actively recruit at the leading business schools around the world.

How many full-time consultants do you expect to hire in the coming year?

The firm's growth in prior years has created a strong demand for talented candidates for associate positions. We have not set a specific target for the coming recruiting year. We extend offers to all candidates who meet our criteria.

Human Resources Practices

Describe your firm's performance appraisal system for consultants. Are there explicit criteria against which an MBA is evaluated before being promoted? How many times a year is there a performance appraisal and hence an opportunity for promotion? Is there an upward evaluation process too?

All consultants are evaluated for performance at approximately six months of employment with the firm and again at one year. Thereafter, consultants are evaluated at the end of each year in a systematic process. Consultants are evaluated after every client engagement as part of our client quality program. Promotion opportunities occur several times throughout the year, based on performance in several areas.

Please describe any initial training programs or ongoing professional development programs for young professionals.

A.T. Kearney provides several professional development programs for its employees. These include new consultant orientation, report writing, proposal writing, presentation skills, business development, and the consulting process training courses.

Does your firm provide for on-site day care? If not, do you provide compensation for day care? Is flextime possible?

A.T. Kearney does not provide for on-site day care, nor does it provide compensation for day care, or flextime.

Bain & Company, Inc.

Two Copley Place
Boston, MA 02116
(617) 572-2000
Web site: www.bain.com

MBA Recruiting Contact(s):
Courtney Kirkland, MBA Recruiting Coordinator

Locations of Offices:
Atlanta, Beijing, Boston, Brussels, Chicago, Dallas, Hong Kong, London, Los Angeles, Madrid, Mexico City, Milan, Moscow, Munich, Paris, Rome, San Francisco, São Paulo, Seoul, Singapore, Stockholm, Sydney, Tokyo, Toronto, Zurich

Total Number of Professionals (U.S. and worldwide):
2,200 worldwide

Company Description

Describe your firm by type of consulting work performed and by types of clients served. What changes are planned in the next few years in terms of services, clients, or locations of offices?

Through its client-Bain team approach, Bain & Company provides innovative strategy consulting and implementation services to help clients achieve significant and measurable results in their financial performance.

Our international client base consists mainly of multi-business, multinational corporations representing virtually all economic sectors: manufacturing, wholesaling, retailing, transportation, financial services, healthcare and services among others.

Describe your organizational structure. Is the firm geographically structured or based around practices? If you have practices, please list them.

Bain is organized as one firm worldwide and looks to hire people to meet the needs of individual offices, not practice areas. However, to maximize its value to clients, individuals may have areas of specialization that address industry sectors and areas of functional expertise.

Who are your competitors, and how does your approach to consulting differ from theirs?

- Competitors for new business: A few major strategy consulting firms

- Competitors for recruits: Primarily other major strategy consulting firms and investment banks

Since its founding, Bain & Company has followed two distinguishing principles. First is an emphasis on measurable results. While many strategy consulting firms talk about adding value, Bain's entire approach is based on it.

Second, Bain establishes a process that strengthens the client's organization. To be effective, this process should not only build consensus and commitment for immediate actions but should also enhance the client's ability to cope with future challenges. By strengthening the organization, Bain builds lasting improvement into the client's performance.

Summarize your growth in terms of revenues (both domestic and international) and professional staff over the past year; over the past five years.

Bain & Company, Inc. was founded in 1973. From the original nucleus of a handful of professionals, the company has grown to a firm of 2,200 people, including a consulting staff of 1,650. The firm has served over 1,500 clients in 90 countries in North and South America, Western Europe, Eastern Europe and the CIS, Africa, the Middle East, and the Pacific.

Approximately how many professionals do you have at each level, i.e., how wide is your pyramid?

There are over 180 officers at Bain, with the balance of the 1,650 total professional staff consisting of associate consultants, consultants, and managers.

Consultant's Job Description

Describe the career path and corresponding responsibilities for an MBA at your firm.

MBA graduates enter as consultants. Typically, the career track progresses to case team manager and finally to vice president, with client management and business development responsibility. Recently named Bain vice presidents are opening regional offices, leading breakthrough business activities in Eastern Europe and the CIS, and developing leading-edge practice areas for the firm. The levels of responsibility are as follows:

- Associate consultants: Do research analysis and client implementation in support of consulting staff.

- Consultants: Execute analysis and become intimately involved in the formulation and implementation of recommendations to improve a client's performance.

- Managers: Plan and manage individual client projects.

- Vice presidents: Manage the firm and client relationships.

As an MBA advances through the firm, how much is he or she required to specialize by level?

During their early years, our people act as generalists. Over time, there exists an opportunity to develop expertise in key practice areas such as competitive strategy, change management, customer retention, logistics/distribution, information technology, manufacturing, marketing, mergers and acquisitions, vendor/supplier relationships, and key industry sectors such as industrial products, consumer goods, retailing, health care, e-commerce, financial services, LBO, technology, and transportation/distribution.

How big is a typical case team? How many cases does a consultant work on simultaneously?

Case teams typically have five to seven members. Each consultant works on two case teams simultaneously.

Discuss the lifestyle aspects of a career with your firm; i.e., average hours per week, amount of travel, flexibility to change offices.

On average, consultants work 60 hours per week. Consultants typically travel two nights per week away from home. We do not move case teams to the client's location for extended periods of time. Every effort is made to accommodate an employee's case assignment preference.

What is your firm's turnover rate for professionals? What careers do your ex-consultants pursue after leaving?

Turnover is consistent with the industry average. People who leave Bain & Company assume impressive positions, including top management positions in companies ranging from small start-up businesses to major corporations. In fact, 40% of consultants who leave Bain go on to pursue entrepreneurial opportunities in private equity or start-ups.

The Recruiting Process

Describe your recruiting process and the criteria by which you select candidates.

An initial interview is conducted with one or two managers/vice presidents. Five to seven interviews normally take place before an offer is made. Candidates can expect a mix of case and non-case interviews.

From which schools do you actively recruit? Do you consider applicants from other schools?

Bain & Company hires the top graduates from leading business schools around the world.

How many full-time consultants do you expect to hire in the coming year?

Our hiring is determined by business need and by the number of exceptional candidates we see.

How many summer interns do you expect to hire? If you have a formal summer program, please describe it. Please be sure to indicate whether the program is in place for all offices or just some.

Over one hundred students worldwide were hired for the 1997 summer program. The program simulates the initial consulting experience. Summer associates are staffed on client teams and become an integral part of the team. All offices recruit for summer associates.

Human Resources Practices

Describe your firm's performance appraisal system for consultants. Are there explicit criteria against which an MBA is evaluated before being promoted? How many times a year is there a performance appraisal and hence an opportunity for promotion? Is there an upward evaluation process too?

Consultants receive semiannual formal performance reviews in addition to ongoing feedback and coaching. Promotion criteria are based on analytical capability, client and team skills, results from upward feedback, and contribution to developing the firm's assets.

What benefits does your company provide for maternity, paternity, or adoption leave?

Bain has a generous paid leave policy for maternity and adoption leaves. The company also has paid paternity leave.

Please describe any initial training programs or ongoing professional development programs for young professionals.

Bain has created a learning environment that manages each employee's professional development. This is accomplished through formal training programs and reinforced through coaching, peer interaction, and individual initiative. Initial training programs acquaint individuals with strategy consulting concepts, build analytical capability, and impart Bain & Company's values. Following the development of basic skills, our training focus shifts to creating client value, managing team performance, and achieving high-impact client relationships.

Describe your firm's outplacement services.

Bain provides customized internal and external support to assist employees looking for future employment outside the firm.

Does your firm provide for on-site day care? If not, do you provide compensation for day care? Is flextime possible?

Bain has an established Dependent Care Assistance Program that enables employees to pay for child care expenses with pretax dollars. In addition, we are participants in a child care referral service that provides guidance and assistance to Bain parents.

To accommodate employees who have family responsibilities, Bain offers part-time employment options.

Booz•Allen & Hamilton

101 Park Avenue
New York, NY 10178
Web site: www.bah.com

MBA Recruiting Contact(s):
Kristina Herbert, HBS Recruiting Manager
Booz•Allen & Hamilton
22 Battery March Street
2nd Floor
Boston, MA 02109

Locations of Offices:
Worldwide Commercial Business: Abu Dhabi, Amsterdam, Beirut, Bogota, Bueños Aires, Caracas, Chicago, Cleveland, Dallas, Düsseldorf, Frankfurt, Houston, Lima, London, Los Angeles, Madrid, Melbourne, Mexico City, Milan, Munich, New York, Paris, Rome, San Francisco, Sãn Paulo, Santiago, Seoul, Sydney, Tokyo, Vienna, Warsaw, Zurich

Total Number of Professionals (U.S. and worldwide):
Commercial Business: over 1,500
Government Business: over 5,000

Company Description

Describe your firm by type of consulting work performed and by types of clients served. What changes are planned in the next few years in terms of services, clients, or locations of offices?

Founded in 1914, Booz•Allen & Hamilton pioneered the business of management consulting. Today, Booz•Allen has grown to 7,000 professionals in offices around the world. Consultants are split between two separate businesses, a commercial business focused on helping top management of leading corporations, and a government business focused on helping the government and other public-sector clients. Booz•Allen generally recruits MBA candidates for its commercial business, which is the focus of this profile.

Booz•Allen's client base consists primarily of companies seeking a new strategy to dramatically increase their economic value. The firm works with CEOs and business unit general managers to help develop the strategy, and then help the client refocus on pursuing that strategy (strategy-based transformation). Booz•Allen's services are performed for leading Fortune 500 companies, as well as selected smaller companies that are undergoing major discontinuous change within their company or industry. The client programs are generally in areas in which answers are not well understood, or where the complexity and scale is substantial.

Across numerous industries, Booz•Allen seamlessly blends diverse perspectives, capabilities, and expertise to deliver results with speed, precision, and certainty in strategically important areas. In order to successfully achieve the type of discontinuous change required, Booz•Allen aggressively partners with its clients. Clients with multiple consulting experiences report that Booz•Allen differentiates itself by truly working with the client, helping them learn the latest business techniques and methodologies, while solving their most challenging problems.

Booz•Allen prides itself on the quality of its work and its people. The culture is one of a diverse community from client, people, and office perspectives. One uniting factor, however, is a passion for ideas and a commitment to results.

Consultant's Job Description

Describe the career path and corresponding responsibilities for an MBA at your firm.

Booz•Allen trains its consultants to lead companies through discontinuous change and become general managers. Consultants must work with both Booz•Allen teams and senior client managers at VP levels and above. The skill mix is analytical, with the ability to drive client teams, and work with senior clients to generate impact. When a consultant first joins the firm, Booz•Allen tries to ensure a variety of client experiences to help the consultant develop as a true professional. As a consultant gains seniority, he or she develops more specific expertise.

The development of expertise in one or more areas is a natural outcome of a consulting career. This expertise is of two dimensions: industry and function. A professional's specialization will depend on his/her interest in a particular business area, and can change over time. Booz•Allen's industry groups are as follows: Communications, Media and Technology; Consumer and Engineered Products; Energy, Chemical and Pharmaceuticals; and Financial and Health Services. Its functional areas include: Strategy; Organization and Strategic Leadership; Operations; and Information Technology.

The post-MBA career path follows a progression from associate to senior associate to principal to partner. Associates are generally responsible for both a discrete piece of work and working with a client team. As staff become more senior, they take on increasing responsibility for overall leadership on an assignment, managing client relationships, managing Booz•Allen teams, and selling work. Associates and senior associates generally work on only one client assignment at a time, while principals and partners spend time on more than one client assignment.

Discuss the lifestyle aspects of a career with your firm; i.e., average hours per week, amount of travel, flexibility to change offices.

The amount of time spent working and traveling varies greatly, depending on assignments and office location. For client assignments that require travel to the client site, consultants may travel 3–4 days per week. Booz•Allen discourages weekend work and tries to schedule client meetings on days other than Monday and Friday in order to avoid travel during the weekend. The work schedules and lifestyles are very free-form, with no "standard." They depend on the client problem and schedule.

Booz•Allen is managed as one firm, and some consultants spend time at multiple offices during their tenure with the firm.

The Recruiting Process

Describe your recruiting process and the criteria by which you select candidates.

Booz•Allen recruits for intellectual and personality traits, rather than technical skills or specific industry/functional experience. Core selection criteria are the candidates' analytical intelligence (for framing/resolving clients' problems), leadership (for convincing clients to act on those solutions), and record of accomplishment.

How many summer interns do you expect to hire? If you have a formal summer program, please describe it. Please be sure to indicate whether the program is in place for all offices or just some.

The summer program consists of a four-day orientation/ training session, followed by immersion in client work. The client assignment offers opportunities to experience client work, interact with partners and team members, develop mentorship relationships, and begin a dialog on students' interests and aspirations and Booz•Allen's longer-term needs.

Booz•Allen summer associates are treated as full-fledged members of the consulting team and are expected to participate on an assignment in a similar manner to new as-

sociates. Summer associates are generally responsible for data gathering and analysis, developing recommendations, and client team management.

Booz•Allen holds a number of activities throughout the summer designed to expose summer associates to a broad range of Booz•Allen professionals. The summer associate class usually numbers around 150–250, and opportunities exist in Booz•Allen offices worldwide.

Human Resources Practices

Describe your firm's performance appraisal system for consultants. Are there explicit criteria against which an MBA is evaluated before being promoted? How many times a year is there a performance appraisal and hence an opportunity for promotion? Is there an upward evaluation process too?

Booz•Allen places a great deal of emphasis on professional development, and differentiates itself through its 360° appraisal system. A principal or partner, with whom the appraisee has never worked, is assigned to perform a composite appraisal. The appraiser interviews a range of partners and both junior and senior staff with whom the appraisee has worked, using formal performance criteria to measure performance against Booz•Allen standards. The appraisal focuses on building a development plan, as well as on evaluating past performance. The appraiser represents the appraisee at a formal appraisal committee meeting, at which a development plan, including promotion, if applicable, is determined. The development plan is subsequently discussed with the appraisee by both the appraiser and the appraisee's mentors.

Consultants have a six-month appraisal check when they first join the firm. Thereafter, appraisals are usually held on an annual cycle. In some circumstances, however, consultants are evaluated semiannually, usually for early promotion. In addition, consultants receive feedback on their performance at the end of each assignment.

Please describe any initial training programs or ongoing professional development programs for young professionals.

Consultants are trained in both craft skills (writing, making presentations, etc.) and the firm's basic approach to problem-solving. The formal training begins in New Hire Orientation (or Summer Hire Orientation) and continues thereafter at all levels, with an increasing focus on leadership and management. The training comes in two forms—firmwide courses and office-level seminars/colloquia.

Training is also available on-line, through Booz•Allen's proprietary, award-winning intranet, Knowledge-On-Line. Consultants may search for training modules in a broad array of areas and analytical techniques. Intellectual capital on service offerings and client work is also available on-line.

In addition, a number of programs build a strong supportive community within the firm. For example, new associates are paired with both junior mentors, normally at the senior-associate level, and senior mentors, normally at the principal/partner level. Mentors provide guidance and support throughout a consultant's career.

If you are excited by Booz•Allen's approach to consulting, and believe that you have the qualities that would make you successful at the firm, we would like to get to know you better. Booz•Allen maintains a relationship-based approach to recruiting; we encourage you to contact our staff to discuss your career objectives and learn more about our firm.

The Boston Consulting Group, Inc.

Exchange Place, 31st Floor
Boston, MA 02109
(617) 973-1006
Fax: (617) 973-1339

MBA Recruiting Contact(s):
Chantel Lindsay, Recruiting Coordinator

Locations of Offices:
44 worldwide offices: Amsterdam, Atlanta, Auckland, Bangkok, Berlin, Boston, Brussels, Budapest, Bueños Aires, Chicago, Copenhagen, Dallas, Düsseldorf, Frankfurt, Hamburg, Helsinki, Hong Kong, Jakarta, Kuala Lumpur, Lisbon, London, Los Angeles, Madrid, Melbourne, Mexico City, Milan, Monterrey, Moscow, Mumbai, Munich, New York, Oslo, Paris, San Francisco, São Paulo, Seoul, Shanghai, Singapore, Stockholm, Stuttgart, Sydney, Tokyo, Toronto, Vienna, Warsaw, Washington, DC, Zurich

Total Number of Professionals (U.S. and worldwide):
Over 2,100

Company Description

Describe your firm by type of consulting work performed and by types of clients served. What changes are planned in the next few years in terms of services, clients, or locations of offices?

The Boston Consulting Group's global reputation in top management consulting derives from more than 30 years' experience helping senior managers discover and achieve their companies' full potential. Our mission is to help our clients attain uncommon success by capitalizing on key opportunities for growth and improvement. We work closely with each client to help set direction, gain organizational buy-in, and realize the full potential of change. For many top managers, we have become their "consultant of choice" on matters of direction and performance, helping address their most significant strategic, managerial, organizational, and operational challenges.

Founded in 1963, The Boston Consulting Group now has more than 1,900 consultants based in 47 offices worldwide. BCG's clients are the world's business leaders.

From automotive to retailing, our professional expertise spans over 50 industries, including consumer and industrial, financial and nonfinancial (including utilities). The vast majority of our clients rank among the 500 largest companies in each of our three major locations—North America, Europe, and Asia. In addition, we work with a number of public and private medium-sized companies and smaller, growing firms.

The success of our assignments has typically led our clients to maintain long-term relationships with us. Over 90% of our top 50 clients continue to work with us from one year to the next, to maintain the momentum for change, and to increase further the bottom line results they have achieved with our help.

We pride ourselves on our fresh thinking. Our evolving ideas have profoundly changed the way most businesses think about competition. Many leading business concepts over the past three decades came from BCG—most recently, time-based competition, Segment-of-One® marketing, and capability-driven competitive strategies. We believe that no other consulting organization has concentrated as thoroughly on understanding business competition and helped companies make the changes needed to succeed in increasingly competitive markets.

Consultant's Job Description

Describe the career path and corresponding responsibilities for an MBA at your firm.

BCG is staffed by professionals who combine industry experience with acute strategic and analytical skills. Most assignments involve one or more teams of three to six BCG professionals, including one or two officers, a project manager, and several consultants, working with a similar group of client staff. The BCG team typically combines consultants with relevant technical and industry backgrounds with others who have functional and strategic skills. The team incorporates a mix of seniority and skills to balance the capabilities needed for the project with an acceptable budget. We create value by customizing our skills and approach to the client's capabilities and the issues at hand.

We believe consulting is a process, not a product. Our goal is to guide, develop, facilitate, and enrich the client's strategy development process. Our consulting process depends on close teamwork between the client's organization and our staff. Clients often remark that a valuable and unusual aspect of working with BCG is the firm's commitment to joint discovery of insights and strategies and to building the experience base and skills of its client's organization. The team interaction centers on intensive analysis of objective data and open discussion of logic and conclusions. This collaborative work is complemented by objective research into the competitive environment, for example, competitor analysis and capability benchmarking.

Our team works with clients from all levels of the organization, in order to integrate our staff's strategy, operational, and industry experience with the client's knowledge of its particular situation, culture, and constraints. To ensure follow-through by a client, we have found it vital to closely link BCG's senior managers to the highest level of the client's organization responsible for acting on the outcomes of our involvement.

Individual assignments can last anywhere from two to twelve months or more, depending on the complexity of the challenges and the client's needs. We usually break each project into modular phases, so that our clients can start seeing some results well before the engagement's end. Typically, assignments proceed through three stages over a period of several months: (1) identifying and analyzing opportunities for change and laying out different options for senior management to consider; (2) fleshing out the best options to create detailed action plans; and (3) assisting in the execution of the plan. We believe in working with a client until results are assured.

The Recruiting Process

Describe your recruiting process and the criteria by which you select candidates.

We seek people with first-rate minds, an ability to lead and persuade, and drive and energy. In selecting people to join the firm, we carry out an intensive interviewing process.

Compensation for consultants entering the firm is extremely attractive and grows rapidly with strong performance.

How many summer interns do you expect to hire? If you have a formal summer program, please describe it. Please be sure to indicate whether the program is in place for all offices or just some.

The summer program is one of our most important recruiting activities. In each recent summer, we have employed 80 to 100 MBA candidates worldwide, many of whom have returned to full-time positions with us after graduation. The aim of the program is to give the summer consultants an opportunity to know our business and our people well. We ask the summer staff to assume responsibilities like those of new permanent consultants and to serve as full members of assignment teams.

Braun Consulting, Business Strategy Group

(formerly Vertex Partners, Inc.)

2 Atlantic Avenue
Boston, MA 02110
(617) 367-7600
Fax: (617) 367-8780
Web site: www.braunconsult.com

MBA Recruiting Contact(s):
Melissa Owens, Recruiting Coordinator

Locations of Offices:
Boston, MA

Total Number of Professionals (U.S. and worldwide):
Braun Consulting: 275
Business Strategy Group: 85

Company Description

Describe your firm by type of consulting work performed and by types of clients served. What changes are planned in the next few years in terms of services, clients, or locations of offices?

Braun Consulting is a leader in delivering strategy and information technology solutions. As business intelligence and data warehousing pioneers, customer relationship management (CRM) experts, and leading-edge business strategists, Braun helps clients navigate emerging electronic business opportunities and drive revenue growth.

Braun Consulting combines expertise in customer-centric strategy and business intelligence with leading information technology and advanced Internet application development skills. Our full services capabilities are represented in eSolutions, an integrated approach to business that leverages the convergence of strategy, knowledge assets, and the Internet to enable electronic commerce, improve customer relationship, and drive revenue growth.

Braun helps clients to identify opportunities and transform their business by leveraging the convergence of:

- Customer-centric strategies that improve relationships with customers;

- Business intelligence capabilities (including CRM and datawarehousing) and analytical applications;

- Internet, intranet, extranet applications; and

- Web integration.

Through our proprietary methodology, we provide eSolutions and leading-edge strategy consulting services to our Fortune 500 and middle-market clients, in order to help them achieve competitive advantage in rapidly changing markets.

The Business Strategy Group of Braun Consulting provides the strategic element to Braun's consulting projects. Past projects of the Business Strategy Group have included corporate strategy and reorganization, sales force optimization, product launch and market entry strategy, design and implementation of internet applications, design and operationalization of customer-focused marketing strategies, and commercialization of breakthrough technologies.

Describe your organizational structure. Is the firm geographically structured or based around practices? If you have practices, list them.

Braun Consulting is organized around four lines of service: Strategy, eSolutions, Business Intelligence, and Web Integration.

Strategy. Braun's Strategy practice is based on our experience with what works in consulting, and focuses on helping clients achieve sustainable, profitable growth by recognizing and realizing value from their customers, knowledge assets, and the Internet. Our approach to consulting strategy can change an organization, enabling it not only to realize short-term strategic potential, but also to gain the capacity to sustain the improvement long after we depart. We also add insights and help mobilize efforts around an existing strategy, increasing speed, adding analytical firepower, providing an objective eye, and enhancing the likelihood of success.

We have incorporated our research and experience into proprietary analytical tools and process management approaches. Our philosophy combines analytical, market-driven strategy development with a unique understanding of organizations and a pragmatism about how to integrate functions, create organizational alignment, and get the job done.

Business Intelligence. Our Business Intelligence services enable clients to use technology to effectively manage knowledge assets to improve growth and profitability.

Our core expertise in Business Intelligence consists of the following services.

Analytical Applications. Our analytical expertise allows our clients to deliver meaningful information to the desktops of business users, enabling them to make improved analyses and insightful decisions concerning

- Market opportunity identifications;

- Customer trends;

- Budgeting and forecasting;

- Product profitability; and

- Financial consolidation.

Customer Relationship Management (CRM). We help clients move closer to their customers by effectively combining data warehousing and analytical applications with innovative marketing approaches. Our CRM expertise enables better assessment of customer value, prospective customer opportunities, and prioritization of customer preferences in new products and services.

Data Warehousing. Data warehouses form the foundation needed to enable disparate sources of data to be leveraged across a business. Effective data warehousing overcomes issues presented by incompatible databases, geographic dispersion, and multiple technology platforms.

eSolutions. eSolutions are integrated new approaches to business that leverage the convergence of strategy, knowledge assets, and the Internet. Braun Consulting helps clients succeed in electronic commerce, improve customer relationships, and grow revenues through our expertise in customer-centric strategies, business intelligence, and advanced information technologies.

Web Integration. Our Web Integration services help clients to effectively manage the interaction between their company and its customers, suppliers, and sales force. Our Web Integration offerings include:

Electronic Commerce and Electronic Business. Our expertise with leading applications helps our customers build and deploy systems that enable online transactions with customers, suppliers, and strategic partners.

Internet, Intranet, and Extranet. We have extensive Web development expertise that spans Internet, large-scale intranets that connect disparate departments and divisions within a company, and extranet systems that allow secured electronic access to proprietary systems.

Sales Force Automation and Call Center. We help clients build and implement systems that enable effective information exchange among geographically dispersed sales executives, which helps our clients effectively capture, store, and utilize volumes of data gathered through large-scale call center applications.

Supply Chain Management. Our expertise in applications provides our clients with leading-edge manufacturing process capabilities that are increasingly tied to CRM and decision-support initiatives.

Core and Extended Enterprise Applications. We bring business expertise and insights to enterprise resource planning (ERP) projects and offer extensive experience in extending the functionality of core applications through our data warehousing, reporting interfaces, and CRM.

Who are your competitors, and how does your approach to consulting differ from theirs?

The Business Strategy Group's competitors fall into two main categories: emerging Web consulting firms that are focused on Internet-based, electronic business and digital business solutions; and other leading strategy and management consulting firms.

While we may address similar strategic challenges for our clients, we are different in the way that we integrate implementation into the strategy consulting process, which enhances our ability to create lasting change for our client organizations. Our philosophy combines rigorous, analytical, market-driven strategy development with a unique understanding of organizations and a pragmatism about how to promote positive change. We work with senior executives to develop strategies targeting the specific competitive and organizational drivers of success. We then build an analytical foundation that, coupled with our expertise in change management, builds understanding and alignment across divisions, countries, and functional areas in an organization.

In addition, we are also distinct in our desire to create an organization that genuinely fosters a desirable quality of life for our employees. We believe the parallel objectives of client and employee satisfaction are not mutually exclusive. In fact, by building a firm that retains its people over the long-term, we have created an experienced and motivated team that enjoys both a positive work environment and a better product for our clients.

Summarize your growth in terms of revenues (both domestic and international) and professional staff over the past year; over the past five years.

Braun Consulting has grown steadily during the past five years, with a 54% compounded annual growth rate in revenues over this period. During this same period, we have added 250 new employees to our firm.

Consultant's Job Description

Describe the career path and corresponding responsibilities for an MBA at your firm.

As a young firm, it is in both the firm's and the consultants' best interest to move individuals along as quickly as their talents will permit. We recognize, however, that different individuals have different strengths. Our challenge is to take advantage of these diverse strengths in the context of client work and of our firm-building. As a result, there is no predefined career path or time frame for advancement within the Business Strategy Group. We want consultants to play a role that best challenges their skills, as long as they continue to contribute and grow.

Consultants are expected to be active team participants from their first day, with a broad set of responsibilities that includes market and financial analysis, strategy development, group leadership and facilitation, case team and client presentation development and delivery, client management, and internal process development.

An interim point in the career path of a consultant is the promotion to senior consultant. Individuals are promoted to the senior consultant position when they have demonstrated proficiency across the broad range of consulting capabilities. In the senior consultant role, individuals begin to develop the management skills that will allow them to transition into the director role.

As an MBA advances through the firm, how much is he or she required to specialize by level?

It is our expectation that consultants will become strong business strategy generalists. For that reason, there is no requirement to specialize at any level. Consultants will typically work on a broad range of projects, from top-level corporate and business-unit strategy, to more tactical projects such as product commercialization and launch, or sales force strategy and management. However, there are opportunities to specialize in areas of interest or expertise as they develop. These may include change management, sales force strategies, data modeling, or more specific industries, like healthcare, financial services, or telecommunications.

How big is a typical case team? How many cases does a consultant work on simultaneously?

A typical case team is headed by a vice president, managed on a day-to-day basis by a director, and staffed with four to six consultants and associate consultants. Consultants typically work on one client team and one internal team dedicated to building our practice. This approach allows for the best client service and the opportunity to manage most effectively a consultant's workload. There are internal teams in areas such as: recruiting, professional development and training, product design, practice development, and marketing.

Discuss the lifestyle aspects of a career with your firm; i.e., average hours per week, amount of travel, flexibility to change offices.

In the Business Strategy Group, we strive to maintain balance—balance between professional and personal lives, between time in the office and trips on the road. The number of hours that an individual works and the number of days that one travels vary depending on the project and its phase. Consulting is a demanding profession, and commitment and a strong work ethic are essential to succeed in our business. However, our experience shows that "camping" at the client site lowers the productivity of the team, carries a tremendous personal cost for the consultants involved, and does not lead to better client results. In the Business Strategy Group, consultants are rarely at the client on Mondays and Fridays and typically spend no more than one or two nights away from home each week.

What is your firm's turnover rate for professionals? What careers do your ex-consultants typically pursue after leaving?

In the Business Strategy Group, we pride ourselves on having created a place where people who enjoy consulting can stay long-term. It is by design that our turnover rate for professionals is lower than industry average. Those who have chosen to leave are currently employed in fields other than management consulting, such as entrepreneurial start-ups, venture capital firms, or small companies.

The Recruiting Process

Describe your recruiting process and the criteria by which you select candidates.

The Business Strategy Group looks for individuals who are capable of becoming integral, contributing members of our team—individuals who not only possess the aptitude and intellectual curiosity to learn and contribute as strategy consultants, but who also desire to contribute to our growing firm.

Consultant candidates should have an MBA degree from a leading graduate school, plus at least two years of consulting, business, or management experience. The Business Strategy Group looks for candidates who possess an ability to learn quickly, a structured approach to problem solving, intellectual curiosity, analytical and quantitative ability, an effective communication style, team skills, and common sense.

All candidates should expect to undergo two or three rounds of interviews and to meet with at least six members of our experienced consulting staff before receiving an offer.

From which schools do you actively recruit? Do you consider applicants from other schools?

The Business Strategy Group recruits on-campus at a select number of top business schools. We do accept applications from students at other schools where we do not participate in the on-campus recruiting process. To meet the demands of our expanding practice, the Business Strategy Group also welcomes applications from candidates working in industry or at other consulting firms throughout the year.

How many full-time consultants do you expect to hire in the coming year?

While the number of new hires will ultimately be based on the number of qualified candidates we interview and the needs of our business, we currently expect to hire between 8 and 12 consultants in the coming year.

How many summer interns do you expect to hire? If you have a formal summer program, please describe it. Please be sure to indicate whether the program is in place for all offices or just some.

We expect to hire 2–3 exceptional students for our summer intern program. The summer intern program is designed to teach consulting basics in a limited time frame and to give interns a realistic preview of what they could expect as a member of the full-time consulting staff in the Business Strategy Group. Summer interns participate on case teams, take part in an abridged version of the Business Strategy Group's Professional Education Program (PREP), and work with a case team mentor. Additionally, a number of social events are planned throughout the summer, which are designed to expose interns to Business Strategy Group professionals, as well as to the city of Boston.

Human Resources Practices

Describe your firm's performance appraisal system for consultants. Are there explicit criteria against which an MBA is evaluated before being promoted? How many times a year is there a performance appraisal and hence an opportunity for promotion? Is there an upward evaluation process too?

The Business Strategy Group employs a comprehensive appraisal process in the evaluation and development of its consultants. Formal performance reviews occur every six months. At each review, the consultant and his or her director discuss the individual's performance in the context of the Business Strategy Group's "Skills Progression Chart" and conclude by developing an action plan for the next six months and discussing the employee's long-term career goals. Two additional formal reviews are held annually—a salary review held on the individual's anniversary date and a bonus review held at year-end.

In addition, consultants also meet with directors for pre-case objective setting, post-case reviews, and performance discussions following major milestones or important events. On-the-job coaching and informal feedback take place on an ongoing basis, as each consultant is assigned a case team mentor.

To be considered for promotion, consultants must meet clearly defined criteria that are laid out in the Business Strategy Group's "Skills Progression Chart." Promotions may occur at any time.

All Business Strategy Group employees participate in a quarterly upward-feedback process, as well. This process gives everyone in the firm the opportunity to provide specific and anonymous feedback and input to the vice presidents and to their directors. This feedback plays a role in management's evaluations and incentives. Firmwide results of the surveys, showing particular strengths or opportunities for improvement, are shared at a firm meeting.

What benefits does your company provide for maternity, paternity, or adoption leave?

Braun Consulting provides 12 weeks for maternity leave. Full benefits extend throughout the entire 12-week period. The portion of the 12 weeks that is paid is determined by length of the consultant's employment. Braun also provides generous paid paternity and adoption leave. Vacation time may be used to extend maternity, paternity, and adoption leave.

Additionally, the Business Strategy Group is extremely flexible in accommodating the lifestyle demands of new parents when they return to work. In the past, consultants have chosen to pursue alternative career paths at Braun or reduced work schedules after returning from maternity leave.

Please describe any initial training programs or on-going professional development programs for young professionals.

Central to the Business Strategy Group's vision is its commitment to continuous learning for all members of the firm. The Business Strategy Group's Professional Education Program (PREP) is a comprehensive training agenda that develops the skills of individuals and ensures that we operate together as a highly effective team.

At the beginning, we offer structured learning covering the skills that will enable new consultants quickly to become effective members of the Business Strategy Group. New consultants participate in formal seminars, rigorous simulations based on actual cases, and a training off-site to develop and enhance core consulting skills. Sessions are interactive and include opportunities to practice new skills in a collegial, nonthreatening environment. Training sessions are conducted by subject-matter experts from inside and outside the firm.

Formal training doesn't stop after the first year with the Business Strategy Group. Experienced members of the consulting staff participate in training sessions to hone the basic consulting skills developed during the initial year. At this point, training becomes increasingly customized and expands to include attendance at professional workshops selected to meet individual developmental goals and the firm's business priorities.

In addition to position-specific training, PREP provides a number of firmwide development forums to maximize cross-firm learning and teamwork. Firmwide training allows us to learn as a company and as such, promotes teamwork and enhances the quality of our client work. Regularly scheduled Idea Exchanges, Brown Bag Lunches, off-site firm development sessions, and periodic training modules disseminate information on exemplary case-team work, business and management topics, and quality of work/life issues. They help to create the atmosphere of continuous learning that distinguishes the Business Strategy Group, and they help the firm maintain its stimulating, supportive environment.

Describe your firm's outplacement services.

We have in the past, and will continue in the future, to offer assistance in any way we can to employees seeking opportunities outside of the firm.

Does your firm provide for on-site day care? If not, do you provide compensation for day care? Is flextime possible?

The Business Strategy Group is committed to creating a work environment that supports a balanced lifestyle for its employees, and is therefore very accommodating in creating flexible work arrangements on an individual basis.

Additionally, Braun participates in a Flexible Spending Program that allows employees to set aside pretax income in a dependent care reimbursement account to cover day care expenses.

The Cambridge Group

30 Rockefeller Plaza, 40th Floor
New York, NY 10112
(212) 218-7250
Fax: (212) 218-7251
Web site: www.thecambridgegroup.com

MBA Recruiting Contact(s):
Howard Shetter
For New York office,
E-mail: recruiting_ny@thecambridgegroup.com
For Chicago office,
E-mail: recruiting_chicago@thecambridgegroup.com

Locations of Offices:
Chicago, IL; New York, NY

Total Number of Professionals (U.S. and worldwide):
50+ and growing

Company Description

Describe your firm by type of consulting work performed and by types of clients served. What changes are planned in the next few years in terms of services, clients, or locations of offices?

The Cambridge Group is a rapidly growing demand strategy consulting firm.

The company was founded on a simple principle—one ought to look at the business through the lens of demand to identify the most rewarding opportunities in the marketplace. Typical consulting projects include identifying critical forces and factors that create current and emerging demand, defining target customer segments and their needs, defining new products and business concepts, making portfolio choices, aligning the organization, assessing and deploying strategic capabilities, developing and extending brands, optimizing positioning strategy, and developing international growth opportunities.

Our work combines fact-based analytics and experienced judgement with proprietary intellectual capital to consistently deliver meaningful and provocative marketplace insights and implications to our clients. We help translate project insights into simplified and prioritized actionable recommendations that gain client buy-in, and then over-see the implementation across the client organization and execution in the marketplace.

Our approach has helped shape the growth agenda and operating decisions of many companies, ranging from start-ups to Fortune 100 incumbents. We consult across a wide range of industries including Apparel, Automotive/Transportation, Food and Beverage, Financial Services, Health and Beauty Care, High-tech, Internet/eCommerce, Media and Entertainment, Pharmaceuticals, Publishing, Restaurants, Retail, and Telecommunications.

Examples of our work include:

- Demand strategies for companies as diverse as Allstate, AT&T, Champion, Hanes, Merrill Lynch, Sears, and United Airlines;

- Internet strategy, target segmentation, positioning and business development across numerous start-up and incumbent brick and mortar clients;

- Strategic and financial value assessments of over 20 acquisition candidates;

- New product annual revenues in excess of $15 billion across clients;

- Five-Year marketing and sales strategy for Disney World;

- Healthy Choice growth strategies for ConAgra;

- Segmentation of the Cough/Cold/Allergy Relief market, identifying opportunities for Johnson & Johnson;

- Ten-year growth plan for Gatorade;

- Turnaround plan for Circle-K; and

- Positionings for brands such as Ford Cars, Healthy Choice, Heinz Ketchup, Pepsi-Cola, etc.

Recently, we have formed a partnership with a money management firm to invest in micro-cap companies. We assist in the screening process and provide consulting services for the companies we invest in. This is particularly exciting since it allows us to shape the future for companies in their nascent years. We are also developing alliances with eCommerce development firms and selected VC/incubator firms in order to provide strategy services to their Internet clients.

Describe your organizational structure. Is the firm geographically structured or based around practices? If you have practices, please list them.

We have offices in Chicago and New York. We are not practice driven, though we encourage "centers of excellence" based on individual skill sets and professional aspirations.

Professionals are typically staffed across industries and across offices.

Who are your competitors, and how does your approach to consulting differ from theirs?

In most instances The Cambridge Group is invited to work with clients on the basis of prior work and/or relationships. On occasion we are asked to compete with other top-tier strategy consulting firms, e.g., McKinsey, BCG, Bain, Booz•Allen.

We differentiate ourselves by focusing singularly on demand strategy and by consistently applying a unique set of proven principles:

- One ought to look at businesses through the lens of demand.

- Strategy driven by the customer is a certain path to growth.

- Businesses have to be both relevant and differentiated to win.

- Successful businesses prioritize market opportunity for higher growth, profitability, and efficiency.

- Understanding and targeting the heavy user, heavy needer is at the core of a successful strategy.

- Businesses have to deliver the brand promise across all facets of customer interactions—not just in their advertising.

- The business system has to be driven by the strategy, not just accommodate it.

- The client has to own and implement the recommendations—not the consultant.

Summarize your growth in terms of revenues (both domestic and international) and professional staff over the past year; over the past five years.

Over the past five years we have had double digit revenue growth.

Approximately how many professionals do you have at each level, i.e. how wide is your pyramid?

The Cambridge Group is biased toward senior hires, in order to provide the maximum value to our clients, given the nature and level of our advice. Therefore, our pyramid is not as wide as some of our competitors who deploy larger teams, especially on reengineering oriented engagements.

Consultant's Job Description

Describe the career path and corresponding responsibilities for an MBA at your firm.

There is no such thing as a typical career path at The Cambridge Group. Consultants advance at their own level and speed. We believe in the "each of us and all of us" principle that allows us to celebrate individual strengths and aspirations.

MBAs usually enter at the consultant level before moving on to become project manager, project director, then partner. Consultants are expected to be adept at structuring problems, identifying issues, gathering and analyzing data, and developing recommendations. Project managers and project directors also have responsibility for managing teams and project schedules.

Impact with clients. Because of the nature of our work, new consultants can very quickly have an impact on clients. Everyone has responsibility for interacting with the client. We all work together with the client in teams—not just the partners. Exposure to the client is immediate.

Impact within the firm. Consultants contribute to the firm's development whether they participate in one (or more) firm initiatives, such as planning social activities, recruiting, training, or intellectual capital creation. The character of our firm is the collection of each individual's own, unique personality.

Supportive, collaborative, internal environment. We learn from one another and succeed as a team. To this end, the entire firm meets quarterly to share new ideas, exchange information, and conduct training. To use a sports analogy, not everyone can, or wants to be, the pitcher, therefore, we take a "team approach" to professional development.

As an MBA advances through the firm, how much is he or she required to specialize by level?

The Cambridge Group does not require consultants to specialize in particular industries or content areas.

How big is a typical case team? How many cases does a consultant work on simultaneously?

Our teams are typically small, consisting of 3–5 professionals. Depending on the nature of a project, consultants can work on one or two cases at a time. New consultants are usually staffed on one assignment.

Discuss the lifestyle aspects of a career with your firm; i.e., average hours per week, amount of travel, flexibility to change offices.

On average, consultants work 50–60 hours per week. Travel varies by project and can run anywhere from 2–3 days per month to 2–3 days per week. We typically do not have teams on-site at the client. We support transfers between offices.

What is your firm's turnover rate for professionals? What careers do your ex-consultants typically pursue after leaving?

Consultants who leave the firm enter a variety of fields, from senior management positions in industry to entrepreneurial ventures. Some consultants who have moved away from our offices have rejoined as freelancers. It is rare for someone to go to another consulting company.

The Recruiting Process

Describe your recruiting process and the criteria by which you select candidates.

The Cambridge Group is looking for proven performers who have significant consulting experience. New consultants are evaluated on their analytical skills, management/leadership potential, communication skills, and their ability to work in teams. We seek out candidates who can demonstrate their achievements, intellectual curiosity, and interpersonal skills. Above all, candidates should have a passion for the work that The Cambridge Group does.

From which schools do you actively recruit? Do you consider applicants from other schools?

In the past, we have recruited from Columbia, Kellogg, and Chicago. We will consider applicants from other schools with an interest in working in either our Chicago or New York offices.

How many full-time consultants do you expect to hire in the coming year?

We expect to hire 4–6 consultants in the coming year. Last year, The Cambridge Group hired 4 full-time MBAs.

How many summer interns do you expect to hire?

The Cambridge Group does not have a summer internship program.

Human Resource Practices

Describe your firm's performance appraisal system for consultants. Are there explicit criteria against which an MBA is evaluated before being promoted? How many times a year is there a performance appraisal and hence an opportunity for promotion? Is there an upward evaluation process too?

Consultants are evaluated against explicit criteria at the conclusion of every project. Longer projects have interim reviews. There is an annual review at year-end as well. We are rolling out an "upward appraisal" process for partners this summer.

What benefits does your company provide for maternity, paternity, or adoption leave?

The Cambridge Group provides a minimum of twelve weeks maternity leave and two weeks paternity leave.

Please describe any initial training programs or ongoing professional development programs for young professionals.

All new consultants participate in an immersion program where they have an opportunity to experience our work firsthand and contribute as members of the consulting team. In addition to immersion, consultants attend quarterly "share & grow" events and training sessions, which are typically led by partners or project directors.

Does your firm provide for on-site day care? If not, do you provide compensation for day care? Is flextime possible?

The Cambridge Group does support flexible working alternatives.

Cambridge Strategic Management Group (CSMG)

One Memorial Drive
Cambridge, MA 02142-1311
(617) 864-0022
Fax: (617) 876-7087
Web site: www.csmgusa.com

MBA Recruiting Contact(s):
Joanna Kamins, Recruitment Coordinator

Locations of Offices:
Cambridge, MA (Headquarters), London, Paris

Total Number of Professionals (U.S. and worldwide):
40 (approx.)

Company Description

Describe your firm by type of consulting work performed and by types of clients served. What changes are planned in the next few years in terms of services, clients, or locations of offices?

The Cambridge Strategic Management Group is an international strategy consulting firm serving clients in the high-technology and telecommunications industries. Our mission, simply put, is to help our clients out-perform their competitors.

The range of our strategy work goes well beyond the recommendations of "what to do." It focuses soundly on "how" the recommendations can be accomplished:

- *Strategy Formation*—Competitive assessment and response, market entry and growth catalysis.

- *Acquisition Evaluation*—International and domestic acquisitions, joint ventures and joint marketing arrangements.

- *Marketing Initiatives*—Service development, competitive positioning and pricing.

- *Technology Assessment*—Product and service oriented assessment of emerging technologies.

We strive to deliver simple, clear, and compelling answers to complex questions facing our clients.

Our clients range from start-ups to Fortune 100 public companies. We interact extensively with all levels of a client's organization to ensure that our work is well-understood, effectively implemented, and useful long after we have left the project.

Describe your organizational structure. Is the firm geographically structured or based around practices? If you have practices, please list them.

The scope of CSMG's practice is global. We, therefore, base our organization, and staff our engagements, largely based on geography. The Cambridge office typically serves clients in North and South America, the London or Paris offices serve clients on the Continent, and all offices serve clients in the Asia-Pacific region. Client service is paramount: it is not uncommon for an engagement team to comprise individuals from more than one office, depending on the needs of the particular client.

Who are your competitors, and how does your approach to consulting differ from theirs?

CSMG typically competes against the other premier strategy consulting firms and has historically enjoyed great success in all competitive situations. While all consulting firms profess a commitment to adding value, CSMG has always delivered it.

As a firm, we have true expertise in the industries with which we work. In every engagement, CSMG begins with a broad and thorough understanding of the high-technology or telecommunications industry in which our clients exist. Our expertise *at the beginning* of a project allows us to absorb and understand immediately the critical issues facing a client as deeply as the client understands them.

Our expertise also allows us to stay on the cutting edge of the industry. We pride ourselves on our ability to anticipate, understand, and create tangible solutions to problems—often before they are recognized. Rigorous qualitative and quantitative analyses support all our solutions, which helps build consensus within an organization. We strive not only to provide answers, but to provide compelling answers.

Summarize your growth in terms of revenues (both domestic and international) and professional staff over the past year; over the past five years.

Over the last few years, our revenues and professional staff have grown at an annual rate in excess of 40%. Given our focus on the world's most dynamic industries, we expect to grow at similar rates into the foreseeable future.

Approximately how many professionals do you have at each level, i.e., how wide is your pyramid?

CSMG prides itself on a flat organizational structure in which all consultants actively participate in the day-to-day work of a client engagement, regardless of level. The actual firm structure is dictated by our growth and our client service needs. We currently have two partners. Principals, associates, and analysts make up the balance of our professional staff.

Consultant's Job Description

Describe the career path and corresponding responsibilities for an MBA at your firm.

An MBA would typically join CSMG as an associate. Associates design and lead major components of client engagements, serve as liaisons to the client, and act as supervisors and mentors to analysts. As business skills and management abilities deepen, an associate is considered for promotion to principal.

Principals oversee project management while having an active role in client relationship management and business development. Principals are also expected to help lead the firm through professional example, involvement in firm initiatives, and development of associates and analysts.

Partners are ultimately responsible for growing and managing CSMG. This includes managing the firm's overall strategic direction while leading business development and building intellectual capital. Partners also maintain close working relationships with all levels of professionals and play a significant role in staff development.

Progress upward within CSMG is determined entirely by an individual's abilities and performance. A successful consultant at any level will consistently enhance delivery of value to our existing clients, contribute to developing new clients, and help make CSMG a more enriching place to work.

As an MBA advances through the firm, how much is he or she required to specialize by level?

Since CSMG consults in the high-technology industry, we expect that all consultants will become knowledgeable in that arena. After that, associates have considerable ownership of their career paths. While some of our consultants are widely recognized experts in particular areas, others are generalists who contribute their broad-based strategy experience and business sense.

How big is a typical case team? How many cases does a consultant work on simultaneously?

The size of a CSMG engagement team is dictated entirely by the needs of the client and may, therefore, vary. While there are no strict conventions defining the number of engagements on which one is assigned, an associate most frequently works on at least two projects.

Discuss the lifestyle aspects of a career with your firm; i.e., average hours per week, amount of travel, flexibility to change offices.

Associates typically work 50–60 hours per week, although this figure varies widely depending on the nature of the client engagements. The amount of travel is also extremely variable, although CSMG consultants, on the average, travel significantly less than their counterparts in other strategy consulting firms—about 1–2 days per week.

At CSMG, our professional responsibility is to render the best consulting services available—and we have ample confirmation that we do. Equally important to us, however, is developing and maintaining an environment in which the brightest and most highly motivated people want to build careers. Our project portfolio represents a diverse array of consistently challenging work—and, of course, we reward results handsomely. CSMG is also a place, however, where top-flight professionals can have fun and feel comfortable with their colleagues. While our consultants are extremely intelligent and motivated, they are also consistently humble and honest.

What is your firm's turnover rate for professionals? What careers do your ex-consultants typically pursue after leaving?

CSMG historically has experienced extremely low turnover. Consultants who leave usually do so to pursue opportunities outside of consulting, often in senior management positions in high-technology or telecommunications firms.

The Recruiting Process

Describe your recruiting process and the criteria by which you select candidates.

MBA candidates must submit cover letters and resumes. After an initial screening, candidates can expect to encounter two to three rounds of interviews. All serious associate candidates will possess a number of basic attributes, including: two or more years of meaningful work experience, well developed communications skills, outstanding quantitative abilities, and computer literacy (i.e., facility with or ability to learn standard software applications, modeling, etc.). Beyond meeting these basic qualifications, successful candidates must exhibit all of the following:

- Creativity, curiosity, and incisiveness

- Leadership and motivation

- Tolerance for ambiguity

- Humility and integrity

- An ability to work effectively in a team-oriented environment

CSMG works primarily with high-technology clients and we therefore favor applicants with some industry or consulting experience. Such experience, however, is not a "gating" factor in our recruiting of associates. Individuals from a wide variety of backgrounds have gone on to become successful CSMG consultants.

From which schools do you actively recruit? Do you consider applicants from other schools?

While we recruit directly from a select group of top graduate business schools and undergraduate institutions, we consider applicants from other programs or from the work force as well. In addition to many MBAs, our professional staff also includes individuals with backgrounds ranging from law to the natural sciences to academia.

How many full-time consultants do you expect to hire in the coming year?

We expect to hire approximately 20 consultants worldwide during 1998. Our growth plans will likely require that we hire at similar rates for the next few years.

How many summer interns do you expect to hire? If you have a formal summer program, please describe it.

Please be sure to indicate whether the program is in place for all offices or just some.

We offer summer internships to one to three exceptionally qualified first-year business students.

Human Resources Practices

Describe your firm's performance appraisal system for consultants. Are there explicit criteria against which an MBA is evaluated before being promoted? How many times a year is there a performance appraisal and hence an opportunity for promotion? Is there an upward evaluation process too?

At CSMG, we place an extremely high emphasis on the development of our professional staff. All CSMG consultants receive structured feedback after each major project. We also have in place an annual review process that covers a number of areas including, but not limited to: performance appraisal/promotions, compensation adjustments, and developmental goals/annual plans. Further, all new professionals are assigned a mentor who is available to provide professional guidance as needed. In addition to these formal programs, all of our professionals have the benefit of both upward and downward day-to-day feedback.

Please describe any initial training programs or ongoing professional development programs for young professionals.

Upon joining the firm, CSMG associates will participate in a training program covering general business skills as well as imparting a strong foundation in the high-technology industry. As we grow, we will continue to invest in ongoing internal and on-the-job training. Our training programs are always evolving to help our professional staff better serve our clients while developing personally and professionally.

What benefits does your company provide for maternity, paternity, or adoption leave? Does your firm provide for on-site day care? If not, do you provide compensation for day care? Is flextime possible?

CSMG firmly believes that consulting can be a richly rewarding long-term career. We offer highly competitive medical and family-oriented benefits. More importantly, we believe that our culture and work style are extremely supportive of a balanced personal and professional life.

CFI Group, Inc.

625 Avis Drive
Ann Arbor, MI 48108
(734) 930-9090
Fax: (734) 930-0911

MBA Recruiting Contact(s):
Jenni Pozar
E-mail: HR@mail.cfigroup.com

Locations of Offices:
Ann Arbor, Atlanta, Bueños Aires, Christchurch, Kuala Lumpur, London, Madrid, Melbourne, Milan, Paris, Porto Alegre, Stockholm, Zurich

Total Number of Professionals (U.S. and worldwide):
170

Company Description

Describe your firm by type of consulting work performed and by type of clients served. What changes are planned in the next few years in terms of services, clients, or locations of offices?

CFI Group assists its clients worldwide to maximize shareholder value by optimizing customer and employee satisfaction. The firm is a pioneer in a methodology that provides its clients with an ability to center all business activities around Customer Asset Management (CAM). The methodology is based on the principle that satisfied customers are economic assets that yield future cash flows and increase the equity of the shareholders. CFI Group helps its clients to establish a monetary measure of the customer asset and to develop action plans and investment strategies for increasing the equity of the customer base.

CAM is a comprehensive system that quantifies the effects of quality improvements on customer satisfaction and economic returns. A version of the same methodology is used in the American Customer Satisfaction Index, for which CFI Group has developed the software. It is also a tool for allocating resources to maximize the equity of the customer base.

CFI Group is an international consulting company structured as a partner-owned holding company. The firm's headquarters are located in Ann Arbor, Michigan, where it houses both consulting staff (typically with MBA or similar educational backgrounds) and the corporate research staff (with doctorates in economics, statistics, operations research, marketing, organizational behavior, and psychology). CFI Group clients are found in over 20 countries. They tend to be large multinational consulting offices, located in Paris, Zurich, Stockholm, Madrid, Melbourne, Porto Alegre (Brazil), Christchurch, Milan, London, Bueños Aires, and Kuala Lumpur (Malaysia). A new office in Atlanta was established in 2000.

On average, CFI Group has grown at a rate of more than 20% in the past several years. It is expected that this growth will continue in the foreseeable future. The basic reason is the increasing reliance that companies are placing on nonfinancial measures, such as customer and employee satisfaction, to supplement traditional accounting data. The core of CFI Group's expertise is its ability (1) to determine the relationship between these nonfinancial measures and economic results and, based on an understanding of this relationship, (2) to develop actions for enhancing shareholder value.

Who are your competitors, and how does your approach to consulting differ from theirs?

We are distinguished from other consulting firms both in focus and approach. We are not a broad-based consulting firm in the traditional sense—all our activities are focused on enhancing the economic value of our clients' customer base and human capital, in order to ensure growth of shareholder value. Our approach is firmly grounded in superior scientific measurement. This means that the CFI Group consultants are involved with issues of the highest order for any business organization and that they always have the backing of the best scientific methodology for their recommendations and action plans.

Consultant's Job Description

Describe the career path and corresponding responsibilities for an MBA at your firm.

The rapidly increasing attention to CFI Group among companies around the world opens up very attractive career opportunities. An MBA with a few years of relevant experience will typically begin as an Associate. There will be immediate client responsibility and work in a team led by a CFI Group program director. The objective at this level is not only to help deliver value added to clients but also to develop as a professional. Substantial effort is devoted to the dissemination of knowledge via mentoring, internal seminars, and actual work experience.

The successful consultant will quickly move into the day-to-day management of one or more accounts.

CFI Group directors and partners are responsible for client acquisition and are accountable for overall engagement results. Program directors and partners are also active in the development of present clients and in the overall strategy of CFI Group.

CFI Group offers a unique opportunity for high-caliber individuals to be involved in shaping tomorrow's business in a new type of consulting firm that blends characteristics of accounting firms, market research firms, stock market analysts, and scientific work with management consulting.

How big is a typical case team? How many cases does a consultant work on simultaneously?

The number of individuals (researchers and consultants) varies from three to more than six, depending on the scope of the work. Initially, a consultant will usually work on one project, expanding to two or three after four to eight months.

Discuss the lifestyle aspects of a career with your firm; i.e., average hours per week, amount of travel, flexibility to change offices.

On average, consultants work 50–60 hours per week. Travel varies greatly across assignments. Because of our international presence, there is always an opportunity to take advantage of international travel. Only on rare occasions do we move client teams for extended periods of time to the location of the client.

The Recruiting Process

Describe your recruiting process and the criteria by which you select candidates.

CFI Group looks for individuals who can succeed in a very demanding and challenging environment. Among our most important criteria in evaluating MBA candidates are

- Superb interpersonal and communication skills;

- Strong academic background;

- High tolerance for change;

- Ability to generate excitement and enthusiasm; and

- Dependability and productivity.

Human Resources Practices

Describe your firm's performance appraisal system for consultants. Are there explicit criteria against which an MBA is evaluated before being promoted? How many times a year is there a performance appraisal and hence an opportunity for promotion?

Compensation and promotion at CFI Group depend on performance. We reward people who make significant contributions in terms of client work and knowledge development. There is a formal performance appraisal on an annual basis.

Please describe any initial training programs or ongoing professional development programs for young professionals.

Since CFI Group is at the forefront in terms of scientific development of analysis and measurement, it is necessary that its consultants have a practical understanding of the implications for client work. CFI Group training programs for new consultants are centered around two major categories: (1) the foundations of the CFI Group system for customer asset management and (2) client applications of the system.

Charles River Associates Incorporated

200 Clarendon Street, T-33
Boston, MA 02116-5092
(617) 425-3000
Fax: (617) 425-3132

MBA Recruiting Contact(s):
Amy Connolly, Recruitment Manager

Locations of Offices:
Boston, MA; Washington, DC; Palo Alto, CA;
Oakland, CA; Los Angeles, CA; Toronto, Canada;
Mexico City, Mexico

Total Number of Professionals (U.S. and worldwide):
224+

Company Description

Describe your firm by type of consulting work performed and by types of clients served.

Charles River Associates (CRA) is a multidisciplinary consulting firm recognized for more than thirty years of experience in the fields of competitive strategy development, diversification analysis, valuation and risk management, legal and regulatory economics, policy impact evaluation, market forecasting, transfer pricing, and technology assessment.

CRA is unique in its ability to bring together highly qualified MBAs and Ph.D.s with specialties in economics, finance, strategy, and technology to address the complex issues faced by companies in today's uncertain global business environment.

The firm is organized into two major consulting groups: Business Consulting, and Litigation and Regulation; however, all staff are part of a common pool of professionals. Our staff help clients make better decisions by providing critical analyses of economic, technological, and management issues. Our professionals include economists, engineers, urban and transportation experts, financial analysts, planners, computer scientists, and senior managers from industry.

The services CRA's Business Consulting Group provides focus on the firm's economics expertise:

- Competitive and game theory

- Finance: valuation, risk management, capital budgeting under uncertainty

- Dynamic pricing strategies

- Competitive market assessments and marketing strategy

- Technology, cost, and competitive assessments and environmental issues

The Business Consulting Group assists high-profile domestic and international clients in a range of industries that includes

- Chemicals and plastics

- Energy

- Environment

- Pharmaceuticals

- Manufacturing

- Natural resources

- Sales management

- Transportation

Two initiatives generate our growth: continued expansion of existing practice areas and addition of new practice areas. In addition to economics, finance, and management professionals, the Business Consulting Group's staff have backgrounds in materials science and engineering, geology, chemical engineering, operations research, transportation, civil engineering, and healthcare. Many have complementary industry experience.

CRA is one of the nation's foremost consulting firms in the area of economic litigation and regulation. The Litigation and Regulation Group provides analysis, support, and testimony involving the use of economics in many legal settings. In addition to traditional antitrust cases, which continue to rely heavily on economic analysis, CRA helps clients with cases involving

- Mergers, acquisitions, and divestitures

- International trade

- Intellectual property rights

- Contractual disputes

- Securities manipulation

- Health Economics

- Telecommunications

- Bankruptcies

- Tax and transfer pricing

The varied skills and experience of our staff members can readily be combined for any project that demands a multidisciplinary approach to problem solving. In addition to our complement of full-time personnel, CRA enlists the consulting services of leading academic authorities and research specialists on the faculties of Harvard, MIT, Stanford, University of California, and others.

Many CRA projects involve the application of advanced quantitative techniques to solve practical problems. However, to be useful, quantitative analysis must be guided by a thorough understanding of the technological and institutional aspects of a problem as well as by the needs of a client. This blend of quantitative sophistication, institutional knowledge, and client orientation is reflected in CRA's work.

Consultant's Job Description

Describe the career path and corresponding responsibilities for an MBA at your firm.

At CRA, MBAs typically enter at the senior associate level. From there, they can progress to principal and then officer. Some brief descriptions of these positions follow.

- **Senior Associate.** Senior-level staff who work on a variety of projects; senior associates also direct projects and undertake business development efforts.

- **Principal.** Senior staff who are responsible for managing large projects in a manner that ensures client satisfaction and meets company profitability objectives; principals maintain a high level of demand for individual services and undertake major business development efforts.

- **Vice President.** Senior staff who manage multiple projects with a high combined dollar value and who generate major business assignments for the firm.

The Recruiting Process

Describe your recruiting process and the criteria by which you select candidates.

CRA seeks highly motivated, articulate individuals with excellent interpersonal skills. We look for individuals with a rigorous academic background, creativity, business insight, and analytical acumen. We offer exceptional opportunities to candidates who

- are attracted to an entrepreneurial environment

- have project management capabilities

- seek a high-visibility position in an interactive client/consultant environment

- are motivated to help us build our practices

CRA recruits from the country's leading business schools and economics departments.

Human Resources Practices

Please describe any initial training programs or ongoing professional development programs for young professionals.

CRA is committed to ensuring a structured internal career development program for our consultants. Our program comprises three general areas—orientation, seminars, and scheduled courses. It is designed to complement on-the-job experience and the independent pursuit of one's own intellectual development. All new staff consultants are introduced to the program through participation in a structured orientation program based on partnership with an assigned mentor.

Through CRA's ongoing seminar program, outside speakers make presentations and conduct discussions with the consultants on various topics. In addition, staff consultants are expected to present papers, discuss significant cases, or outline new analytical techniques or marketing opportunities periodically at in-house seminars. CRA also provides scheduled courses designed to improve an employee's professional skills, such as presentation, marketing, and project management skills. Consultants are also encouraged to pursue their academic interests by authoring articles for economic and other journals.

Cornerstone Research

1000 El Camino Real
Menlo Park, CA 94205
(650) 853-1660
Web site: www.cornerstone.com

MBA Recruiting Contact(s):
Associate Recruiting Director

Locations of Offices:
Cambridge, MA; Menlo Park, CA; New York, NY;
Washington, DC

Company Description

Describe your firm by type of consulting work performed and by types of clients served. What changes are planned in the next few years in terms of services, clients, or locations of offices?

Cornerstone Research is a consulting firm specializing in the analysis of complex financial, economic, accounting, and marketing issues. Cornerstone Research staff and its nationally prominent academic and industry experts provide clients with state-of-the-art analysis that has earned us a reputation for excellence and effectiveness. Attorneys often choose to rely on our work as the foundation for testimony in complex business litigation.

In recent years, Cornerstone Research has grown quickly to become one of the nation's leading finance and economics consulting firms with more than 120 full-time staff members across our four offices and an extensive network of experts. Our culture of growth and collegiality provides a challenging and dynamic work environment.

Cornerstone Research attributes its success to the unique combination of resources we bring to client engagements. We work with faculty and industry experts in a distinctive "partnership" that combines the strengths of the academic and business worlds. The faculty experts come from the nation's leading business schools, economics departments, and law schools and keep us on the forefront of academic research. Industry experts add practical experience and business acumen. Our consultants employ innovative problem-solving approaches, cutting-edge technology and research, and unparalleled analytic depth.

Cornerstone Research has consulted on a wide variety of projects involving numerous industries. Our clients have included over 100 established and start-up Silicon Valley high-tech companies, nearly all major Wall Street investment banking firms, many multinational consumer product companies, and several large telecommunications providers. These companies often have a large percentage of their net worth at stake when they seek our services. As such, our projects receive focused attention from client chief executive officers and boards of directors.

Cornerstone Research has diverse experience across many types of issues, which enables us to provide clients with a unique breadth of perspective and expertise. For instance, securities projects employ analysis of stock prices, options, junks bonds, and other debt instruments. Cornerstone Research has also assessed issues arising from high-profile mergers and acquisitions, insider trading, and share repurchases. In antitrust and intellectual property cases, we have analyzed industry structure, the nature of purchase decisions, and the commercial value of innovation and technology. A more complete list of the types of issues that Cornerstone Research frequently addresses includes:

Securities
Valuation
Intellectual Property
Antitrust
Derivatives
Real Estate
Oil and Gas
Financial Institutions
Auction Strategy/Game Theory

Consultant's Job Description

Describe the career path and corresponding responsibilities for an MBA at your firm.

The professional consulting staff at Cornerstone Research is comprised of analysts (graduates from leading undergraduate programs), associates, managers, and officers. A newly hired MBA enters Cornerstone Research as an associate and participates in a training program designed to introduce the new consultant to the litigation process and the role of the litigation consultant. This training includes learning the software and analytical methods used at Cornerstone Research, case structure and issue analysis, and the firm's core values. Immediately afterward, the new associate is placed on a project team.

Associates are central to casework at Cornerstone Research, and are involved in all phases of a project. Initially, associates actively participate in the formulation of the work plan and the analysis of issues. As work progresses, associates handle the complex aspects of a case directly, while managing and advising analysts. They work with senior staff, experts, and clients to develop case strategy and to determine how best to communicate our findings. An associate's responsibilities include:

- Identifying key economic and financial issues

- Conducting in-depth research and analyzing relevant data

- Creating analytical frameworks, and building economic and financial models

- Presenting complex findings to counsel

- Participating in the preparation of expert reports, declarations, and other work product

In addition, associates have responsibilities extending beyond client work, and have the opportunity to play active roles in the development of our practice areas, as well as shaping and implementing the firm's recruiting, training, and marketing strategies.

Over time, associates work on a variety of cases across numerous industries. This experience allows associates to take on increasing responsibility for client and expert interaction, case strategy conceptualization, and project management. The path to manager is expected to take three years; and consideration for promotion to officer four to five years later.

How big is a typical case team? How many cases does a consultant work on simultaneously?

A typical case team is comprised of two analysts, one associate or manager, and an officer. An associate will generally be assigned to two cases at one time; however, it is quite possible that a large complex case may necessitate full-time commitment. Case assignments vary considerably in length: some may be as short as a month, while others may last as long as a year or more.

Discuss the lifestyle aspects of a career with your firm; i.e., average hours per week, amount of travel, flexibility to change offices.

Cornerstone Research places great emphasis on its consultants enjoying a high quality of life. While client needs occasionally require extra effort from our consultants, associates generally work 55 to 65 hours per week. Travel for casework is limited; however, assignments that ultimately end up in trial will often lead to opportunities for travel.

The Recruiting Process

Describe your recruiting process and the criteria by which you select candidates. From which schools do you actively recruit? Do you consider applicants from other schools?

We seek MBAs and Ph.D.s with an interest in tackling business issues spanning the areas of finance and economics. The ideal candidate should have the ability to apply academic research to real world problems, present concise explanations of complex analyses, and independently manage projects and junior staff. Candidates should have a strong background in finance, accounting, or economics, as well as strong analytical and communication skills.

Our associates have Ph.D.s in economics, finance, and accounting from schools including Stanford, MIT, Princeton, and Northwestern, and MBAs from Wharton, Stanford, NYU, and Duke.

Interested candidates should send a cover letter that includes their location preference and a resume to the Associate Recruiting Director in the Menlo Park Office. The recruiting process begins with a highly selective resume screen and is followed by two to three rounds of interviews with senior-level consultants at the office where the candidate desires to work.

How many full-time consultants do you expect to hire in the coming year?

We expect to hire eight to ten new associates and fifteen to twenty new analysts in the coming year firmwide.

How many summer interns do you expect to hire?

We expect to hire three to four summer associates and four to six summer analysts firmwide.

Human Resources Practices

Describe your firm's performance appraisal system for consultants. Are there explicit criteria against which an MBA is evaluated before being promoted? How many times a year is there a performance appraisal and hence an opportunity for promotion? Is there an upward evaluation process too?

Consultants receive a formal performance review every six months. Associates are reviewed in the following categories: research skills, thought leadership, personal effectiveness and delivery of work product, management skills, faculty/client relationships, experience in litigation process, and presentation skills. Critical to the review process is the completion by each consultant of a six-month development plan that formally indicates his or her future development interests. Promotion decisions are made in January and July of each year. Upward reviews are also an integral part of the semiannual review process.

What benefits does your company provide for maternity, paternity, or adoption leave?

Cornerstone Research provides up to ten weeks paid maternity leave and three days paid paternity leave.

Corporate Directions, Inc.

Hirakawa-cho Kaizaka Bldg.
1-6-8 Hirakawa-cho
Chiyoda-ku, Tokyo 102
Japan
(03) 3221-0211
Fax: (03) 3221-6335
Web site: www.cdi-japan.co.jp

MBA recruiting contact(s):
Yasunori Nakagami, Vice President & Director

Location of Offices:
Tokyo, Japan

Total Number of Professionals (U.S. and worldwide):
40

Company Description

Describe your firm by type of consulting work performed and by types of clients served. What changes are planned in the next few years in terms of services, clients, or locations of offices?

Corporate Directions, Inc. (CDI) works with high-level management of major foreign and domestic companies to plan strategies for success and to assist clients in implementing strategic change. CDI analyzes the competitive positioning and environment and then maps out the optimal strategic direction for the client. Our consultants develop and test assumptions against the realities of the Japanese market. Through this process we recommend workable, unbiased strategic solutions for our clients.

CDI is one of the leading strategic management consulting firms in Japan. Our staff of highly skilled professionals work with over 300 Japanese and foreign clients, in fields ranging from high-technology, manufacturing, and utilities, to finance and service industries. CDI consultants have valuable functional expertise in three key areas.

• Business performance: developing strategies that enhance competitive position and profitability

  – Corporate strategy
  – Market entry strategy
  – Marketing strategy
  – Strategic alliances and acquisitions

  – Information-systems development
  – Operations

• Organizational effectiveness: creating organizations that make the best possible use of resources consistent with strategic objectives and operating realities

  – Organizational streamlining
  – Total quality management
  – Customer service engineering
  – Performance management

• Human resource management: designing ways to achieve long-term competitive advantage through managing and motivating people

  – Human resource strategy
  – Compensation and benefits
  – Employee communication

Who are your competitors, and how does your approach to consulting differ from theirs?

CDI differentiates its consulting services by incorporating Western ideas and practices into the Japanese market. Our approach applies Western business strategy to the Japanese market while accounting for the influence of the Japanese culture and environment.

We further leverage our local knowledge and accumulated consulting skills by drawing on our network of affiliations with other management consulting firms. Our affiliates throughout Asia, North America, and Europe give CDI a global range of consulting resources to draw on. Examples of our coverage include an Asia/Pacific regional strategy for a North American conglomerate, and a global strategy for a Japanese multinational.

Consultant's Job Description

Describe the career path and corresponding responsibilities for an MBA at your firm.

MBA graduates generally enter CDI at the consultant level and are promoted according to their performance. Rather than focus on a functional specialization immediately, consultants are initially encouraged to gain experience in different areas to increase their general skills in gathering and analyzing information, and developing recommendations.

Consultants who demonstrate exceptional performance, leadership qualities, and a high degree of commitment are given increasing responsibilities and promoted to the managing consultant level.

Managing consultants take on more responsibility within project teams and in developing client relationships. Managing consultants are also expected to develop an area of specialization or participate in one of the industry-specific consulting groups.

Principals take overall responsibility for multiple consulting projects, from initial client contact to project follow-up, and take on an increasing role in the management of the firm.

Vice presidents and directors are responsible for managing the firm and leading sales development and project management.

How big is a typical case team? How many cases does a consultant work on simultaneously?

A typical case team consists of four to five consultants and varies according to the scale of the project. CDI consultants divide their time between an average of two cases. All new employees are assigned a mentor from the managing consultant level or higher who will supervise new employees to develop their abilities as consultants and managers.

Discuss the lifestyle aspects of a career with your firm; i.e., average hours per week, amount of travel, flexibility to change offices.

Consultants work long hours and are encouraged to spend time on-site with clients. Hours worked and travel time vary with project schedules, but because the Japanese economy is over-centralized, extended travel is limited.

What is your firm's turnover rate for professionals? What careers do your ex-consultants typically pursue after leaving?

Our turnover rate is comparable to that of other firms in the industry. Former consultants often find management work in private industry.

The Recruiting Process

Describe your recruiting process and the criteria by which you select candidates.

CDI recruits regularly at the top business schools in the United States. We recruit intelligent, creative individuals who demonstrate cultural adaptability, sound analytical and interpersonal skills, and a high degree of self-motivation. Japanese–English bilingual ability is a key requirement before we consider a candidate.

From which schools do you actively recruit? Do you consider applications from other schools?

We recruit primarily from the top ten business schools in the United States, from the top six universities in Japan, and directly from industry.

How many full-time consultants do you expect to hire in the coming year?

CDI expects to continue growing at a steady pace and will hire about three MBA candidates this coming year.

How many summer interns do you expect to hire? If you have a formal summer program, please describe it.

The summer internship program is considered a major recruiting activity and will be offered to two or three students. Through the summer internship, students will gain a full understanding of CDI's corporate culture and approach to management strategy consulting by taking on the responsibilities of a full-time consultant. The program lasts two to three months, depending on the student's schedule, and serves as an ideal opportunity for the summer interns and CDI to mutually evaluate each other.

Please describe any initial training programs or ongoing professional development programs for young professionals.

Newly hired MBAs undergo an intensive training program that covers basic consulting skills, client relations practices, and the firm's philosophy. Employee education is an ongoing process at CDI, and semiannual off-site retreats are held for employee development. The firm also provides financial assistance for the continued educational development of its employees.

CSC Consulting

Strategic Services

5885 Landerbrook Drive, Suite 300
Cleveland, Ohio 44124
(216) 449-3600

MBA Recruiting Contact(s):
Janet Shields, Recruiting Specialist
Heather Gotlesman, Recruiting Specialist-
Business Strategy
200 Clark Avenue
32nd Floor
New York, NY 10166
(212) 251-6230

Location of Offices:
Cleveland, Ohio; New York, NY

Total Number of Professionals (U.S. and worldwide):
400 in Strategic Services
Over 4,000 in the Consulting Group

Company Description

Describe your firm by type of consulting work performed and by types of clients served. What changes are planned in the next few years in terms of services, clients, or locations of offices?

CSC's Strategic Services is a 400+ member management consulting unit of Computer Sciences Corporation (CSC). Headquartered in El Segundo, California, CSC is a multibillion-dollar company recognized as a world leader in the strategic use of information technology to achieve business results. No other company offers the range of professional services at the level of quality we provide in management consulting, information systems consulting and integration, and outsourcing.

CSC works with the world's leading organizations to create and implement innovative solutions to their most complex business problems in the areas of operations, change management, technology, strategy, and corporate culture. CSC uses technology to automate and streamline processes and to leverage information as a way to create new strategies, markets, and customer relationships. CSC helps companies grow by designing and implementing business strategies and change programs that clarify their customer strategies, energize and mobilize the workforce,

and leverage emerging technologies like the Internet to create new business opportunities.

Strategic Services capabilities combine leading expertise from several best-in-class management and e-business consultancies acquired by CSC over the past decade, such as the world-renowned CSC Index organization, the Weston Group, Kalchas Group, DiBianca-Berkman, and Cleveland Consulting Associates (CCA).

Describe your organizational structure. Is the firm geographically structured or based around practices? If you have practices, please list them.

CSC's Strategic Services Practices have been organized to support CSC's three market solution focus areas (e.g., Business Growth, Operational Excellence, and Technology Agility). The following is a brief overview of the practices within Strategic Services.

Business Strategy originated from The Kalchas Group, an international strategy consulting firm that provides senior managers with an effective resource to help them resolve complex strategic issues.

CSC's Business Strategy experts give senior managers a comprehensive understanding of the "external" environment (e.g., market structure, customers' needs and segmentation, competitive landscape) integrated with "internal" analysis (e.g., sources of profit, drivers of costs, customer profitability). Our commitment is to deliver value to our clients by defining strategic solutions that achieve results and then partner with clients to implement targeted solutions.

Growth Strategy helps boardroom-level executives meet the formidable challenge of managing the people, processes, and technology at the core of enhanced shareholder and customer value. In a time when Wall Street rewards profit from growth twice as much as profit from cost-cutting, effective sales, marketing, and customer service strategies can mean the difference between merely surviving and thriving in the competitive landscape.

By defining the target markets, businesses, brands, and customers that represent the best market growth opportunities, CSC's seasoned Growth Strategy experts deliver swift and measurable business results. Proven services include CustomerConnectSM, Technology-Enabled Marketing (TEM), and Growth Strategy.

I/T Strategy experts help clients get their I/S organizations back on track. Working with senior-level business and technology executives across all industries, I/T Strategy delivers pragmatic solutions in four defined areas: I/T

Strategy, Agile I/T Architecture Design, I/S Organization Transformation, and I/T Program Management. We assist clients with achieving the maximum corporate business value by helping them gain the appropriate view of I/T, prioritizing their systems investments, executing their systems well, and using the appropriate technologies.

Supply Chain Solutions helps companies leverage supply chain excellence to improve marketplace performance. We serve clients by increasing efficiency and streamlining/integrating key processes that comprise tangible and virtual supply chains. We work with clients to grow their business by leveraging the supply chain as a vehicle for increasing revenues in a profitable manner. In addition, our methods, tools, and approaches to clients focus on their individual needs, with an emphasis on speed to business results.

Procurement enhancement services provide clients with proven solutions to reduce costs and increase efficiencies throughout their procurement processes. We have worked with Senior Executives from major organizations across the globe in the areas of Value Sourcing, Process Enhancement and Implementation Change Management, Electronic Procurement, and Procurement Process Outsourcing.

Financial Management helps clients greatly enhance their ability to obtain and utilize financial and operational information in a way that creates enterprise-wide value. CSC has worked with senior level executives on a broad range of solutions with particular emphasis in the areas of Financial and Managerial Process Redesign, Cost and Profitability Measurement System Design, Development and Implementation, Activity-Based Costing/Management, Strategic Cost and Profitability Analysis, and Performance Measurement. Working with organizations across a wide industry spectrum to provide swift results, CSC has delivered pragmatic business solutions to clients such as GATX, McDonald's, and Wells Fargo.

Product Information Management (PIM) refers to the control and organization of information related to a manufactured product. This includes data on product definition, product process, information relationships, and workflow. For many companies, computerized PIM solutions, when combined with business process changes and organizational change management, can substantially reduce product time-to-market and non-value-added effort. CSC's experts have worked with many organizations to deploy PIM strategy development, planning, and implementation.

Supply Chain Planning focuses on helping clients effectively plan the process of buying, making, delivering, and forecasting products in the most customer effective way with the least expenditure of resources. CSC provides "end-to-end" supply chain planning consulting, implementation, and systems integration. To better serve our customers, we have formed strategic alliances with two software vendors, i2 Technologies and Manugistics. Both of these software vendors have demonstrated numerous successful implementations and receive high marks from their customers for service and support.

Supply Chain Execution has helped clients improve and enhance their physical distribution process by working with senior executives in the following disciplines: Assessment and Optimization, Information Systems, Material Handling Systems, and Enabling Warehouse Technologies. The proper application of these disciplines can significantly improve quality, accuracy, and productivity of the distribution process.

Alignment & Change, formerly The DiBianca Berkman Group, helps organizations map the true characteristics of their capabilities, marketplace, and competition. We have worked with senior executives across many industries to assist with companywide business process reengineering. CSC experts assess the client's current operating state and are able to make actionable recommendations that achieve breakthroughs and foster relationship building among team members. CSC's methods and approach focus on the client's needs with an emphasis on speed to business results.

Operational Excellence has enabled senior-level executives from organizations across all industries to accelerate and restructure operations initiatives, streamline/consolidate corporate center functions, and transform product-focused companies to services-based operations. We work with clients to adapt their organization to the changes within their environment for optimal results. CSC's Operational Excellence experts have assisted companies in areas such as Information Technology Turnaround, Operations Restructuring and Reengineering, and Operations Productivity Enhancement.

Consumer Industrial Products (CIP)—spanning a channel from industrial manufacturer to consumer packaged goods to wholesale/retail—focuses on the Consulting Group's largest industry. As an industry practice, its primary objective is to identify the leading consumer channel business forces of both today and the future, and to create demand in our channel for all of the Consulting Group. To achieve this, the practice concentrates on building CSC's Consumer channel visibility and reputation. Practice experts suggest and recommend the next generation of industry capabilities and solutions, tailor the strategic offerings of other practices, and selectively provide senior expertise on both opportunity pursuits and significant engagements containing substantial strategic leverage.

Chemical, Oil & Gas focuses predominantly on commodity companies in the oil, gas, and chemical industries. The issues that the companies in these industries face are cyclical markets, asset and company consolidation, globalization, cost reduction, creating customer value, and attracting and retaining people. CSC serves the needs of the market through the following service offerings: Advanced Supply Chain Management, Asset Consolidation Acceleration & Technology Value Realization, Cash Flow Measurement Systems & Valuation of ERP, SG&A Cost Reduction, and the CEO Playbook (Strategy and Mobilization). Clients include companies like DuPont, Occidental Chemical (OxyChem), El Paso Energy Company, Zeneca, Amoco, Elf Atochem, BP/Mobil, and MAPCO.

Utilities focuses on the three dominant issues that electric and gas companies face as the last major North American industry undergoes restructuring: deregulation, new competitive markets, and mergers and acquisitions. Compelling events in this industry include preparing for open competition, maintaining/improving shareholder value, realizing full value from M&A, and meeting financial challenges. Having served the majority of the top utilities, we focus on Strategy, growth, and new ventures, customer care, and distribution operation solutions. Clients include firms such as Duke, Florida Power & Light, Southern California Edison, Cinergy, Commonwealth Edison, and Baltimore Gas & Electric.

Who are your competitors, and how does your approach to consulting differ from theirs?

CSC's Strategic Services competes successfully with operations management units of the world's largest consulting firms. Among the most famous competitors are Andersen Consulting, Coopers & Lybrand, and A.T. Kearney. Our approach is collaborative, flexible, strategy-focused, visionary, and comprehensive. Teamed with seasoned industry professionals, our solutions are tough to beat.

Summarize your growth in terms of revenues (both domestic and international) and professional staff over the past year; over the past five years.

CSC, a company with 50,000 employees worldwide and boasting over $7 billion annual revenues, has continued its rapid growth in the marketplace. Strategic Services continues to grow tremendously, and promises to achieve remarkable growth in the years to come, due in part to

recognition by mainstream business executives as a viable means for competitive strategy, operational excellence/cost management, IT strategy, strategic architecture, supply chain issues, and sales/marketing/customer service techniques.

Consultant's Job Description

Describe the career path and corresponding responsibilities for an MBA at your firm. As an MBA advances through the firm, how much is he or she required to specialize by level?

Fundamental to our goal of excellent service to clients is our policy of hiring, retaining, and promoting the best-qualified people we can find. Translating this policy into action means that we measure performance according to exceptionally high standards of integrity, professional competence, and conduct. We provide generous benefits and compensation for outstanding performance. We treat our staff as mature, responsible, self-managing business professionals. We expect them, in turn, to dedicate themselves to meeting the needs of our clients and to acting in the best interests of the firm.

Because of our smaller size, the career path at Strategic Services is more flexible than at most firms. An individual's contributions to the firm, and thus his or her rewards, are measured both quantitatively and qualitatively. Unlike many professional organizations, we do not base salaries or other professional rewards primarily on the amount of revenue generated by an individual.

Strategic Services provides financial support to staff members for seminars, university course work, professional societies, and conferences. There are an increasing variety of internal programs for skills development and continuous opportunities for on-the-job learning.

Because our firm is already specialized, an individual's decision to join us reflects an interest and background in supply chain management operations or marketing disciplines in consumer oriented industries. Associates and consultants join a pool and can expect to be assigned to a wide variety of projects initially. They can choose to develop as generalists or migrate to or between practice areas over time. In assigning staff to projects, we try to balance the individual's skills and interests with the needs of our clients and of the firm. Staff is expected to utilize the resources and archives of the firm to learn and work on new projects.

Strategic Services officers handle most of the interaction with senior executives in a client organization, while day-to-day management of a consulting project is usually the responsibility of a principal or a senior consultant. Throughout the life of a typical project, principals, consultants, and associates will all work closely with client management.

Early in their careers at Strategic Services, consultants participate in all aspects of assignments for clients, including problem identification, development of an analytical approach, organization of the work effort, motivation of client personnel through project leadership, and communication of study findings and recommendations. Those new to the firm normally work on one assignment at a time. More experienced staff may work on several projects at once and supervise other professionals on selected assignments.

We try to create a working climate in which creativity, individuality, and teamwork flourish. We believe this requires an unregimented but not unstructured environment where working relationships and individual responsibilities are more important than titles and prerequisites. We encourage every member of the firm to create and share innovative ways to solve problems and exploit opportunities. Ours is an idea-intensive business: clients come to us for practical recommendations that we believe are most likely to be generated by people who are encouraged to make their own judgments and articulate them clearly.

Experience has taught that "creativity," "freedom of thought," "individuality," and "client-centered teamwork" are not just pleasant, abstract slogans. They are the foundation of CSC Strategic Services' service to clients, whose satisfaction is essential for our growth and success.

Discuss the lifestyle aspects of a career with your firm; i.e., average hours per week, amount of travel, flexibility to change offices.

At the management consultant level, a 45–60-hour workweek is standard. Travel varies by assignment, and may be anywhere from three to five days a week. As our alignment with CSC continues, we may have more movement to the 14 other cities where CSC maintains offices. As a firm, we have found that many of our top producers work very well out of "virtual" Strategic Services offices in other cities.

What is your turnover rate for professionals.? What careers do your ex-consultants typically pursue after leaving?

Employee turnover at CSC Strategic Services averages 10% per year. With very few exceptions, consultants who leave the firm do so either to go into the business for

themselves, or to move into management positions in industry. A few move to other consulting firms.

The Recruiting Process

Describe your recruiting process and the criteria by which you select candidates.

CSC Strategic Services invites students to forward a letter of interest with a resume to our office. Candidates are selected from those students who contact us as well as through selected on-campus visits by former graduates.

Selected students are invited to our offices for a day of interviews with representatives of each of CSC Strategic Services' consulting levels. Time spent with peer discussions are especially valuable, because it gives candidates a chance to hear a peer discuss 1) what the work really entails, and 2) their impressions of how well their prehiring expectations were met by the actual position.

How many full-time consultants do you expect to hire in the coming year?

CSC Strategic Services expects to hire more than 35 full-time staff within the next 12 months.

How many summer interns do you expect to hire? If you have a formal summer program, please describe it. Please be sure to indicate whether the program is in place for all offices or just some.

CSC Strategic Services expects to hire several summer interns to work in our Strategic Services office. While this is not a formal program, consulting interns are often given challenging assignments that hold much value for the firm and for the personal development of the individual.

Human Resources Practices

Describe your firm's performance appraisal system for consultants. Are there explicit criteria against which an MBA is evaluated before being promoted? How many times a year is there a performance appraisal and hence an opportunity for promotion? Is there an upward evaluation process too?

Consulting staff employees are assigned directly to a partner who acts as their resource manager and mentor. This system is fluid to allow for exposure to a variety of expertise and management styles.

Promotion criteria are outlined on a consulting staff matrix. Promotions are based on the completion of satisfactory project work and project reviews, the annual review, and reputation in the firm and the professional community. Currently, the annual review is completed and promotions are announced at the end of the fiscal year.

What benefits does your company provide for maternity, paternity, or adoption leave?

CSC Strategic Services grants six weeks of paid maternity leave. Eligible employees may be granted a leave of absence for paternity or adoption, as permitted under family and medical leave legislation.

Please describe any initial training programs or ongoing development programs for professionals.

New employees are introduced to CSC Strategic Services with a full-day orientation program and the "New Employee Survival Guide." We also sponsor a semiannual "Day for CSC Strategic Services" to encourage cross-project learning exchanges. Additional programs are available in written and oral communications and functional (industry-oriented) training.

Describe your firm's outplacement services.

CSC Strategic Services' severance program includes a separation package.

Does your firm provide for on-site day care? If not, do you provide compensation for day care? Is flextime possible?

Because CSC Strategic Services is a relatively small business unit, on-site day care, day care compensation, and flextime are not currently available.

CSC Healthcare Payor/ Provider Consulting

1325 Avenue of the Americas, 6th Floor
New York, NY 10019
(212) 401-6000
Web site: www.csc.com/industries/healthcare

MBA Recruiting Contact(s):
Diane Owens, Recruiting Manager

Locations of Offices:
New York, Chicago, and San Francisco

Company Description

Describe your firm by type of consulting work performed and by types of clients served. What changes are planned in the next few years in terms of services, clients, or locations of offices?

Payor/Provider Consulting was founded in 1974 to bring a vision, management expertise, and business discipline to the healthcare industry. The firm grew rapidly because of the success we bring to our partnerships with clients, becoming the largest U.S.–based management consulting firm dedicated to healthcare. In July 1996, Payor/Provider Consulting joined Computer Sciences Corporation (CSC) to expand our ability to help providers, suppliers, and health plans make the industrywide transformation to managing health instead of sickness. In addition to our own leading-edge strategic and operational expertise, Payor/Provider Consulting now has additional capabilities in information systems and outsourcing, including both business process and information technology outsourcing.

Today, Payor/Provider Consulting is a leading force in the full-service powerhouse CSC Healthcare Group, a CSC division that brings together Payor/Provider Consulting's and CSC's extensive healthcare experience with providers and health plans. Our sole commitment to healthcare has led to an industry-wide recognition of our leadership in helping clients set standards for excellence while creatively managing change. That same exclusive commitment allows us to continually invest significant resources in creating new system models—in strategy, operations, managed care and disease management, and information management—which continually push forward what is possible in improving the healthcare delivery system.

Payor/Provider Consulting has achieved our leadership position in a competitive industry by attracting professionals and clients with a common vision to improve healthcare in the communities where they live. More than 190 consultants work from offices in New York (CSC Healthcare Group's headquarters), Chicago, San Francisco, Atlanta, and Toronto. We plan to maintain our rapid growth rate and to continue developing new business solutions to further help our clients set high-performance standards in this changing industry.

Describe your organizational structure. Is the firm geographically structured or based around practices? If you have practices, please list them.

Because of the duration of our involvement with clients, we strive to staff people close to their home offices. The firm itself is structured around the two broad sectors of healthcare—providers and health plans—and the services they need.

Strategic services are developed to meet the needs of each sector and include Managed Care Strategy (contracting, HMO/PPO development, network development and management, network data sharing, provider profiling, and provider-payer integration); Consumer Linkage (internet/ intranet strategies, health information, health promotion, and care management); General Strategy (strategic planning, mergers and acquisitions, integrated delivery network development, new business development, product line management, and organizational development); Physician-Hospital Linkages (managed care management, PHO/MSO formation, primary care development, packaged pricing, integrated delivery system development, group formation, and integrated data systems); and Supplier Strategy (clinical trial management and value networks).

Performance improvement services include practices covering Disease Management and Clinical Resource Management (quality improvement, clinical pathways, LOS management, ancillary utilization, data sharing networks, case management, and outcomes tracking); Operations Restructuring (unit cost reduction, work restructuring/reengineering, patient-focused care, service improvement, organizational restructuring, patient satisfaction); Supply Chain Management; Organizational Development and Business Process Outsourcing.

Information Technology services include Systems Integration (information technology planning and systems implementation support); Application Solutions and IT Outsourcing.

Who are your competitors, and how does your approach to consulting differ from theirs?

While our competitors include the healthcare divisions of the major general management consulting and accounting companies plus the smaller boutique healthcare firms, CSC Healthcare's size and single-industry focus allow us to develop resources and approaches others are unable to match. Our consulting staff has an unusually high mix of professionals who have had significant line operating experience in their careers in addition to those who are highly experienced consultants. We can relate practically and immediately, therefore, to the real-world concerns of healthcare executives and can provide the perspective, strategic analysis, and insight necessary for helping them build sustainable competitive capabilities. In addition, our colleagues in CSC Healthcare bring systems integration, management consulting, systems outsourcing, and business process outsourcing capabilities that give us a broader service offering that is more complete that our competitors'.

Summarize your growth in terms of revenues (both domestic and international) and professional staff over the past year; over the past five years.

Our professional staff of consultants operate from our New York, Chicago, and San Francisco offices. Growth in revenues and staff over the past five years has averaged 16 percent. Due to the exciting opportunities resulting from our CSC relationship, Payor/Provider Consulting is expecting fiscal 2000–2001 to mirror this rapid growth.

Consultant's Job Description

Describe the career path and corresponding responsibilities for an MBA at your firm.

The recently graduated MBA would join the firm as an associate and work closely with Payor/Provider Consulting team members and the client in formulating and executing action plans to achieve desired goals. We develop new associates rapidly by providing a wide range of projects in which they contribute to the management of change directly at the client. Because all client work is performed in teams, Payor/Provider Consulting values information exchange and mutual support, which translates into an intensive learning opportunity for new associates. In the typical team structure, the associate joins senior associates, principals, and directors in a task force with client executives in an intense, focused effort to resolve specific business problems.

Payor/Provider Consulting's approach emphasizes on-the-job learning with direct client contact at every level of the consultant's career path. Formal training programs supplement the process, emphasizing technical and analytical skills early in the consultant's career and managerial and relationship-building skills later. As associates master analytical skills, they are given increasing opportunities for managing client engagements and demonstrating potential for advancement to senior associate. Given our rapid growth rate, advancement to senior associate is achievable after two to four years with the firm.

The potential role of first- and second-year associates can be quite rewarding in a specialized consulting firm like CSC Healthcare. According to recent associates surveyed about their experiences, new associates quickly develop an industry knowledge base that can be leveraged either with the client or in the development of the firm. In addition, associates become "functionally literate" by getting hands-on experience with all levels of running the business of healthcare.

How big is a typical case team? How many cases does a consultant work on simultaneously?

A Payor/Provider Consulting project team for operations assignments usually includes a director, a principal, a senior associate (who is the on-site manager), one to two associates, one to two research associates, and a specialist. The client also has a team, including analysts, that is dedicated to the project. Project teams for strategy assignments are smaller and include a partner, a senior and an associate, with assistance from specialists as needed.

Given CSC Healthcare's "whatever it takes" philosophy, associates are usually assigned to one project and can expect a fairly rigorous work schedule.

Discuss the lifestyle aspects of a career with your firm; i.e., average hours per week, amount of travel, flexibility to change offices.

CSC Healthcare strives to provide a working environment in which our consultants can fully develop as individuals in a personal as well as a professional sense. Associates work more than 55 hours per week, with three to four days at the client site. There is some movement between offices.

The Recruiting Process

Describe your recruiting process and the criteria by which you select candidates.

CSC Healthcare's objective is to work with healthcare leaders, building long-term relationships. As part of this orientation, we recognize the necessity of building a consulting staff of a caliber that can continually provide value to senior managment of successful healthcare organizations. The qualifications we seek in our consulting staff member are problem-solving skills, an ability to build working relationships, a demonstrated pattern of accomplishment, and a strong interest in healthcare.

From which schools do you actively recruit? Do you consider applicants from other schools?

CSC Healthcare actively recruits at Harvard, Kellogg, Stanford, University of Chicago, Wharton, and Yale.

How many full-time consultants do you expect to hire in the coming year?

Our recruiting efforts this year will concentrate on the leading business management programs we have targeted, from which we will seek at least 15 to 20 hires.

How many summer interns do you expect to hire? If you have a formal summer program, please describe it. Please be sure to indicate whether the program is in place for all offices or just some.

We will hire up to 10 outstanding first-year MBAs for our summer associate program. The summer associates from our six targeted schools are divided among our main offices. Our objective is to provide a realistic and meaningful consulting experience to the summer associate. We therefore make every effort to offer the summer associate exposure to both analysis and implementation as a mem-ber of a client team. Summer associates function as an associate on client projects.

Human Resources Practices

Describe your firm's performance appraisal system for consultants. Are there explicit criteria against which an MBA is evaluated before being promoted? How many times a year is there a performance appraisal and hence an opportunity for promotion? Is there an upward evaluation process, too?

Consultants are appraised using the following criteria: work management, client management, team interaction, conceptualization and analysis, and firm development. The consultant is assigned to a partner or senior project manager, who gathers data and develops a comprehensive appraisal encompassing the consultant's client work, internal firm development, and contributions to the advancement of the firm's consulting technology. Promotions occur in July and January. (Upward appraisals have been introduced on a pilot basis.) After the appraisal, the partner/manager is responsible for overseeing the implementation of the consultant's development plan.

Please describe any initial training programs or ongoing professional development programs for young professionals.

New MBAs and undergraduates attend a two-week orientation program to provide a foundation in the following: general consulting skills, industry knowledge, CSC Healthcare technology. The firm has ongoing training in new product areas and analysis, client team skills, and communications skills for all members of the firm.

Dean & Company

8065 Leesburg Pike, Suite 500
Vienna, VA 22182-2738
(703) 506-3900
Fax: (703) 506-3905
Web site: www.dean.com

MBA Recruiting Contact(s):
Recruiting Coordinator

Location of Offices:
Washington, DC

Total Number of Professionals (U.S. and worldwide):
60

Company Description

Describe your firm by type of consulting work performed and by types of clients served. What changes are planned in the next few years in terms of services, clients, or locations of offices?

Dean & Company is a strategy consulting firm that works with large corporations (Fortune 100), equity funds, and technology start-ups. Our clients are senior managers seeking to improve their companies' bottom-line performance and facing complex business challenges to which neither conceptual nor practical solutions are evident. Our fact-based, analytical, and customized approaches combined with a commitment to creating actionable solutions and working with our clients to drive implementation provides our clients with a compelling value proposition for their consulting investment.

Founded in 1993 by several senior partners of Strategic Planning Associates, Dean & Company has experienced rapid expansion in terms of both professionals and revenues. We currently have over 60 professionals and expect approximately 20 new hires in 2001. We are located in the Washington, D.C. area.

Dean & Company provides support to CEO's and senior management of select companies in the following core areas:

- Business development and expansion (including acquisition assistance)

- Shareholder value expansion programs

- Business unit strategy development

- Competitive analysis and positioning (including benchmarking and best practices)

- Market segmentation, customer targeting, pricing, and customer retention

- Growth and new product/service development

- Restructuring and turnarounds

- Business process reengineering/operational enhancements

Dean & Company competes in the top-tier of strategy firms. Methodologically, we distinguish ourselves primarily through our state-of-the-art, fact-based, analytical approach, which focuses on understanding and realigning the fundamental value-added structure of a business. Most often, we seek to improve basic business economics by understanding and developing the key set of performance "drivers" of a business or industry.

Dean & Company's expertise spans a variety of industries:

- Telecommunications

- Financial services

- Utilities

- Equity Funds

- Internet (especially e-commerce)

- Computing and software

- Distribution

- Retailing

Our clients have come to expect nonstandard, well documented, and well socialized solutions to their high-stakes, complex issues. Our fact-based approach utilizes analytically rigorous frameworks that drive the generation of powerful insights. This approach also provides an objective platform for clarity of thinking, which allows us to translate insights into practical, sustainable solutions that enhance bottom-line performance.

Consultant's Job Description

Describe the career path and corresponding responsibilities for an MBA at your firm.

Dean & Company consultants are called on to meet a wide array of challenges faced by our clients. Their careers are guided by the dual objectives of deriving solutions to complex, high-stakes problems and assuring that these solutions are implemented and that bottom-line improvement is achieved. Successful applicants will demonstrate the following qualities:

• Strong analytic and problem-solving skills;

• Communications proficiency;

• Ability to guide fundamental client change in a challenging yet supportive manner;

• Capability to learn rapidly and to structure problem-solving approaches efficiently; and

• Possess the ultimate goal of thinking and acting like a CEO.

During the first year or two, most consultants will work on several types of problems (e.g., product strategy, M&A, cost analysis, turnarounds), in multiple industries, and will have the opportunity to specialize as they move into a managing role. Associates are quickly exposed to senior Dean & Company consultants and key decision makers in the client organization, and are given broad responsibility from the outset.

Associates at Dean & Company work within case teams, both internal and client staffed, and take responsibility for a significant module of the casework. Case team sizes vary according to project, but generally consist of four to six Dean & Company professionals. Associates usually work on one case at a time, though more experienced associates and managers may split time across cases.

Associates typically travel two to three days per week, dependent on client needs. The office culture is non-hierarchical; all consultants are encouraged to play an active role in driving client solutions and work regularly with the senior partners. The office attire is casual, in keeping with the open culture.

Turnover is consistant with industry standards. Those who have departed have leveraged their experience at Dean & Company to attain senior positions in industry or "ground floor" opportunities in emerging companies.

The Recruiting Process

Describe your recruiting process and the criteria by which you select candidates.

The company plans to hire 15 to 20 full-time consultants this year (associates and analysts) and to continue to grow its staff rapidly to meet demand. We recruit MBA candidates from top business schools such as Chicago, Harvard, Sloan, and Wharton. Our process includes resume screening and a series of case interviews on campus, as well as subsequent office visits. We also actively consider candidates from other schools (including those in law and Ph.D. programs), and from industry. Compensation is competitive with other top-tier strategy firms.

How many summer interns do you expect to hire? If you have a formal summer program, please describe it. Please be sure to indicate whether the program is in place for all offices or just some.

We have a summer program for a select number of outstanding business school candidates. Summer associates participate as full case team members, providing an excellent opportunity for experiencing actual casework and Dean & Company's culture.

Human Resources Practices

Describe your firm's performance appraisal system for consultants. Are there explicit criteria against which an MBA is evaluated before being promoted? How many times a year is there a performance appraisal and hence an opportunity for promotion? Is there an upward evaluation process too?

Promotion is based on a "speedometer" vs. an "odometer" philosophy. It is the individual's skills and drive rather than tenure that determine career path. As a result, top performers at Dean & Company will achieve levels of responsibility and compensation more quickly than at most larger consulting firms. Because ultimate movement into management at Dean & Company involves equity participation, all consultants are expected to take responsibility for an aspect of the firm's management.

The performance review system is structured to provide frequent, open feedback. Consultant's case performances are reviewed every three months, according to specific criteria. Career reviews are conducted twice per year, and provide an opportunity to consolidate case experiences into a career message highlighting the individual's strengths and development objectives, with an emphasis on continued career growth. Promotions and salary/bonus adjustments are determined during career reviews.

Additionally, Dean & Company has an upward review process, whereby consulting teams review the case management's performance, identifying management best practices and areas for improvement.

Please describe any initial training programs or ongoing professional development programs for young professionals.

Dean & Company's new hires participate in an initial training and orientation program, as well as ongoing training developed to address individual and firm needs. The emphasis, however, is on senior management involvement, coaching, and feedback on an individual basis, rather than reliance on a structured training schedule.

Deloitte Consulting

John Hancock Tower
200 Clarendon Street
Boston, MA 02116
(617) 850-2000
Fax: (617) 850-2001
Web site: www.dc.com

MBA Recruiting Contact(s):
Tina Ege
(617) 850-2600
E-mail: tege@dttus.com

Locations of Offices:
Global locations

Total Number of Professionals (U.S. and worldwide):
Over 5,000 in the United States
Over 8,000 worldwide

Company Description

Describe your firm by type of consulting work performed and by types of clients served. What changes are planned in the next few years in terms of services, clients, or locations of offices?

Deloitte Consulting is a global management consulting firm, helping organizations define their strategic positions and working with them at all levels to execute their strategies, implement meaningful operational improvements, and transfer our expertise so they gain lasting value from their relationship with Deloitte Consulting. In short, our approach delivers results that our clients can build on because these improvements make their organization more robust and adaptable to future shifts in the global environment.

We have built strong ongoing client relationships with premiere companies around the globe, 75% of which we have served before. In fact, last year we generated worldwide revenues of 2.4 billion, representing a 35% growth over the previous year.

In addition, Deloitte Consulting is an integral part of Deloitte Touche Tohmatsu, a global leader in professional services, offering consulting, audit, tax, and related services to clients worldwide.

The industries we serve:

Manufacturing: Deloitte Consulting helps clients in the manufacturing industry compete—and win—in volatile and increasingly complex markets. While we provide diverse consultative services, our engagements focus on four critical business issues: developing and deploying a global manufacturing strategy; achieving rigorous control of companywide cost structures; shaping business operations to ensure that companies can always meet or exceed customer expectations; and applying advanced technology to achieve superior business results. In this practice, you'll focus on supply chain challenges, warehousing, logistics, distribution issues, systems integration, and other manufacturing processes.

Consumer Business: Today, consumer businesses face extraordinary marketplace challenges—heightened competion, global threats and opportunities, tighter margins, technology-driven innovation, and acute sensitivity to cost. With a wealth of industry expertise and experience, Deloitte Consulting helps clients confront these strategic challenges. In working with mass merchants, department stores, specialty retailers, wholesale distributors, and trade associations, you'll address all dimensions of the consumer products lifestyle—from factory floor to check-out line—with a focus on supply chain issues.

Telecommunications & Media: Rapid growth, change, innovation, competition, and market convergence are defining today's telecommunications industry. Looking to you for strategic advice and implementation support will be local and long-distance telephone companies, cable television operators, multimedia software providers, electronic publishers, interactive video and data services, equipment manufacturers, and direct broadcast satellite operators. We offer clients in these areas a full range of strategic, process, and information consulting services.

Financial Services: In the financial services industry, regulatory changes, technology-driven service platforms and solutions, a changing customer base, a burgeoning portfolio of new products and services, and a constant blurring of distinctions between financial institutions all converge to create a climate of both uncertainty and exciting growth potential. To help clients turn these forces to their advantage, we have built a strong financial services consulting practice that serves money center banks, securities firms and investment banks, credit unions, and five of the ten largest insurance companies in the United States. We assist these clients in defining their strategies, developing solutions, and implementing change that will help them compete in the 21st century.

Health Care: Perhaps no industry today is buffeted by such rapid and unrelenting change as health care. Pricing and cost containment pressures, new delivery channels, a profound shift to managed care, and uncertainties regarding the role of the public sector combine to create a new complexity. In our large and broadbased health care practice, you'll advise insurers, medical and pharmaceutical manufacturers, academic medical centers, integrated delivery systems, managed care organizations, large physician groups, and every type of service provider. We are the eminent strategy, process, and change leadership firm serving the health care industry.

Utilities & Energy: Among the fundamental and far-reaching shifts in the marketplace challenging the utilities and energy industry are the rapid pace and dramatic scope of deregulation, consolidation among energy companies, escalating demands for lower prices, and novel power production options (including cogeneration, independent sourcing, and retail wheeling). All of these create a dynamic business environment of tremendous risk and potential reward. Here, you'll help companies exploit these new options for growth and success.

Public Sector: Sweeping legislative reform in welfare, education, and health care is compelling federal, state, and local governments to radically transform their service delivery systems and processes. Deloitte Consulting is superbly positioned to help these public sector entities as they reengineer and—in some cases—reinvent their operational, financial, and strategic ways of doing business. In the public sector practice, you'll work closely with governmental bodies, agencies, and authorities on a wide spectrum of management issues.

The type of work we do:

We are a full-service consulting firm. Our consulting services span all aspects of enterprise transformation. Depending on your background and interests, you will build on a deep understanding of a client's business issues to work on:

Strategy: We help clients define and develop strategies—including competitive strategies, value solutions, and growth strategies—to achieve corporate and business unit objectives. Braxton Associates, an integral element of Deloitte Consulting, is the brand name of our global strategy service line.

Processes: Our reengineering, change leadership, financial management, and reorganization services enhance clients' operational effectiveness and build their capacity for sustainable change.

Technology: Our work in technology transformation, software package implementation (SAP, Baan, Oracle, PeopleSoft), networking, and client/server solutions—which focuses on technical, application, and data architecture solutions tailored to specific industries or business functions—enables quantum leaps in organizational performance.

People-Transformation: Successfully implementing sustainable change requires that we focus not only on "hard" technical solutions, but also on the subtle human factors—organizational design, training, team building, behavior changes—that are critical to our clients' success in the marketplace.

In the next few years, we plan to continue to invest heavily in these major transformation areas as well as continue to look for new areas of growth. We also plan to continue our global initiatives, working towards becoming a truly seamless global organization.

Who are your competitors, and how does your approach to consulting differ from theirs?

Deloitte Consulting offers its clients a very different approach—a highly respectful, flexible, and collaborative working style with an unmatched ability to transfer knowledge and skills and to generate employee buy-in. In addition, our firm focuses on the realization that changing business processes is necessary to achieve the promised returns from strategy and technology. This unique strategy enables the firm to deliver very different results. Clients can build on our results, because their people buy into the need for continued change and have the ability to lead the next change. And finally, not only do we create business processes that deliver improved performance today, we also design processes that can adapt to shifts in the environment, continuing to deliver results in the future.

Consultant's Job Description

Describe the career path and corresponding responsibilities for an MBA at your firm.

MBAs with significant prior work experience join the firm as senior consultants. The natural career progression leads to manager, senior manger, and partner opportunities. There are significant opportunities for rapid professional growth. You can go as fast and as far as your abilities take you. Many of our partners joined the firm as senior consultants and advanced to partner following outstanding performance and consistent professional growth.

While most of our senior consultants receive a broad-based exposure to industries and functional service lines over the first few years, all are encouraged to select an area of specialization upon promotion to senior manager, if not before. For people who are convinced that immediate specialization is right for them, we offer this option as well.

How big is a typical case team? How many cases does a consultant work on simultaneously?

Engagements range in scope from multiyear projects to those lasting six to twelve months. There is, therefore, a corresponding variation in the size and complexity of each engagement team. Each team is led by a partner. All members of the team are active participants in the project and work closely with each other and with top client management. Actual case team size can range from two to twenty people. In a typical first year, a senior consultant might work on one or two project engagements, often representing different industries and/or functional areas.

Discuss the lifestyle aspects of a career with your firm; i.e., average hours per week, amount of travel, flexibility to change offices.

A career in consulting is demanding, often requiring long hours and out-of-town travel. While the average workweek for senior consultants is 50 to 60 hours, project deadlines and client requirements have an impact on the actual time spent on a job. Most of your work will be performed at a client's place of business, not in your office.

At Deloitte Consulting, we work to strike a balance between our client's needs and the need for our consultants to have satisfying, well-rounded personal lives. Therefore, while travel time varies by assignment, the burdens will be carefully considered, and no consultant will be asked to shoulder more than a fair share. We also have a number of initiatives in place (regional staffing, the 3-4-5 initiative) to help minimize travel demands. Our 3-4-5 program means spending three nights away from home in an average week and four days at the client site. Client work is continued from a regional office on the fifth day, giving consultants the opportunity to network with colleagues. Office meetings and training programs are formally held every third Friday of each month to further develop our consultants.

We have received national recognition for our commitment to establish programs that help our staff maintain a successful balance between a satisfying, well-rounded personal life and a challenging professional career. We have received particular recognition for our Women's Initiative. Our leaders believe that "we cannot exceed the expectations of our clients without the best people and we can't have the best people without advancing people of both genders to all levels." The results have been impressive. The number of women in leadership positions has tripled since 1993, with women now holding positions on the Board of Directors and Management Committee, and serving as Managing Directors of practice offices and leaders in many emerging service areas. We have also eliminated the gap between male and female turnover. Our firm has received awards from Working Mother Magazine as "Champion of the Year" and "100 Best Companies for Working Mothers." These initiatives, and the work/life balance we promote, recently earned us recognition from *Fortune* magazine as #8 of the Best 100 Companies to Work for in America.

What is your firm's turnover rate for professionals? What careers do your ex-consultants typically pursue after leaving?

The turnover rate for Deloitte Consulting is less than the industry average. The majority of our ex-consultants pursue rewarding opportunities either in their industry of expertise or with a client with whom they have consulted in the past.

The Recruiting Process

Describe your recruiting process and the criteria by which you select candidates.

Deloitte Consulting does not look for a "typical" consultant. Each person we hire is unique, but all share certain qualities, such as:

- The ability to think clearly, logically, and with insight

- A quick mind and a high level of energy

- Common sense and judgement

- Skill and sensitivity in dealing with people

- The ability to secure the cooperation of others and persuade them to act

- Flexibility and a sense of humor

- The desire to broaden one's career focus beyond specific technical or functional skill

- The self-confidence to work effectively with people at all management levels

- Initiative, drive, and persistence

Our interview process is a blend of case and "behavioral" questions. While we do probe candidates' ability to analyze and grasp business situations, we also must get to know them and why they have succeeded in the past.

How many full-time consultants do you expect to hire in the coming year?

We recruit over 30% of our hires through referrals. In addition, we actively attract talent through our experienced and global campus recruiting efforts.

How many summer interns do you expect to hire? If you have a formal summer program, please describe it. Please be sure to indicate whether the program is in place for all offices or just some.

No distinction is made between a summer associate and a new full-time senior consultant in either the role played or our expectations of performance. Accordingly, client contact and exposure is an important element of the typical experience. We recruit summer associates for all of our global recruiting locations.

Human Resources Practices

Describe your firm's performance appraisal system for consultants. Are there explicit criteria against which an MBA is evaluated before being promoted? How many times a year is there a performance appraisal and hence an opportunity for promotion? Is there an upward evaluation process too?

The Consulting Career Continuum (C3) is our professional development process, which leads consultants to the appropriate education and experience-based programs that they need to reach their goals. At Deloitte Consulting, senior consultants are formally evaluated after each client engagement and career planning is formally done on an ongoing basis. These programs encourage informal feedback throughout the client engagement so that our staff can be aware of areas needing improvement. Performance is evaluated through certification exams and performance appraisals, with the results establishing an individual's compensation and promotion path.

What benefits does your company provide for maternity, paternity, or adoption leave?

Our firm provides short-term disability benefits for up to 65 days for women who are delivering children. In addition, the firm provides family leave in increments of up to one year for parents facing child adoption, birth, or childrearing needs. Similar leaves are also available for elder care and other relevant personal reasons.

Please describe any initial training programs or ongoing professional development programs for young professionals.

All newly hired senior consultants will attend a two-week course entitled "Fundamental Consulting Skills." As a new hire, professional development is ensured because:

- You are continually coached and encouraged on the job.

- You participate in all aspects of an assignment: project review meetings, engagement development, and project control.

- You strengthen your capabilities and build a general business perspective through a diversity of projects and experiences and by working directly with clients.

- You receive recognition for developing others.

- You continually receive evaluations of your performance throughout the engagement, and formal reviews occur frequently.

Each year, your development and growth will be supplemented by additional global education programs that you will attend with the firm's management group and your peers from around the world. These programs provide specialized education in various disciplines such as strategy, process, technology, and people, as well as broad business issues and consulting skills education. They are an important part of what we do, providing an opportunity for learning new skills, discussing meaningful issues, developing relationships with peers, and having fun.

Describe your firm's outplacement services.

It is our policy and philosophy to hire and develop people for the long term. We do, however, provide counseling and job search assistance to individuals who are leaving the firm.

Does your firm provide for on-site day care? If not, do you provide compensation for day care? Is flextime possible?

We do provide referrals to our staff when day care is needed and offer emergency day care arrangements when primary care arrangement is problematic. We also offer a variety of flexible arrangements for our staff who are proven high performers. This is only one of many ways we put our resources to bear to benefit our people.

Delta Consulting Group

1177 Avenue of the Americas
New York, NY 10036
(212) 403-7500
Fax: (212) 221-5882
Web site: www.deltacg.com

Recruiting Contact(s):
Jennifer Tarlow, Director of Human Resources
E-mail: Careers@deltacg.com

Locations of Offices:
New York, San Francisco

Total Number of Professionals (U.S. and worldwide):
50

Company Description

Describe your firm by type of consulting work performed and by types of clients served. What changes are planned in the next few years in terms of services, clients, or locations of offices?

Delta Consulting Group works with CEOs and other senior executives on the design and leadership of large-scale organizational change. It focuses on the areas of strategy development, organizational architecture, change management, and the development of effective leadership and executive teams.

Since its founding in 1980, Delta has worked closely with more than 200 organizations, including nearly 150 Fortune 500 companies. The firm brings this broad and deep experience to bear in all of its client engagements and relationships.

Delta's clients, including the CEOs of more than 90 public companies, tend to be involved in large-scale change in response to major changes in their business environment. Some must change because their enterprise has outgrown its existing strategy or organizational structure. Many are attempting to reshape their organizations in the wake of an acquisition, merger, spin-off, or major divestiture. Whatever their circumstances, all seek assistance in dealing with both the human and organizational aspects of change.

Delta helps its senior-level clients address the challenges of change by combining two perspectives. On one hand, we understand organizations in strategic terms as economic enterprises. We also have a deep understanding of organizations as complex systems of human behavior. Whether on the level of the individual, the small group, or the large enterprise, we have had years of experience in helping leaders manage the social and behavioral dynamics of organizational change.

Working in close collaboration with our clients, we have helped major U.S.–based enterprises, such as Bristol-Myers Squibb Company, Chase Manhattan Corp., Corning Incorporated, The Limited Inc., Lucent Technologies, and Xerox Corporation, transform their businesses in fundamental ways. We have also worked with smaller, high-growth companies, sharing with them the benefit of our years of collaboration with some of the most accomplished leaders of change.

Along with expertise in each of our practice areas, we also deliver certain intangibles that may be equally valuable to our clients.

First, we bring insight. Because of our experience, training, and objectivity, we help clients perceive their situation from a new vantage point. Second, we bring energy, in the sense that our work helps motivate clients to change. Third, we focus on impact and we help to produce interventions that actually result in major change. And fourth, we provide the support of a trusted confidant. In both a technical and emotional sense, we support our clients through difficult decisions and adjustments.

Describe your organizational structure. Is the firm geographically structured or based around practices? If you have practices, please list them.

All Delta consultants are expected to be capable of consulting with CEOs and other senior executives in each of these areas: organizational diagnosis; strategy development; organizational architecture; strategic selection (assessment and placement of candidates for senior positions); operating environment/culture; executive teams; executive leadership; change management; and strategic combinations (mergers, acquisitions, joint ventures, etc.).

In 1996, responding to the increasing demand for our consulting services by companies in the western U.S., Delta opened a San Francisco office. The New York and San Francisco offices both offer the same full range of Delta offerings.

Who are your competitors, and how does your approach to consulting differ from theirs?

Our direct competitors tend to be the large, first-tier consulting companies. Delta's offering is unique in several ways.

Our primary client is the CEO. Although we collaborate closely with others throughout the senior levels of the organization, our experience shows that the CEO must personally own and lead the overall change.

We specialize in the four practice areas (strategy development, organizational architecture, change management, and leadership and executive team effectiveness) that lie at the intersection of strategy and organization.

We employ only experienced consultants who combine a distinguished academic background with years of experience in working with the senior leaders of major organizations. We deploy small teams of senior consultants who understand the executive point of view.

Because our consultants are engaged in more than one client relationship, they have the independence necessary to speak candidly and to constructively challenge the client by raising issues that others might be unwilling to discuss.

We operate at the intersection of "expertise" and "facilitation." We are experts in change management, rather than in any particular industry. Our role is to enable our clients to arrive at informed decisions about the best way to run their own businesses.

We believe in "technology transfer"; we work hard to educate our clients about the principles and processes of change management so that they do not become dependent on consultants.

We make extensive use of accessible, client-friendly products that capture our state-of-the-science intellectual capital.

We leverage our experience and insights to provide customized interventions rather than off-the-shelf solutions.

Summarize your growth in terms of revenues (both domestic and international) and professional staff over the past year; over the past five years.

During the 1990s Delta has experienced consistent, significant, but managed growth. During the past five years, growth in revenues has averaged 20% compounded. Growth in number of professionals has been approximately 15% per year.

Approximately how many professionals do you have at each level, i.e., how wide is your pyramid?

There are only two professional levels within Delta's consulting staff: directors and senior directors, with roughly half the consultants at each level. The formal governing group, the Management Committee, includes approximately half of the senior directors, who are designated as managing directors. The professional levels are used only internally, indicating accomplishment and a level of responsibility within the firm. As a matter of policy, we avoid the use of such designations with our clients.

Consultant's Job Description

Describe the career path and corresponding responsibilities for an MBA at your firm.

Delta recruits only senior-level consultants who typically combine a superior academic background in management and behavioral science with an established record of consulting and management-level operating experience. Successful candidates have earned an MA/MBA and/or Ph.D. degree and have counseled senior managers for at least five to ten years. The firm has hired a small number of outstanding MBAs who have had at least three to five years of relevant job experience.

How big is a typical case team? How many cases does a consultant work on simultaneously?

We generally have two or three consultants assigned to a specific project, though it's not unusual for a half dozen or more Delta consultants to be working simultaneously on various projects within a client organization where we have a long-standing relationship. Each consultant usually has either two or three clients at any given time.

Discuss the lifestyle aspects of a career with your firm; i.e., average hours per week, amount of travel, flexibility to change offices.

Work pressures at Delta can be fairly demanding and travel tends to be extensive. Most consultants are involved in two to three different clients' systems at one time, so the travel does not usually involve full weeks away from home. An effort is made to assign consultants to at least one client in the same metropolitan area as the office to which they are assigned. The firm is deeply sensitive to the problems—both personal and professional—that often result when work demands become excessive. Managing directors carefully monitor the deployment of each consultant and work to help them maintain a healthy balance between their private and professional lives.

The Recruiting Process

Describe your recruiting process and the criteria by which you select candidates.

Delta interviews candidates throughout the year, but generally hires in groups, with newly-hired consultants beginning their work with us in June of each year. Consultants are hired directly into either the New York or San Francisco office.

How many full-time consultants do you expect to hire in the coming year?

At present, Delta plans to hire approximately eight consultants in the coming year.

Human Resources Practices

Describe your firm's performance appraisal system for consultants. Are there any explicit criteria against which an MBA is evaluated before being promoted? How many times a year is there a performance appraisal and hence an opportunity for promotion? Is there an upward evaluation process too?

Performance at Delta is assessed on the basis of both client work and internal firm-building activities. Consultants work with their assigned managing director to develop a set of individual goals in January, and progress toward those goals is monitored regularly throughout the year.

Diamond Technology Partners Incorporated

875 N. Michigan Avenue
Suite 3000
Chicago, IL 60611
(312) 255-5000
Fax: (312) 255-6000
Web site: www.diamtech.com

MBA Recruiting Contact(s):
Jill Marie Rupple, Director of Recruiting
Christa Setterlund, Campus Recruiting Manager
E-mail: setterlund@diamtech.com

Locations of Offices:
Chicago, San Francisco, and London. Consultants at the associate level or above can live anywhere within the continental U.S.

Total Number of Professionals (U.S. and worldwide): 433

Company Description

Describe your firm by type of consulting work performed and by types of clients served. What changes are planned in the next few years in terms of services, clients, or locations of offices?

Diamond Technology Partners is an e-commerce services firm that develops Digital Strategy business strategies that leverage information technology to improve our client's competitive positions. More and more companies are realizing that technology is not just the solution, but also the problem. Our consultants serve as the CEO's guide to e-commerce by working closely with our client's senior management to explore how the digital age will change the company's products, services, organization, and competition. At Diamond, we help clients identify and create bold, winning business strategies and then help clients build and operate these new e-businesses. Our aim is to help create "killer apps"—those category-transforming solutions that place our clients in the winner's circle.

Diamond Technology Partners was founded on the premise that strategy and technology together create a new "marketspace" and that experts across these disciplines work together. We have been delivering "killer app" solu-

tions since our founding in 1994 and are leaders in this space.

Describe your organizational structure. Is the firm geographically structured or based around practices? If you have practices, please list them.

On our client engagements, we create multidisciplinary teams composed of consultants with complementary skills and various backgrounds. These teams may reflect a focus on a particular industry, a certain skill set, or a mix of competencies. A team typically consists of one partner, at least two or three senior principals or principals, and several associates and analysts. We rely heavily on small teams. In fact, we view our small-team approach as one of our competitive advantages. The small-team approach allows us to provide value-added, cost-effective services to our clients in a timely fashion. Small, highly experienced teams work well together and enable us to identify and execute solutions quickly.

Who are your competitors, and how does your approach to consulting differ from theirs?

Diamond is a unique firm in a new and emerging category that isn't well defined and where information about providers is still pretty scarce. So, as an e-business services firm, we have no competitors because we deliver breakthrough *killer apps,* while our competitors tend to be more Web enablers who help you go "faster, better, and cheaper."

Typically though, those who track the industry suggest there are a number of potential competitors. In the past, the marketplace has been segmented into strategy firms, design/creative firms, and technology implementation firms. These days those definitions are blurring as buyers and providers seek to deliver end-to-end solutions. (We think the need is for killer apps.) In the strategy space, we compete with traditional strategy firms like McKinsey, Booz•Allen, Bain, and BCG. In the implementation area, we face a number of traditional firms like AC, PWC, KPMG, and D&T. A number of newer entrants in the field include start-up e-business services providers like Scient, Viant, and Zefer. They also include firms that have been involved with creative Web design and implementation like Razorfish, iXL, Proxicom, US Web/CKS, and others.

Consultant's Job Description

Describe the career path and corresponding responsibilities for an MBA at your firm.

Exact tasks and responsibilities of a consultant will vary from one engagement to the next because of industry and client differences. However, from the start of an individual's first engagement, he/she is a member of a team.

Diamond currently recruits at the top business schools to seek out MBA candidates to enter the firm as associates. Associates are expected to take an active role in all aspects of client engagements, from defining the problems through identifying, evaluating, and implementing solutions. With Diamond, associates work closely with clients to help them set the right goals, initiate the right programs, and make the appropriate decisions to translate their strategy into concrete business solutions.

Consultants develop core business and technical skills through Diamond's engagements, which offer opportunities in the areas of project management, business development, and client relations. These are the critical activities by which our professionals are evaluated for promotion to higher levels of our organization. The steps leading to partner are analyst, associate, principal, and senior principal. With our foundation based upon the expectation that all employees share in the wealth and growth of the firm, a new associate has the opportunity to be a partner within six years.

How big is a typical case team? How many cases does a consultant work on simultaneously?

A project team's composition generally reflects the shape of a diamond and represents Diamond's commitment to provide services to its clients through small, multidisciplinary teams of highly skilled and experienced professionals. The size and composition of a "diamond" is determined by the particular needs of a given project and is generally comprised of a partner, who serves as the project leader, three to five senior principals or principals, and two to four associates or analysts. Each of our experienced consultants and analysts are dedicated to a single engagement at any given time to provide the best possible environment in which to learn and perform. However, our consultants often provide remote support for other engagement teams in order to provide our clients with the highest level of service.

Discuss the lifestyle aspects of a career with your firm; i.e., average hours per week, amount of travel, flexibility to change offices.

Our clients face increasing competition in the marketplace and require timely and effective service if they are to achieve their business objectives. We believe that a maximum presence at the client site increases our ability to help clients achieve their business goals. To help our consultants balance work/life issues, we are currently implementing a 5-4-3 travel policy: five days of work, four days at the client site, and three nights away. However, all client engagements are unique, and the amount of time spent traveling varies by engagement.

Diamond understands the amount of stress a consultant may face from client demands and travel schedules, and we work to ensure that our consultants maintain a balanced lifestyle. To achieve this goal we provide the following: we allow our consultants to choose where they live in the United States rather than require that they live in Chicago; we equip all of our consultants with the technology to allow them to work from home, when possible; and we give all of our consultants four weeks of vacation.

Due to our client focus, we require a high degree of commitment from each of our professionals, from partners through analysts. However, because we require such commitment, Diamond offers highly competitive career advancement opportunities.

The Recruiting Process

Describe your recruiting process and the criteria by which you select candidates.

Diamond actively recruits individuals directly from top graduate MBA, MS, and undergraduate programs, as well as talented, experienced individuals looking for a challenging career change. Our business is built upon our ability to develop, communicate, and implement business strategy. Obviously it is important for our people to possess the skills to analyze and clarify complex issues, reach sound conclusions, develop winning solutions, and effectively communicate with our clients.

Within the schools from which we recruit, candidates are encouraged to attend Diamond's corporate presentation and to proceed through their school's placement office for interviews. Diamond pre-selects candidates based on initial meetings at presentations and receipt of resumes expressing interest. First-round interviews are held on-campus. These interviews allow Diamond to assess the candidate's credentials while providing time for the candidate to learn more about Diamond. Candidates are then invited to Diamond's Chicago office for the second round of interviews, which consists of four interviews focusing on problem solving, teamwork, experience, and analytical ability.

Diamond is looking for highly motivated individuals who believe that the future of business is inextricably intertwined with technology. We are looking for talented, motivated, and entrepreneurial individuals who have the ability to provide outstanding client service and the desire to lead our firm into the future. We desire dedicated individuals who believe that learning is an ongoing process, are highly adaptable, and have both the desire and aptitude to work in a collaborative environment. Qualified candidates should expect to undergo two or three rounds of interviews, speaking with five to six of our experienced consultants and partners.

From which schools do you actively recruit? Do you consider applications from other schools?

We seek students from a broad range of educational backgrounds and work experience to work as consultants on our multidisciplinary teams. Therefore Diamond actively recruits at leading MBA, MS, and undergraduate programs, and will consider letters from qualified individuals from other leading institutions.

How many full-time consultants do you expect to hire in the coming year?

Diamond has experienced tremendous growth in its first years of existence and remains committed to expanding its recruiting presence at the leading graduate institutions. For the 2000–2001 recruiting year, Diamond expects to hire approximately 100 MBA candidates.

How many summer interns do you expect to hire? If you have a formal summer program, please describe it. Please be sure to indicate whether the program is in place for all offices or just some.

Diamond's summer associates are contributing members of the engagement teams, performing the role of new associates, and reporting to the engagement partner. As active team members, the summer associates gain valuable insights about Diamond through their peer group who help to act as advisers to the summer associates, answering their questions and introducing them to Diamond's people and culture. For one week during the summer, all summer associates participate in a training course designed to provide insight and guidance into what it means to be a consultant at Diamond, while imparting a deeper knowledge and understanding of the company. Diamond expects to hire approximately 35 summer associates.

Human Resources Practices

Describe your firm's performance appraisal system for consultants. Are there explicit criteria against which an MBA is evaluated before being promoted? How many times a year is there a performance appraisal and hence an opportunity for promotion? Is there an upward evaluation process too?

All consultants are evaluated through engagement performance appraisals and annual performance reviews. The engagement performance appraisals are given every four months or at the completion of an assignment. The performance criterion used in the engagement performance appraisals has been developed to establish performance expectations at each level. Each employee is also given an annual performance review during which his/her performance appraisals, development needs/opportunities, promotion, and compensation adjustment are discussed.

Please describe any initial training programs or ongoing professional development programs for young professionals.

All new hires participate in Diamond's Assimilation Program, which introduces them to our approach to consulting through a simulated case study. This initial training is highly interactive, involving partners and principals with extensive engagement experience. As the new hires progress through the program, they develop their skills in research, business writing, and presentation development.

To augment the "on-the-job" training our consultants receive while on client engagements, we require all of our consultants to participate in a number of training programs throughout their careers at Diamond. These programs are uniquely designed using the concept of "goal-based scenario training," which promotes learning through doing.

Our diverse engagements and innovative training programs provide an ideal environment for our professionals to engage in the full range of business issues from strategy formulation to implementation. Diamond offers recruits the opportunity to utilize and expand upon their management, analytical, and technical skills in a variety of industry settings. In addition, our professionals make significant contributions to build an entrepreneurial business and share in the success of that business.

Digitas LLC

800 Boylston Street
Boston, MA 02199
(617) 867-1000
Web site: www.digitas.com

MBA Recruiting Contact(s):
Peggy Novello
E-mail: pnovello@digitas.com

Locations of Offices:
Boston, New York, San Francisco, Salt Lake City, Miami, London

Total Number of Professionals (U.S. and worldwide):
1,400+

Company Description

Describe your firm by type of consulting work performed and by types of clients served.

Digitas is a leading Internet professional services firm that provides integrated, Internet-based strategic, technological, and marketing solutions to Fortune 100 and other industry-leading companies. We develop large-scale, long-term, strategic relationships with a select group of clients who have embraced the Internet as a principal means of business transformation. We help our clients leverage their existing infrastructure and the Internet to develop stronger and more profitable customer relationships. We employ approximately 1,400 professionals and are headquartered in Boston, with offices in New York City, San Francisco, Salt Lake City, Miami, and London.

We believe there is a need for an innovative Internet professional services provider, which has the scale, breadth of experience, and expertise to help companies understand and capitalize on the potential of the Internet as a part of their overall business strategy. This includes leveraging the power of their existing assets to drive growth, maximizing customer value, and building a sustainable competitive advantage. As we work with clients to redefine their business model, we draw on our comprehensive Internet professional services capabilities and marketing experience to provide a fully integrated, end-to-end solution with the following key elements:

- **Define digital business strategy:** We work with clients' senior management to define new business strategies that are broad-based and grounded in a thorough understanding of our clients' overall business and competitive environment.

- **Create enterprise-wide customer value propositions:** We employ a customer-centric approach to develop value propositions that enhance customer loyalty and generate new business opportunities by leveraging our clients' existing assets, such as distribution channels, customer service networks, and customer information systems.

- **Build new technology and marketing infrastructure:** We build this infrastructure for our clients, including Web sites that enhance our clients' brands. We also develop electronic customer relationship management (eCRM) systems that develop and strengthen customer relationships across all channels and touchpoints.

- **Implement solutions on an enterprise-wide basis:** We provide training, organizational alignment, and operational support to help our clients implement solutions across their enterprises. We also coordinate the efforts of various client businesses to create customer-oriented applications with a consistent corporate message.

- **Develop integrated marketing plans:** We design integrated marketing plans that typically involve identifying customer segments, developing marketing strategies, and optimizing on-line media planning and channel allocation, including mix, messaging, and frequency.

- **Execute across marketing and service channels:** We leverage our on-line media buying, design, and creative services and event sponsorships to market seamlessly across multiple channels to help our clients build relationships with their customers.

- **Measure performance:** Through every step of our solution, we measure the value being delivered to our clients by determining relevant metrics and tracking our performance against those measures. We collect data frequently and use it to continually refine our solution and maximize our clients' return on investment.

Consultant's Job Description

Describe the career path and corresponding responsibilities for an MBA at your firm.

93

Career path and responsibilities are a function of specific, expert departments within Digitas. While MBA candidates are welcome to seek positions within any Digitas practice area, the majority of MBA applicants in recent years have entered the following areas:

Integrated Marketing: Candidates hold responsibility for the strategic design and flawless implementation of on-line, off-line, and cross-channel marketing programs for clients. Marketing team members are typically staffed against a single client, and may hold responsibility for several distinct streams of client deliverables. Candidates typically serve as the key contact between Digitas and clients, and hold overall responsibility for timeliness and quality of client deliverables, as well as client financial management.

Digital Strategy: MBA candidates may be considered for one of three distinct areas of the Digital Strategy Group.

- *Strategy Generalists:* Responsible for determining the role of interactive marketing in a client's overall strategy, reviewing opportunities to transform existing operations, as well as engineering new business concepts and models afforded by the digital channel.

- *Economic and Financial Modeling:* Responsible for financial modeling and analysis used to inform strategy, including forecasting potential value of marketing campaigns, assessing potential contribution of new ventures, and determining optimal allocation of marketing budget across channels.

- *Measurement/Customer Analytics:* Responsible for designing measurement strategies that provide client teams with the ability to track performance of marketing efforts, spanning both on-line and off-line channels.

Integrated Technologies: Candidates are sought for a full range of technology development functions, including Web site engineering and development, database integration, marketing operations, and technology visioning.

ECRM (Electronic Customer Relationship Management): Candidates are responsible for designing, implementing, and optimizing customer service systems delivered through live and technology-automated support. Specific areas of focus include inbound and outbound email-based support, as well as inbound and outbound call centers, leveraged for both sales and servicing purposes.

The Recruiting Process

Describe your recruiting process and the criteria by which you select candidates.

Digitas conducts a year-round recruiting program from both on-campus and open-market candidates. Résumés submitted from MBA program candidates are reviewed against the needs of individual Digitas departments. First-round, on-campus interviews are used to explore specific areas of expertise and work experience, and identify potential fit for specific departments. Candidates selected for second-round interviews are invited to a Digitas office, where they will meet a combination of Digitas team members from several practice areas, probing the ability to deliver against specific departmental needs, but also assessing the ability to work across multiple departments in a collaborative fashion.

Digitas is an equal opportunity employer.

From which schools do you actively recruit? Do you consider applicants from other schools?

Digitas participates in on-campus recruiting at select MBA programs including Harvard, MIT, Kellogg, Columbia, Stanford, Tuck, Boston University, Boston College, Carnegie Mellon, and Babson. In addition, we welcome qualified candidates from other institutions, as well as individuals with strong track records in management consulting, marketing, and technology.

How many full-time consultants do you expect to hire in the coming year?

We anticipate hiring between 20 and 25 MBA-level candidates in 2000.

Human Resources Practices

Describe your firm's performance appraisal system for consultants. Are there explicit criteria against which an MBA is evaluated before being promoted? How many times a year is there a performance appraisal and hence an opportunity for promotion? Is there an upward evaluation process too?

Each employee receives a review after six months, examining progress in four competencies: thinking, influencing, managing, and orchestrating. These competencies are applied against strategic planning, client service, project management, and communication skills. Thereafter, employees receive reviews on an annual basis, tracking the same review criteria that serve as a basis for promotion and salary advancement. Input to these reviews is gathered through a multi-lateral process, where data is gathered from managers, clients, peers, direct reports, as well as through the employee's self-assessment. This process also allows employees to provide input into the reviews of their managers, forming a complete system of checks and balances.

Please describe any initial training programs or ongoing professional development programs for young professionals.

- Digitas believes in a commitment to formal, firmwide training initiatives, coupled with individually designed training programs. All new employees across each discipline participate in a two-day orientation program to review the firm's capabilities, history, and operating procedures. Recent MBAs also participate in a custom-designed, intensive four-day session that provides a detailed, in-depth understanding of all of Digitas's capabilities and an introduction to a set of management tools and methodologies. In addition, individuals have access to topic-specific training courses, some held interactively, some held on a weekly basis, thus permitting them to tailor coursework to their particular needs and experience. Additionally, firmwide "shared learning sessions" are held on a monthly basis, each covering an agenda designed by senior management, in order to review the most salient topics in digital marketing. Employees also have the ability to attend external training courses and conferences relevant to their individual practice areas.

Edgar, Dunn & Company

847 Sansome Street
San Francisco, CA 94111
(415) 397-5858
Fax: (415) 397-0142
Web site: www.edgardunn.com

MBA Recruiting Contact(s):
Tom Jarman
E-mail: tjarman@edgardunn.com

Locations of Offices:
San Francisco, Atlanta, London, and Sydney

Total Number of Professionals (U.S. and worldwide):
Approximately 50 (includes professional and support staff)

Company Description

Describe your firm by type of consulting, work performed, and by types of clients served. What changes are planned in the next few years in terms of services, clients, or locations of offices?

Edgar, Dunn & Company is a boutique strategy consulting firm, founded in 1978. Our areas of focus include some of the most exciting specialties in the business world today—electronic commerce; payment products including credit, debit, and smart cards; brand strategy and positioning; and energy/telecommunications services. Our clients range from Internet start-ups to large, global corporations and financial institutions. We provide original, practical solutions to our clients that are only possible from a firm that combines an entrepreneurial mindset, a collaborative workstyle, and a "can do" attitude with the knowledge, objectivity, and expertise of an established firm. We are committed to creating recommendations with an eye toward implementation. We work with clients to develop practical strategies and help them develop the resources to implement them.

The EDC culture is deeply rooted in a set of values that serves as a foundation for all that we do. We have a growth mindset that requires each of us to be entrepreneurial in developing thought leadership, in expanding and developing client relationships, and encouraging responsible risk-taking. We enjoy a collaborative environment that values both individual contribution and teamwork.

Describe your organizational structure. Is the firm geographically structured or based around practices? If you have practices, please list them.

EDC is a global firm and has offices in Atlanta, San Francisco, London, and Sydney. While most firms operate their physical locations as separate entities, EDC has maintained an integrated, "one firm" perspective that allows us to quickly and easily combine our domestic and international experiences to the benefit of our clients.

We are focused and small with practice areas in e-Business, Financial Services, Marketing/Brand Strategy, and Energy Services/Telecommunications.

Who are your competitors and how does your approach to consulting differ from theirs?

For 20 years, we have leveraged our expertise and unique approach to provide our clients with innovative solutions to complex problems. EDC is different from most consulting firms in that

- **We have a point of view**—EDC takes a stand on what actions should be taken, and we support our recommendations with facts and analysis.

- **We customize solutions**—Each client has a unique set of competencies and challenges that EDC incorporates into our consulting approach. In responding to client issues, EDC does not employ "cookie-cutter" methodologies; instead, we tailor solutions to fit the particular engagement. The focus is on outcomes, not project activities.

- **Partners lead and actively participate in each assignment**—While partners at most firms spend much of their time selling, EDC's partners concentrate on consulting. As a result, EDC clients receive advice and counsel from the firm's most experienced consultants.

Consultant's Job Description

Describe the career path and corresponding responsibilities of an MBA at your firm.

Consultants assume increasing responsibility over time, including managing engagements and project teams, and participating in the firm's practice development activities. At EDC, MBAs are initially hired into the firm rather than a specific practice area. Consequently, consultants have the opportunity to work across functions in multiple industries. Over time, a consultant will begin to focus on one or two practice areas. Through these experiences,

EDC consultants develop a comprehensive set of management and consulting skills, and ultimately have the opportunity to become a partner in the firm.

The roles and responsibilities of each consultant vary upon experience level and aptitude. Generally, EDC consultants are expected to

- Design and conduct primary and secondary research using research tools and interviews

- Develop and execute qualitative and quantitative analyses of industries, customers, and competitors

- Interpret complex data in order to create and test hypotheses

- Present strategic recommendations to client management

- Manage EDC and client project teams

- Assist in practice development areas

How big is a typical case team? How many cases does a consultant work on simultaneously?

Typical engagement teams consist of one to three consultants along with a partner of the firm, allowing the consultants to learn directly from the professionals in our firm with the most experience—our partner group. In addition, because our project teams are small, consultants are ensured of comprehensive project involvement, significant responsibility, and client visibility. Consultants most often are working on one to two projects at the same time.

Discuss the lifestyle aspects of a career with your firm; i.e., average hours per week, amount of travel, flexibility to change offices.

Because we understand that consulting is an extremely demanding profession and are sensitive to our consultants' personal needs, we work with our professionals to most effectively balance their private and professional lives. We try to achieve a balanced environment so that consulting as a career choice can be a reality.

The Recruiting Process

Describe your recruiting process and the criteria by which you select candidates.

EDC actively recruits top MBA candidates with demonstrated analytical and problem-solving skills, quantitative abilities, and strong interpersonal and management skills. Because we place a great deal of emphasis on versatility and dedication to the consulting profession, we look for individuals who have the ability to develop a diversity of skills and the potential to become partners. Successful candidates are those who flourish in an unstructured professional environment, know how to work collaboratively, and display independence, creativity, and a drive to succeed.

From which schools do you actively recruit? Do you consider applicants from other schools?

We recruit MBAs from a limited number of schools; however, we do consider applicants from other top business schools. If you are a second-year student interested in career opportunities with EDC, please forward a cover letter and resume via e-mail, fax, or standard mail to our recruiting contact.

Human Resources Practices

Describe your firm's performance appraisal system for consultants. Are there explicit criteria against which an MBA is evaluated before being promoted? How many times a year is there a performance appraisal and hence an opportunity for promotion? Is there an upward evaluation process too?

Informal, verbal performance reviews are conducted after each engagement by the project manager or partner who has worked most closely with the consultant during the assignment. Written, formal annual performance reviews are conducted at year-end and incorporate all work completed during the year. Explicit evaluation criteria are described in EDC's Employee Orientation Manual.

Ernst & Young LLP

Web site: www.ey.com

MBA Recruiting Offices(s):
Atlanta (Charlotte): 600 Peachtree St., Atlanta, GA 30308

Chicago (Minneapolis, Milwaukee): 233 South Wacker Drive, Chicago, IL 60606

Cleveland (Detroit, Pittsburgh, Cincinnati, Indianapolis, Columbus): 1300 Huntington Building, 925 Euclid Avenue, Cleveland, OH 44115

Dallas (Ft. Worth, Irving): 104 Decker Court, Irving, TX 75201

Houston Area: 1221 McKinney St., Suite 2400, Houston, TX 77010

Los Angeles (Irvine, Phoenix): Pacific Corporate Towers, 200 North Sepulveda Blvd., El Segundo, CA 90245

New York (Boston): 750 Seventh Avenue, New York, NY 10019

Philadelphia (Fairfax, D.C., Baltimore): Two Commerce Square, Suite 4000, 2001 Market Street, Philadelphia, PA 19103

St. Louis (Kansas City, Denver): 701 Market St., Suite 1400/Gateway 1, St. Louis, MO 63101

San Francisco (Seattle): 555 California St., Suite 1700, San Francisco, CA 94104

Locations of Offices:
89 offices in the U.S., 670 worldwide

Total Number of Consulting Professionals (U.S. and worldwide):
8,000 in U.S., 13,000 worldwide

Company Description

Describe your firm by type of consulting work performed and by types of clients served. What changes are planned in the next few years in terms of services, clients, or locations of offices?

Ernst & Young LLP is one of the largest integrated professional services firms in the world. Ernst & Young LLP is also a member firm of Ernst & Young International (EYI). Its Consulting Services (CS) practices had 1998 global revenues of $4 billion. Ernst & Young LLP provides assurance and advisory business services, tax services, and consulting for domestic and global clients. The CS practice of Ernst & Young LLP works with companies to quickly solve mission-critical problems by identifying, designing, and operating high-value changes in their strategies and global operations. We deliver integrated, innovative solutions to help our clients achieve significant improvements in revenue growth, operating efficiencies, and the management of capital throughout the business. Our services include:

- Strategy

- E-Commerce

- Financial Advisory Services

- Systems Development and Technology

- Systems Integration/Enterprise Resource Planning

- Business Transformation Management

Our client base encompasses virtually all industries and represents those corporations included in the Fortune 500. In addition, the firm focuses on clients who represent those emerging corporations that today are under $2 billion in sales. Ernst & Young LLP is considered a premier firm in the consumer products, financial services, health care, manufacturing/high technology, media and entertainment, telecommunications, and real estate industries.

Ernst & Young's LLP CS practice is well along a major initiative to quadruple revenues within six years. This initiative is called Global State 2002. It is the firm's blueprint for locking in our position as one of the top consulting firms worldwide by integrating the extensive range of resources that allow us to implement quantum improvements to our clients' business processes.

Describe your organizational structure. Is the firm geographically structured or based around practices? If you have practices, please list them.

CS is integrated globally, but continues to promote national practices, multicultural values, and service integration. The structure of the CS practice is consistent with that of a worldwide organization and is aligned globally around industries and services lines. CS has four market focuses that are referred to as sectors within the practice:

- Product-based companies

- Service-based companies

- Health-based companies/institutions

- Middle market companies

Senior managers and partners that have particular industry experience are usually aligned to work with clients in these markets.

The following, key business solutions are aligned with our markets:

- customer connections

- e-commerce

- materials requirement ordering

- new product development

- shared services

- supply chain

- post-merger integration

- value exchange

- clinical integration

- revenue cycle

In addition to the four sectors previously described, Core is the sector within the organization in which the majority of consultants through managers reside. Core is not industry specific, but rather it allows for our staff to build deep competencies in either systems development and technology, systems integration/enterprise resource planning, or business transformation management. The competencies within Core are set up to serve all of our target markets.

Who are your competitors, and how does your approach to consulting differ from theirs?

Competition comes from both general management consulting groups and boutique specialty firms. Clients have identified several key differentiators setting us apart from other firms:

Thought Leadership. Research facilities such as our Centers for Business Innovation (CBI) are continually developing new ideas, methodologies, and solutions for our clients.

Acceleration. Techniques have been developed to move an organization through major work efforts.

Centers of Excellence, such as our Accelerated Solutions Environment (ASE) and Advanced Development Center (ADC), have been established to facilitate rapid solutions and development for our clients in the following areas: business strategy, operations strategy, custom software, rapid design, and business transformation. This process includes Ernst & Young LLP professionals and our clients working in a collaborative setting.

Service Integration. Our fusion philosophy brings together individuals with the functional and industry expertise to quickly craft effective solutions for many business situations.

Knowledge Transfer. Support groups such as the Center for Business Knowledge (CBK), allow our consultants to quickly access our national skills database, research recent project profiles, and identify internal resources in key subjects. Our consultants are all equipped with PCs that allow for remote access to the Lotus Notes network and the technology infrastructure of the firm.

Implementation. Dedicated to providing a wide array of services to our clients, we can deliver integrated solutions starting at the high end with an analytical, sound strategy and then carry it through to implementation. The bulk of our time is focused on making solutions work for our clients. The four critical ingredients in our approach to business improvement are:

Our account-centric view. We center our thinking and activities on our clients, wherever they are located. From consulting groups in North America, Europe, Asia Pacific, and Latin America, we offer our clients a single point of contact and consistent, high-quality global service.

Our total-solution focus. We deliver complete solutions regardless of the size of the client's business. Each solution we craft is comprehensive, customized, and built to generate tangible improvements quickly.

Our teamwork. To solve clients' problems, we assemble virtual teams of professionals that have the knowledge, skills, and tools to bring the strategy, performance, and technology elements together. Whatever the team, you'll always have a home base in the area office to which you're assigned.

Our value-added emphasis. We build our reputation on the economic and operational value that our clients get from our work.

Approximately how many professionals do you have at each level, i.e., how wide is your pyramid?

In the U.S., Consulting Services has approximately 600 partners, 3,100 management members (senior managers and managers), and 3,800 professional staff members (senior consultants and consultants).

Consultant's Job Description

Describe the career path and corresponding responsibilities for an MBA at your firm.

Almost 90% of MBAs are either assigned to strategy, business transformation management, or enterprise resource planning and implementation projects. Assignments may vary depending upon the candidate's interests, prior experience, and expertise. Qualified MBAs typically come in as either consultants (less than one year work experience) or senior consultants (three to five year's work experience). Those with five or six years of work experience may be hired as managers. The career progression leads to manager, senior manager, and partner. Every staff member is expected to effectively contribute to delivering high quality, value-added services, managing client relationships, and helping develop other team members.

Exact roles for MBAs in their first several projects are difficult to predict, but could easily include financial analysis, focus and work group facilitation, vendor evaluations, project management, organizational change management, interviews of client service personnel from shop floor to president, new/improved processes and implementation plans development, process modeling, and proposal writing and presentation. There is significant involvement in non-engagement activities such as recruiting, continuing education, and counseling. Strong performance is recognized quickly and new MBAs will take on additional responsibilities in project management and ultimately business development as soon as they are ready.

Consultants and senior consultants are usually responsible for deliverables or parts of a project. Managers and senior managers delegate assignments and prioritize work engagements. Partners are responsible for developing and maintaining relationships with our clients.

How big is a typical case team? How many cases does a consultant work on simultaneously?

An engagement team usually consists of anywhere from three to ten people. Larger projects are typically subdivided into groups that function concurrently. Consultants and senior consultants normally work on one engagement at a time.

Discuss the lifestyle aspects of a career with your firm; i.e., average hours per week, amount of travel, flexibility to change offices.

Consulting is a demanding profession, requiring travel and time commitment. The usual workweek for consultants is 45 hours, with project deadlines defining periods of lighter or heavier intensity. Consultants usually travel about 80% of the time, depending upon where the client's operations are based. Our global structure, use of technology, and multiple office locations help staff members to manage the amount and distance of out-of-town work. We have a voluntary transfer policy—if there is a need at the office, you are welcome to transfer locations.

What is your firm's turnover rate for professionals? What careers do your ex-consultants typically pursue after leaving?

Turnover averages from 15% to 20% per year, lower than the industry norm. The majority of consultants who leave Ernst & Young LLP pursue rewarding opportunities either in their area of functional or industry expertise or with a client with whom they have consulted in the past.

The Recruiting Process

Describe your recruiting process and the criteria by which you select candidates.

Critical success factors at Ernst & Young LLP are intellectual competence, flexibility, communication skills, teamwork and interpersonal skills, leadership, motivation, time management, and technical competence. We are always looking for individuals who are strong team players and are willing to "go the extra mile" to get the job done. Most new staff members have outstanding records of achievement in academic, social, and community activities.

The recruiting process generally consists of an initial campus interview followed by a half-day office visit. Throughout the process, you will have the opportunity to meet partners, managers, and other consultants who will evaluate your fit with the firm, and ensure you have a solid grasp of what it means to be a part of Ernst & Young LLP.

From which schools do you actively recruit? Do you consider applicants from other schools?

Ernst & Young LLP actively recruits at leading MBA and undergraduate programs. We seek a diverse community of professionals; therefore, we hire from a broad range of educational backgrounds and experience.

How many full-time consultants do you expect to hire in the coming year?

Ernst & Young LLP anticipates hiring over 1,200 college graduates for its upcoming fiscal year, of whom close to 300 will be MBAs.

How many summer interns do you expect to hire? If you have a formal summer program, please describe it. Please be sure to indicate whether the program is in place for all offices or just some.

Ernst & Young LLP will hire approximately 100 first-year MBAs for summer internships in CS in our nine area offices around the country. The exact number of internships varies from location to location. Interns are collectively part of an internship program, but are assigned individually to either client engagements or special projects (benchmarking, methodology upgrade teams, national planning activities, etc.).

Human Resources Practices

Describe your firm's performance appraisal system for consultants. Are there explicit criteria under which an MBA is evaluated before being promoted? How many times a year is there a performance appraisal and hence an opportunity for promotion? Is there an upward evaluation process too?

Our goal is to provide all professional staff with at least four engagement update reviews during the year (at the end of an engagement or at stated intervals during a long project). These are conducted by the individual's engage-

ment manager. Each staff member also has assigned to him/her a counselor to serve as a permanent "coach" regardless of project assignment. The counselors meet semiannually to review performance and rate all staff members in a round-table format. These discussions and the periodic reviews are the input for the individual's mid-year update and annual performance review. The ratings directly impact compensation and individual performance bonuses.

Our performance reviews are not simply the distribution of report cards. They are designed as a two-way discussion of an individual's strengths, and how to leverage them, weaknesses and how to address them, continuing education needs and how to plan for them, and long-term potential and how it can be realized.

Promotion candidates are also identified during the round-tables. Promotions are based solely on merit—demonstrated ability and readiness to take on additional responsibilities. Ernst & Young LLP is a meritocracy where top performers are rewarded with faster promotions, significantly increased compensation adjustments, and higher individual bonuses.

What benefits does your firm provide for maternity, paternity, or adoption leave?

All new parents have up to sixteen weeks of family leave available. More time can be taken as a leave of absence for up to an additional five months.

Please describe any initial training programs or ongoing professional development programs for young professionals.

Ernst & Young LLP places strong emphasis on the professional development of our employees' technical and management capabilities. MBAs entering the firm begin their first week of employment by attending a three-day program designed to assist the individual on assimilating to his or her new surroundings and to prepare the new hire for the five-day Consulting Services Entry (CSE) program. During the CSE, the firm's methods and techniques are applied to solving problems, producing deliverables, and presenting results. These sessions, along with Firmwide Orientation and Technology Basics, are the first components of the Consulting Services Entry Learning System, a six-month process designed to prepare you for your career at Ernst & Young LLP. Professionals in the firm are required to attend a minimum of 40 hours per year of professional development classes throughout their careers and can select from a wide variety of in-house seminars, external programs, and interactive desktop learning.

Does your firm provide for on-site day care? If not do you provide compensation for day care? Is flextime possible?

Several of our offices in large cities have facilities available to care for sick children during the normal working day. Additionally, all employees are able to set aside pretax income in a dependent day care reimbursement account to cover day care expenses. Flexible work arrangements are possible with reduced workweeks. Consultants often have wide latitude in managing their time to meet project schedules.

The Farrell Group

21311 Hawthorne Boulevard, Suite 230
Torrance, CA 90503
(310) 316-4420

MBA Recruiting Contact(s):
Nancy K. Vanitvelt

Location of Offices:
Los Angeles

Total Number of Professionals (U.S. and worldwide):
10

Company Description

Describe your firm by type of consulting work performed and by types of clients served. What changes are planned in the next few years in terms of services, clients, or locations of offices?

The Farrell Group, an international management consulting firm based in Los Angeles, develops and implements Integrated Management Systems to enhance clients' business performance and growth. We focus on assisting clients to achieve superior, sustainable operating results. We developed our Integrated Management System by using a Golden Thread process that weaves through all aspects of the organization to set direction and monitor daily performance. The Golden Thread aligns strategic direction with day-to-day business activities. Our client list includes organizations in a variety of industries, including manufacturing, high-tech and telecommunications, health care, financial institutions, and government.

The Farrell Group is dedicated to assisting clients to define and achieve their business objectives. The Farrell Group integrates proven techniques for strategic planning and strategy implementation with a methodology for linking strategy to operations through performance measurement systems. We help client organizations produce improved bottom-line results through redesigning business processes, market assessments, and positioning. In addition, The Farrell Group conducts studies on customer and employee satisfaction to provide clarity and understanding of how these indicators relate to customer and employee productivity.

The Farrell Group staff has extensive management experience at many Fortune 50 firms. Additionally, our client consulting team brings to our clients the knowledge and experience gained from working with some of the largest and most prestigious consultancies in projects with private sector organizations in Canada, South America, Asia, and Africa.

The design, development, and implementation of Integrated Management Systems forms the foundation of The Farrell Group's consulting services. We work closely with our clients to identify the key drivers of their businesses and industry, to plan for the future, and to operationalize the strategic plans throughout every level of the organization. We provide senior management with the tools to monitor and manage the effectiveness of the business units in meeting strategic goals. Components of our Integrated Management System include:

- Strategic Planning

- Strategy Implementation

- Performance Measurement Systems

- Business Process Reengineering

- Change Management

- Supply Chain Management

- Voice of the Customer

- Voice of the Employee

- Business Recovery

The philosophy we employ is that of establishing a value-based partnership with our clients. We keep the needs of the client foremost as we propose the right mix of consultants' skills and technology for each engagement. We realize that different clients, and even different engagements for the same client, require varying degrees of complexity and will demand a particular level of involvement on our part. We tailor our approach to each engagement, ranging from consultative to collaborative. Our ultimate goal is to transfer our expertise to our clients and assist them in achieving their business objectives. Establishing a long-term relationship with our clients, through repeat engagements as well as ongoing dialogues with senior management, is a hallmark of The Farrell Group's client philosophy.

Describe your organizational structure. Is the firm geographically structured or based around practices? If you have practices, please list them.

The firm is organized around three primary practice areas, strategic management services, stakeholder satisfaction, and business recovery. We do not organize around geography.

Who are your competitors, and how does your approach to consulting differ from theirs?

Competition comes from both general management consulting firms and specialty firms.

Summarize your growth in terms of revenues (both domestic and international) and professional staff over the past year; over the past five years.

The revenue and professional staff growth over the past several years has been significant and in line with our growth plans.

Consultant's Job Description

Describe the career path and corresponding responsibilities for an MBA at your firm.

The career path is as follows:

- Consultant—execute research and analysis and participate in the formulation of recommendations to improve client performance

- Senior Consultant—in addition to consultant's responsibilities, lead project assignments and case teams

- Manager—plan and manage client casework and teams

- Vice President—responsible for business development and client relationships

As an MBA advances through the firm, how much is he or she required to specialize by level?

Consultants are provided with the opportunity to work in a variety of industry and case assignments. Consultants will work in all practice areas prior to selecting a practice area of primary focus.

How big is a typical case team? How many cases does a consultant work on simultaneously?

Our project teams range in size in accordance to the scope and duration of the client work. Depending on the type of project, a consultant can expect to work on one to three projects at one time.

Discuss the lifestyle aspects of a career with your firm; i.e., average hours per week, amount of travel, flexibility to change offices.

Consultants on average work 50 hours per week and generally travel two to three days per week.

What is your firm's turnover rate for professionals? What careers do your ex-consultants typically pursue after leaving?

Our turnover rate is very low. Consultants who leave generally assume senior management positions in industry.

The Recruiting Process

Describe the recruiting process and the criteria by which you select candidates.

The firm recruits and selects candidates with the requisite academic and professional skills who can work well within a collaborative environment. We seek candidates who will provide a primary focus on the client's expectations and outcomes and demonstrate the ability to build client relationships. The Farrell Group focuses its recruiting efforts on finding individuals who bring strong problem-solving abilities, good communication skills, and whenever possible, previous management or consulting experience.

From which schools do you actively recruit? Do you consider applicants from other schools?

The firm recruits MBA graduates annually on campus at leading business schools in the United States.

How many full-time consultants do you expect to hire?

The firm plans to hire three to five MBA graduates this year.

How many summer interns do you expect to hire? If you have a formal summer program, please describe it. Please be sure to indicate whether the program is in place for all offices or just some.

Summer intern hiring is based on business need and applicant skills and experience.

Human Resources Practices

Describe your firm's performance appraisal system for consultants. Are there explicit criteria against which an MBA is evaluated before being promoted? How many times a year is there a performance appraisal and hence an opportunity for promotion? Is there an upward evaluation process too?

The Farrell Group has an annual review process. We work with each consultant to agree on individual professional as well as personal growth goals and objectives.

Please describe any initial training programs or ongoing professional development programs for young professionals.

Consultants are provided with an orientation program and participate in the design of an individual development program.

First Annapolis Consulting, Inc.

900 Elkridge Landing Road
Suite 400
Linthicum, MD 21090
(410) 855-8500
Fax: (410) 865-8899
Web site: www.1st-annapolis.com

MBA Recruiting Contact(s):
Sandra L. Westervelt, Director of Recruiting

Location of Offices:
Suburban Baltimore, MD

Total Number of Professionals (U.S. and worldwide):
45 Professionals

Company Description

Describe your firm by type of consulting work performed and by types of clients served. What changes are planned in the next few years in terms of services, clients, or location of offices?

First Annapolis Consulting, Inc. is a full-service, general management consulting firm specializing in financial services. We serve clients nationally and internationally. Our services include planning, financial analysis and management, marketing and market research, operations, and management. An affiliate, First Annapolis Capital, provides merger and acquisition adviser services.

Our clients generally include (1) domestic and international financial service companies, such as commercial banks, special purpose banks, foreign banks, thrifts, securities firms, and mortgage companies; (2) technology companies such as credit card processors, EFT networks, other processors, hardware and software vendors, and telecommunications companies; (3) retail and industrial companies, such as credit card divisions and other payment services divisions; and (4) other interested parties, such as credit card associations, trade associations, regulators, and investors.

Our major practice areas include: credit card issuance, merchant card processing, electronic banking, mortgage banking, and to a lesser degree, retail banking. We operate both as full service management consultants as well as merger and acquisition advisers through our affiliate, First Annapolis Capital. Our offices are located in Linthicum, Maryland, just south of the city of Baltimore, near the Baltimore-Washington International Airport.

Describe your organizational structure. Is the firm geographically structured or based around practices? If you have practices, please list them.

The organizational structure is flat and informal; we have avoided creating inhibiting structure and hierarchy. MBA candidates are recruited as associate consultants. We currently employ the titles principal, senior associate consultant, and associate consultant to describe our professionals.

Our practices include credit card issuance, merchant card processing, electronic banking, mortgage banking, and retail banking.

Who are your competitors and how does your approach to consulting differ from theirs?

Our competitors range in size from other small niche providers to the big six consulting firms.

Our professionals have a unique combination of consulting skills, specialized industry knowledge, and practical experience. Several have been senior officers of major financial services companies. Others have extensive experience as vendors to the financial services industry. All are committed to providing our clients with sound, practical advice. Each project is managed by a small team of experienced professionals who draw on their individual skills and experiences as well as our firm's knowledge base to provide innovative, customized solutions. We are not an ivory tower consulting firm; instead we focus on practical, executable advice. We tend to have greater depth and greater staffing in our niches than the larger general management consulting firms have.

Summarize your growth in terms of revenues (both domestic and international) and professional staff over the past year; over the past five years.

Our revenues are growing at planned projected rates, and the proportion of our revenues from international clients' markets has increased to more significant levels in the past two years. Our international projects (concentrated in Canada, Mexico, the Caribbean, and Europe) accounted for up to 15 percent of our total revenue last year.

Approximately how many professionals do you have at each level, i.e., how wide is your pyramid?

The consulting firm currently has one principal and senior consultant for every two consultants and analysts. Of our 60 total staff, some 50 are generalist and technical staff.

Consultant's Job Description

Describe the career path and corresponding responsibilities for an MBA at your firm.

Successful consultants work under the direction of the firm's principal consultants on a wide variety of projects. They quickly assume responsibility for managing key tasks and projects and supervising analysts. Consultants also play an active role in business development efforts.

There is ample opportunity for professional growth in a fast paced environment. Our consultants are provided the opportunity to develop a breadth and depth of expertise in an industry far more quickly than their peers. Many of our consultants have found that they have surpassed their fellow MBA peers who elected to become employed at larger consulting firms in terms of skill level and marketability.

As an MBA advances through the firm, how much is he or she required to specialize by level?

Consultants generally develop a specialty in one of our practice areas, or in certain functional areas (e.g., information management, risk management), although all consultants may have the opportunity to work on a variety of assignments across our practice areas at a given time.

How big is a typical case team? How many cases does a consultant work on simultaneously?

The size of a case team depends on the size and scope of the individual project. The average engagement requires two to four personnel in some combination of consultants and analysts, and the average engagement is three to six months. A consultant will normally be working concurrently on two primary engagements, and two to three smaller assignments.

Discuss the lifestyle aspects of a career with your firm; i.e., average hours per week, amount of travel, flexibility to change offices.

Unlike many consulting firms whose personnel travel extensively and remain on client sites for protracted periods of time, our consultants travel an average of 30 to 40 % of the time. The majority of our work is prepared in our offices using our professional and research personnel. Travel is necessitated by initial interviews, client meetings, data gathering, and presentation of deliverables. In a deadline driven environment, work schedules vary. However, a workweek is in the range of 50 to 60 hours and, if necessary, includes weekend work.

What is your firm's turnover rate for professionals? What careers to your ex-consultants typically pursue after leaving?

The turnover rate for consultants is very low. Of the consultants who have left us, many have taken positions with our clients and with other industry players.

The Recruiting Process

Describe your recruiting process and the criteria by which you select candidates.

First Annapolis recruits through the use of the career offices at a number of top business schools, through advertising in trade and business publications, as well as referrals. Candidates are selected on the basis of technical skills, intellectual competencies, interpersonal competencies, motivation and goal orientation, as well as overall impressions. We specifically assess candidates in areas such as experience in banking-related industries, analysis and problem solving, flexibility, team building skills, communication skills, professionalism, management and planning capabilities, career focus and aspirations, customer orientation, and leadership aptitude. Typically, our professional staff members visit campuses and conduct interviews with candidates through open and closed schedules. Selected candidates are then invited to interview further at our office in Maryland.

From which schools do you actively recruit? Do you consider applicants from other schools?

Currently the firm recruits from the following business schools: Harvard, Kellogg, Chicago, Wharton, Carnegie Mellon, and Darden. We have also recruited from Tuck, Duke, Michigan, Stern, Kenan-Flagler, and Cornell. We consider applicants with outstanding academic credentials from other business schools.

How many full time consultants do you expect to hire in the coming year?

We expect to hire a minimum of four to six consultants from the 2000 graduating classes.

How many summer interns do you expect to hire? If you have a formal summer program, please describe it.

Please be sure to indicate whether the program is in place for all offices or just some.

The firm does not conduct a summer intern program.

Human Resources Practices

Describe your firm's performance appraisal system for consultants. Are there explicit criteria against which an MBA is evaluated before being promoted? How many times a year is there a performance appraisal and hence an opportunity for promotion? Is there an upward evaluation process too?

Performance evaluations of consultants are generally conducted in writing once a year, in December, followed by verbal reviews in June. The categories used in professional performance reviews include analytic skills, communication skills, client and project management skills, teamwork skills, business development skills, along with management's assessment of their overall contribution to the firm. During the evaluation process, consultants work with management to plan individual development goals that lead to promotion within the organization.

What benefits does your company provide for maternity, paternity, or adoption leave?

Our firm currently has provisions for leave for a number of reasons that are in compliance with the Family and Medical Leave Act.

Please describe any initial training programs or ongoing professional development programs for young professionals.

We assess training needs individually. The firm sponsors a tuition reimbursement program for graduates and undergraduates, as well as nondegree directed study. Specialized training on- and off-site is also provided for staff members. Further, in our view, candidates we hire from MBA campuses generally do not lack formal training; on the other hand, our candidates typically tend to benefit greatly from practical consulting experiences, and we try to involve new colleagues in the project work of the firm immediately. Each fall the firm conducts a series of orientation training seminars for new professionals.

Describe your firm's outplacement services.

On a case by case basis, the firm has made use of professional national outplacement services, generally over a three-month period.

Does your firm provide for on-site day care? If not, do you provide compensation for day care? Is flextime possible?

The firm does not provide compensation for day care, but does have a Flexible Spending plan that allows employees a pretax pay deduction of up to $5000 per year for day care.

First Manhattan Consulting Group

90 Park Avenue, 18th Floor
New York, NY 10016
(212) 557-0500
Fax: (212) 557-0163
Web site: www.fmcg.com/career

MBA Recruiting Contact(s):
Human Resources

Location of Office:
New York

Total Number of Professionals (U.S. and worldwide):
80

Company Description

Describe your firm by type of consulting work performed and by types of clients served. What changes are planned in the next few years in terms of services, clients, or locations of offices?

FMCG is dedicated to serving the financial services industry on a wide range of top-management issues with one very specific goal: increasing clients' shareholder value.

We have built expertise in strategy, finance, technology, productivity, and other areas necessary to enable our clients to meet the challenges now facing the industry. As key issues for the industry emerge, FMCG invests in practice development to provide thought leadership. For example:

- Pioneering work on shareholder value in the early to mid 1980s

- Introducing banks to Customer-Knowledge-Based Management™, a technique that uses behavioral data and research aids to identify customer needs

- Developing benchmarks for the businesses that banks operate, including perspectives on achievable ROE and growth

- Assembling "best practices" for post-merger consolidation and bankwide productivity programs

- Helping banks manage the transition to Web enabled e-commerce

- Helping banks assess and contract outsourcing of major parts of their infrastructure

Since 1980, FMCG has completed over 2,000 assignments. Our clients include:

- 80 percent of the 50 largest bank holding companies

- Over 40 regional banks with assets of between $1B and $25B

- Major foreign banks headquartered in 11 different countries

- Half of the leading investment banks

- Most of the major national brokerage firms

- Leading regional brokerages

- Major finance companies, guarantee companies, and diversified financial firms

- Over 25 technology and other vendors to the industry

At any time, over three-quarters of FMCG's current projects are repeat engagements requested by clients who have been previously served by the firm. Over 50 client institutions have been served more than 10 times and several over 100 times.

Describe your organizational structure. Is the firm geographically structured or based around practices? If you have practices, please list them.

FMCG is organized around practice areas. While most of our work is within the United States, we do have a strong presence in Australia, Canada, Latin America, and South America, with some work in Europe.

Our practice areas include:

Clients' Lines of Business

- Retail Banking

- Investment Management

- Brokerage Services

- Private Banking and Trust

109

- Mortgage Banking

- Insurance Services

- Corporate Banking and Finance

- Corporate and Institutional Trust

Functional Practice Areas

- Corporate and Business Strategy

- Marketing and Segmentation

- Business/Product/Customer Profitability

- Benchmarking and Process Reengineering

- Distribution Strategy/Design

- A/L Management

- Risk Management

- Systems Architecture

- Joint Ventures/Outsourcing

- Organizational Design

- Incentive Compensation

Who are your competitors, and how does your approach to consulting differ from theirs?

FMCG seeks to be the consulting firm of choice for senior managers of large financial service institutions or corporations. We will achieve this position by:

1. Addressing top-level issues and providing solutions that add significant value to clients
2. Building long-term relationships with senior managers in clients and prospects
3. Developing and communicating thought leadership in our chosen functional and line-of-business practices

The firm is distinctive in four respects:

1. Our specialization in the financial services industry enables us to relate to the special needs of these businesses.
2. All our recommendations are driven by a focus on maximizing our clients' shareholder value and a strong bias toward insights based on analysis of the facts and application of modern finance.

3. We have proven management skills useful on broad initiatives related to growth and diversification strategies, merger planning and integration, expense control, and line-of-business management.
4. We invest in building leading-edge viewpoints on the financial services industry and the requirements for players to win.

Summarize your growth in terms of revenues (both domestic and international) and professional staff over the past year; over the past five years.

FMCG has had a steady growth in staff and revenues over the last 16 years. As of April 2000 we had approximately 80 consulting and 30 support staff.

Consultant's Job Description

Describe the career path and corresponding responsibilities for an MBA at your firm.

Entering MBAs begin in either the associate or the consultant position, depending on their experience prior to entering business school. FMCG's career path is based on performance. Individuals can move up through the ranks as quickly as their performance merits. The factors that influence advancement are:

1. Project management skills—i.e., planning, organization, report writing, and managing analysts
2. Client management skills—e.g., ability to handle different client situations, structure and run client meetings with appropriate content and style
3. Client-based experiences that enable the individual to function with minimal supervision in creating client deliverables
4. An expert knowledge base that combines a broad-based knowledge of the financial services industry (especially banking and/or insurance) and a thought-leadership position in a particular practice area
5. Professional deportment

How big is a typical case team? How many cases does a consultant work on simultaneously?

A consultant can expect to work on one to three projects at a time, usually two.

Project team size and an individual's role and responsibility vary with project type and practice area. On average project teams are relatively small. They can range from two (officer and analyst) to three (officer, consultant, and analyst) to seven (officer, senior consultant, two consultants, and several analysts). On smaller teams individuals have a wide range of responsibilities that provide opportunities to "stretch" beyond current performance levels. This may include more client interaction, a larger role in developing and writing documents, or managing analysts.

Discuss the lifestyle aspects of a career with your firm; i.e., average hours per week, amount of travel, flexibility to change offices.

The workload and time demands at FMCG are determined by client commitments. Our entrepreneurial culture reinforces the push for insights and thought leadership that drives our workday. A minimum workweek is 60 hours and may include time traveling to a client. Although some assignments are local, travel is an integral part of the consultant's life. Travel to other cities can be for the day; however, some projects require several days a week at the client site. Weekend work is sometimes required.

What is your firm's turnover rate for professionals? What careers do your ex-consultants typically pursue after leaving?

Consulting staff turnover is difficult to quantify. Most of our hires have historically been undergraduates. Many of these analysts leave the firm to go to business school. Some return to FMCG after gaining a year or two of experience in another environment. Some of our analysts never pursue an MBA, but stay on and progress within the firm. While individual promotion is based on merit and varies accordingly, typically a strong performer may become a senior consultant after two years, a senior engagement manager after three to four years, and a vice president after four to six years. Of the few consultants who have left FMCG, a roughly equal number have left for industry experience as have gone to other consulting firms that do not specialize in financial services.

The Recruiting Process

Describe your recruiting process and the criteria by which you select candidates.

FMCG does not have a formal recruiting program for MBAs. However, we are always looking for smart, driven individuals with financial services experience to join our team. Interested individuals should submit a résumé (including grades and GRE or GMAT scores) with a cover letter.

In the initial interview session, candidates meet with a peer (i.e., an FMCG Associate or Consultant) and a Senior Consultant. Subsequent interviews are with officers.

Candidates can expect to meet with a minimum of four members of FMCG.

Human Resources Practices

Describe your firm's performance appraisal system for consultants. Are there explicit criteria against which an MBA is evaluated before being promoted? How many times a year is there a performance appraisal and hence an opportunity for promotion? Is there an upward evaluation process too?

FMCG does not require its consultants to hold an MBA, nor do we have an "up or out" policy.

The firm recognizes that our employees are our primary assets. FMCG's entrepreneurial environment offers smart and driven MBAs and undergraduates a uniquely challenging career opportunity by:

- Ensuring that individuals' advancement within FMCG is based on meritorious criteria related to the underpinnings of success listed above

- Providing an environment that stimulates everyone to do their best and offering myriad opportunities for growth

- Rewarding exemplary performance with financial compensation that surpasses competitors

FMCG is committed to providing growth opportunities for analytically minded individuals who have a willingness to work hard.

Consulting staff members are reviewed at the end of each project. Annual reviews occur in April. Salary increases are effective April 1, and bonuses are paid out in April, based on the previous calendar year. There is a brief mid-year "check-in" in October. Promotion decisions are made twice a year, once during the annual review period and once in October.

There is an upward review process that corresponds with the project review process.

For all reviews, consulting staff are evaluated on the five criteria noted in the section on the consultant job description.

Please describe any initial training programs or ongoing professional development programs for young professionals.

While most consultant training is on-the-job, there is a formal orientation program for the consulting staff that addresses administrative areas necessary for success at FMCG. There are training videos and documents for all practice areas. Continuing professional development is supported by:

- Formal training sessions for writing and presentation skills

- Individual mentors that assist in identifying areas and steps for development

- Consultants' lunches that provide an arena to share project experience/industry knowledge, address firmwide issues, and discuss common development goals

Gemini Consulting

A Division of Cap Gemini America, Inc.

1114 Avenue of the Americas
35th Floor
New York, NY 10036
Web site: www.gemcon.com

MBA Recruiting Contact(s):
Diane Provini
Recruiting Manager, North America

Locations of Offices:
Barcelona, Berlin, Brussels, Bucharest, Cambridge, Cologne, Frankfurt, Helsinki, Johannesburg, Lisbon, London, Lyon, Madrid, Milan, Morristown, Munich, New York, Oslo, Paris, Riga, Petersburg, Singapore, Stockholm, Tokyo, Utrecht, Vienna, Warsaw, Zurich

Total Number of Professionals (U.S. and worldwide):
More than 1,300

Company Description

Describe your firm by type of consulting work performed and by types of clients served. What changes are planned in the next few years in terms of services, clients, or locations of offices?

Gemini Consulting is a global management consulting firm dedicated to helping business leaders design and implement change through people and technology. With 27 offices throughout Europe, Asia, Africa, and the Americas, we are able to deploy people, knowledge, and capabilities rapidly around the globe. Team members with expertise in strategy, operations, information, and change management bring together state-of-the-art analytical skills and methodologies that enable clients to position their businesses effectively for future growth.

The Gemini approach to e-business is unlike that of any other consulting firm. We view the Internet and technology as not only business solutions, but also as driving forces that continuously redefine boundaries. Gemini in the U.S. has launched an E-Business Unit, which will integrate traditional business strategy with e-strategy, allowing clients to analyze, develop, prioritize, and im- plement flexible business solutions that will deliver sustainable value creation.

Gemini commits to measurable results in advance with its clients, and then helps them implement the actions necessary to achieve those results. We work in teams with our clients in a variety of industries, including automotive, banking, chemicals and the environment, computers, consumer and durable goods, electronics, energy, financial services, healthcare, insurance, pharmaceuticals, securities, telecommunications, transportation, travel, tourism, and utilities.

Gemini consultants apply a dynamic range of industry and business expertise to meet the needs of complex client engagements. Strong academic ties further enhance our depth of experience and knowledge base; our faculty affiliates include leading-edge business thinkers and strategists from top universities and business schools around the globe.

Who are your competitors, and how does your approach to consulting differ from theirs?

Gemini's major competitive advantage rests on our reputation for consistently delivering results to our clients. We work directly on-site. We analyze the strengths and weaknesses of the client organization, create a blueprint for change, and assist the client in implementing sustainable, measurable change, leading to profitability, and growth.

Consultant's Job Description

Describe the career path and corresponding responsibilities for an MBA at your firm.

At Gemini, consultants manage their careers along specific paths of work and achievement that they, their mentors, and Gemini officers have identified as meaningful and appropriate. Self-motivated, high-energy people have unlimited potential for professional growth at Gemini. We are a meritocracy. Compensation and career advancement depend on performance and productivity. We reward and promote those who create profitability, growth, and a winning culture for our clients—and for Gemini.

Working on a Gemini team means working in a close-knit group of MBAs and experienced professionals from around the world. Such diversity puts a premium on adherence to our shared values. Our consultants work closely with top management at the client site and take on highly visible roles that carry extensive responsibilities.

Discuss the lifestyle aspects of a career with your firm; i.e., average hours per week, amount of travel, flexibility to change offices.

At Gemini, the client always comes first. We believe in having Gemini presence full-time at the client's key work site for visibility and impact, and in order to deliver results to our clients faster than they expect. Consultants often travel to client locations on Monday and return home on Friday.

We understand the challenges that frequent travel can cause and realize the importance of a strong personal and family life. We do our best to ensure that our consultants have ample time to spend with their family and friends away from the workplace. Further, Gemini offers a confidential employee assistance program to help teammates maintain a sense of balance between work and personal interests.

Gemini's culture brings together excellent people from all over the world. Market- and client-based meetings and firm-sponsored recreational events promote close, harmonious working relationships. Among our many benefits are sabbatical and reduced work schedule programs that offer flexibility in supporting our people's needs and those of our clients.

The Recruiting Process

Describe your recruiting process and the criteria by which you select candidates.

Gemini consultants come both from universities and industry. MBA candidates participate in multiple interviews, both on campus and in our offices.

To succeed in this demanding and stimulating environment, Gemini consultants need to have certain key skills and core attitudes:

- A rigorous academic background, preferably including a second language

- Sturdy individuality and a strong ethical core

- Creativity and a high tolerance for change, travel, and challenge

- Exceptional interpersonal and communications skills

- Business insight and analytical acumen

- Demonstrated business process expertise

- Ability to generate enthusiasm in a team environment

- A record of success in leadership roles

Human Resources Practices

Describe your firm's performance appraisal system for consultants. Are there explicit criteria against which an MBA is evaluated before being promoted? How many times a year is there a performance appraisal and hence an opportunity for promotion? Is there an upward evaluation process too?

All Gemini consultants participate in a development review process two times a year. Consultants are also reviewed at the completion of each engagement. To be considered for promotion, our people must meet clearly defined criteria that measure the ability to learn and use new consulting skills and refine existing ones, and assess our contribution to the success of our clients and our firm.

Please describe any initial training programs or ongoing professional development programs for young professionals.

Initially, consultants receive a two-week intensive basic skills course in Gemini tools and techniques. Because we believe that the best people working together create the best results, we strive to provide many ways to advance, learn, and grow. Consultants may choose to expand their knowledge in a specific field, or in engagement management, or along geographical and cultural lines. Both region-based and engagement-based training programs supplement cross-industry training and interaction. In addition, Gemini University regularly provides consultants with the opportunity to upgrade and expand their skills and knowledge base.

Greenwich Associates

8 Greenwich Office Park
Greenwich, CT 06831-5195
(203) 629-1200
Fax: (203) 629-1229
Web site: www.greenwich.com

MBA Recruiting Contact(s):
Lisa Caravello, Director, Human Resources
James A. Bennett, Jr., Partner

Location of Offices:
Greenwich, Sydney

Total Number of Professionals (U.S. and worldwide):
29, with staff of 136 total

Company Description

Describe your firm by type of consulting work performed and by types of clients served. What changes are planned in the next few years in terms of services, clients, or locations of offices?

Greenwich Associates is a leading strategic consulting firm specializing in professional financial services. In over 25 years of service development, we have originated—and continue to deliver—more than 100 research and consulting programs worldwide. Our client engagements include virtually all major financial service organizations in the United States, Canada, and the United Kingdom, and many of those in continental Europe, Japan, Asia, and Australia. In number of clients, London is now our largest city.

We anticipate rapid development of our proprietary research platform through several e-commerce initiatives currently in process.

Who are your competitors, and how does your approach to consulting differ from theirs?

Because we are specialists in financial services and because our services involve a unique combination of strong, continuing, high-level relationships and extensive proprietary research and expertise, we have no direct competitors. Our major indirect competitors are the nation's largest consulting firms and market research vendors. Our relationships with clients are sustaining; more than 95% of our work is with regularly repeating clients.

Summarize your growth in terms of revenues (both domestic and international) and professional staff over the past year; over the past five years.

We consistently emphasize qualitative growth in the value of our services to clients. As a private partnership, our revenues are confidential. In the past few years, several associates, vice presidents, and one partner have joined the firm. We continue to look for two to three MBAs with several years' experience in financial services or consulting to join our practice areas.

Consultant's Job Description

Describe the career path and corresponding responsibilities for an MBA at your firm.

We seek consultants who will become partners, so the development process is designed to enable the most capable consultants to advance as rapidly as possible to partnership.

Consultants join us as associates. Each associate will work in a one-to-one relationship with a partner who is responsible for the associate obtaining broad exposure to the firm's overall consulting practice, mastering our proprietary research methodology, learning consulting skills, and developing a clientele.

Successful individuals will take increasing responsibility for client consulting and for the strategic and business planning of the firm as a whole. Associates are expected to become experts in selected industry sectors over a three- to five-year period and to manage one or more of the firm's consulting and research programs within two years of joining the firm.

As an MBA advances through the firm, how much is he or she required to specialize by level?

Our clients expect our consultants to be specialists—with the resulting expert knowledge—and so we all specialize in one or two major businesses within financial services—investment banking, corporate and commercial banking, equity brokerage, bond dealing, foreign exchange, derivatives, and investment management. On the other hand, because each of us works with several clients around the world, we have diverse engagements in our consulting. The degree of specialization is similar for consultants at all levels.

Discuss the lifestyle aspects of a career with your firm; i.e., average hours per week, amount of travel, flexibility to change offices.

Our consultants typically spend 60% of their time working directly with clients. Most consultants have international client engagements.

Working directly with senior executives at client organizations on specific strategic and tactical issues typically represents 50–75% of each experienced consultant's time. Other time is spent at our offices.

Several lifestyle aspects of this work are important. Because our relationships are unusually long-lived, our work is with friends. And because we act as principals rather than agents, we set our own schedules and almost never get a "command summons" that might interfere with personal time.

Most consultants work regularly with clients abroad, particularly in London, Frankfurt, Paris, Toronto, Tokyo, Sydney, and Hong Kong. This international experience is an important opportunity for professional growth. Trips often last a week, and six to eight weeks a year abroad is typical.

Teamwork and friendship are valued and important characteristics of the firm. We enjoy working together.

Consultants are encouraged to take long vacations. We work harder than most during peak periods and expect everyone to rest and play more than most at other periods. Consultants find their ability to plan vacations and to be sure of not being interrupted are both important to their families.

What is your firm's turnover rate for professionals? What careers do your ex-consultants typically pursue after leaving?

Turnover is normal. Most ex-consultants enter the financial services industry working with existing clients of the firm.

The Recruiting Process

Describe your recruiting process and the criteria by which you select candidates.

We are looking for associates who will become partners in our firm, so standards are unusually high. Candidates must have distinctive competence in quantitative analysis; skill in writing, persuasion, and consultation; and a strong sense of inner direction and high professional standards.

Candidates typically have six to eight interviews with our consultants.

From which schools do you actively recruit? Do you consider applicants from other schools?

We welcome candidates from all major business schools and now actively recruit from Harvard, Wharton, and Northwestern. While our compensation strategy emphasizes equity ownership, our salary and bonus levels are highly competitive with other consulting and investment banking firms.

How many full-time consultants do you expect to hire in the coming year?

We plan to hire two to three associates.

Human Resources Practices

Describe your firm's performance appraisal system for consultants. Are there explicit criteria against which an MBA is evaluated before being promoted? How many times a year is there a performance appraisal and hence an opportunity for promotion? Is there an upward evaluation process too?

Competence and performance standards are established in writing for each level of promotion, and the appraisal process is designed to enable each consultant to progress as rapidly as he or she is able. Each new consultant is paired with a partner mentor, and because they work extensively together, informal feedback is virtually continuous. Formal written reviews are conducted annually for all consultants and twice a year for associates. Using the written standards, each consultant prepares a two- to five-page written review of his or her achievements and identifies next steps for professional development.

The partners collectively review each consultant—also in writing—and discuss differences in appraisals privately with the consultant, who writes a brief summary of what he or she has learned.

Each pre-partner consultant prepares a year-ahead development plan with his or her partner mentor to ensure explicit agreement on each consultant's professional career development.

Please describe any initial training programs or ongoing development programs for young professionals.

New associates train with partners and other senior consultants.

Describe your firm's outplacement services.

So few consultants leave that we can design a customized process for each one—and do.

Does your firm provide for on-site day care? If not, do you provide compensation for day care? Is flextime possible?

Our consultants manage their own schedules.

Hamilton•HMC

A Division of Kurt Salmon Associates

1355 Peachtree Street, NE, Suite 900
Atlanta, GA 30309
(404) 892-3436
Fax: (404) 253-0388
Web sites: www.hamiltonhmc.com;
www.kurtsalmon.com

MBA Recruiting Contact(s):
Marian N. Crandall, Principal, Director of Recruiting

Locations of Offices:
Headquartered in Atlanta, with offices in Minneapolis,
New York, San Francisco, and Los Angeles

Total Number of Professionals (U.S. and worldwide):
Approximately 80 professionals in the U.S. within
Hamilton•HMC; over 600 worldwide within Kurt
Salmon Associates

Company Description

*Describe your firm by type of consulting work performed
and by types of clients served.*

Hamilton•HMC, the Health Services Division of Kurt
Salmon Associates (KSA), is one of the most prominent
specialized health care consulting practices in the nation,
serving providers and a variety of other health care organizations.

Hamilton•HMC is a respected name with a national and
international reputation. Over the last 50 years, the organization has served more than 2,000 health care clients in
all 50 states and eight foreign countries. The strength of
the firm centers on the depth and experience of its staff,
who provide expertise in virtually every aspect of the
health care industry.

*Describe your organizational structure. Is the firm geo-
graphically structured or based around practices? If you
have practices, please list them.*

The firm's organizational structure is designed to deliver
integrated services to the client. Because of the nature of
the problems and solutions with which we deal, our organization must remain flexible and responsive. We are organized in geographic regions to ensure attention to professional development. Also, we have functional service
teams, which are focused on assembling the best consultants the firm can offer to meet an individual client's
unique challenges.

As health care specialists, Hamilton•HMC offers a full
range of services to a client base comprising the entire
spectrum of organizations operating in the health care
sector. Our staff of talented professionals—representing a
wide range of consulting, operational, and educational
experience—provides clients with many types of consulting services, including the following:

• Strategic Planning

• Information Technology

• Managed Care

• Facility and Capital Asset Planning

• Physician Planning and Implementation

Strategic Planning and Implementation Services

Hamilton•HMC works with the client's senior leadership
on a wide range of activities, from drafting a high-level
organizational vision statement to tactical action steps,
such as identifying optimal locations for primary care
clinics. We assist clients in developing rationale to support specific business and product-related decisions.

Information Technology Services

The Division's IT services offer comprehensive assistance to clients in the complex arena of information technology, an increasingly essential prerequisite to making a
successful transition into the competitive arena of integrated delivery systems. We assist clients with IT strategic planning, system selection, vendor evaluation and selection, and implementation project management. Using
proven methodologies, we protect our client's information technology investment.

Managed Care Services

Managed care services provide assistance to clients in every aspect of strategy, development, and the operation of
managed care organizations. Our consultants help these
managed care providers to be market leaders in terms of
demonstrable high-quality, low-cost performance and
competitive position.

Facility and Capital Asset Planning

Facility planning services help clients achieve the highest and best use of their existing resources and manage the total cost of housing the delivery system. The operations services guide clients as they improve efficiency and eliminate costs through thoughtful, principled improvement in the way they arrange, provide, track, and support health care delivery. Facility and operations services combine to ensure that a client's physical plant can support the redesign processes.

Physician Planning and Implementation Services

Physician services assist clients as they look to develop a physician organization or a network of physician practices. Hamilton•HMC works with clients to develop strategies, select and adopt an operations model, restructure compensation plans to reward productivity and control expense, develop recruiting approaches that attract physicians who will grow the practice, and create a managed care strategy to take advantage of opportunities in the market.

Who are your competitors, and how does your approach to consulting differ from theirs?

Hamilton•HMC competes with consulting divisions from the top firms, including CSC/APM, the Big 5, McKinsey & Company, Inc., and specialty health care consulting firms. Our organization defines itself by both a client focus dedicated to implementing practical solutions, and a concern for the larger issues affecting health care institutions today. This balance of customer-directed services and a broad forward-looking perspective gives the firm a special identity in the health care consulting field. Approximately 85% of our work is in assignments with ongoing clients.

An essential component of our approach to consulting is the combination of active involvement of senior consultants and full participation by staff consultants in client engagements. Senior consultants, who have a wealth of experience to contribute, regularly participate in client interviews, brainstorming and decision-making sessions, strategic and implementation planning meetings, and boardroom presentations. Hamilton•HMC staff consultants are involved in all aspects of an engagement from research and analysis, to on-site client presentations at the boardroom level. New consultants have frequent interaction with clients.

Our approach to consulting begins with our hiring philosophy. KSA's hiring philosophy may be considered quite different from other firms in the industry: We hire future principals. The firm invests in the long-term development of its people because of the desire to see consultants grow with their experiences. Immediately upon joining KSA, consultants play an integral role within a project team. New consultants will have significant exposure and develop close working relationships with highly experienced consultants. Someone familiar with KSA, a former senior manager of a top strategy consulting firm, may have stated the view of our firm the best. She remarked, "You can have a great consulting experience at my former firm, or you can join KSA and have a great consulting career."

Summarize your growth in terms of revenues (both domestic and international) and professional staff over the past year; over the past five years.

Kurt Salmon Associates has sustained an average growth rate of 21% over the last five years.

Approximately how many professionals do you have at each level, i.e., how wide is your pyramid?

Hamilton•HMC has a principal-to-staff ratio of 1:3.

Consultant's Job Description

Describe the career path and corresponding responsibilities for an MBA at your firm.

All hires from campus recruiting have MBA, MHA, or similar degrees. The career path runs from consultant to manager to principal. An unusual aspect of working at Hamilton•HMC is the consultant's rapid development and assumption of responsibility. Consultants with as little as one or two years of experience often find themselves working directly with senior managers or CEOs of client organizations. The typical challenge involves translating recently learned principles of business management into practical solutions for demanding, sophisticated clients.

After three to five years, the consultant progresses to manager, assuming greater responsibilities in the management of individual client engagements. Specific responsibilities include managing multifunctional projects and further developing a functional or submarket specialization within health care. Business development efforts also become more important.

After six or more years with the firm, the manager may be promoted to principal with an ownership stake in the firm.

(The firm is solely owned by its active principals.) The primary responsibilities of principals are business development and relationship management. Principals may be asked to manage a functional or geographic portion of the practice. These assignments rotate periodically.

As an MBA advances through the firm, how much is he or she required to specialize by level?

Individual consultants tend to develop expertise centered around a particular functional area as they progress in their careers. All new consultants, however, are involved in the full array of projects in which Hamilton•HMC participates. This exposure to, and knowledge of the full range of, functional areas help our consultants to increase their skill sets and to bring greater value to client engagements.

How big is a typical case team? How many cases does a consultant work on simultaneously?

Typically, consulting teams range in size from small teams made up of two to three individuals to multi-office teams of five to six consultants. The size of each team depends on the size of each engagement, the length of the project, and other factors that contribute to the success of an engagement.

A consultant typically works on one to two projects simultaneously, and may work on up to four or five projects at the same time. This depends on his or her degree of involvement in each project.

Discuss the lifestyle aspects of a career with your firm; i.e., average hours per week, amount of travel, flexibility to change offices.

The average hours per week that Hamilton•HMC consultants work is comparable to other prominent consulting firms. Consultants' travel varies by client assignment, with an average of 50% of business nights spent away from home. Changing office locations is not a frequent occurrence, but may be discussed with the firm leadership should a change in office assignments be desired.

What is your firm's turnover rate for professionals? What careers do your ex-consultants typically pursue after leaving?

As a result of careful selection and the nature of the firm and the practice, Hamilton•HMC's annual turnover rate is quite low for a consulting firm, approximately 17%. We believe this reflects our healthy balance between the intense demands of consulting and the equally important demands of family and personal commitments. Health

care consultants who have left pursue a wide variety of opportunities, including hospital planning and administration, staff and line positions in health care provider networks, positions with health care suppliers, and entrepreneurial ventures.

The Recruiting Process

Describe your recruiting process and the criteria by which you select candidates.

Hamilton•HMC is very selective in its recruiting process. We seek special people who respond eagerly to professionalism and independence in an environment encouraging participation. We expect low turnover and target recruiting efforts accordingly. Our goal is to select and develop satisfied, contributing, productive consultants who have the potential to become principals of the firm. To do so, our health care staff conducts in-depth interviews at a select group of campuses offering MBAs, MHAs, as well as with other sources.

Our MBA candidates are very familiar with the markets served by Hamilton•HMC, having at least two years of full-time work experience in health-care-related businesses and/or consulting. They tend to be at the top of the class. In addition to intelligence, drive, tact, and judgement, all candidates must have solid analytical, creative, and communication skills. Also important is a specific interest in the health care industry and the unique issues it faces, along with an interest in management consulting and rapid professional development.

From which schools do you actively recruit? Do you consider applicants from other schools?

In recent years, Hamilton•HMC has recruited at the following schools, among others: University of Michigan Business School, the Anderson School of Management at UCLA, the Haas School of Business at UC Berkeley, the Darden School of Management at University of Virginia, the Carlson School of Management at the University of Minnesota, and the Goizueta Business School at Emory University. We encourage candidates from other graduate programs who have an interest in health care consulting to write to our director of recruiting for employment consideration.

How many full-time consultants do you expect to hire in the coming year?

Our recruiting needs vary from year to year. In 2000, we plan to add fifteen to twenty consultants to our Health Services Division.

How many summer interns do you expect to hire? If you have a formal summer program, please describe it. Please be sure to indicate whether the program is in place for all offices or just some.

In recent years, we have not hired summer interns in our health care practice, but we are continually evaluating opportunities to create a valuable summer experience that would include interns as members of project teams.

Human Resources Practices

Describe your firm's performance appraisal system for consultants. Are there explicit criteria against which an MBA is evaluated before being promoted? How many times a year is there a performance appraisal and hence an opportunity for promotion? Is there an upward evaluation process too?

Performance is the sole basis for success at Hamilton•HMC. At every level, our consultants continually develop their skills to provide the best service to our clients. Performance is reviewed against published criteria for promotion to the next level and against individually established development objectives. Formal performance reviews are scheduled at the end of each project. In addition, service group directors also conduct year-end and career reviews to assess each consultant's readiness for promotion. During these reviews, new goals are established for future development and progress is monitored and discussed with the consultant on a periodic basis.

Please describe any initial training programs or ongoing professional development programs for young professionals.

Within their first year, new health care consultants participate in a one-week company orientation program and receive additional training covering their particular service group. Professional development for KSA is a career-long commitment, made mutually by the firm and each consultant, and monitored annually. Consultants devote at least 60 hours per year to professional development activities. Throughout the career of a consultant, emphasis is placed on the broad and deep professional development required to be an effective account executive, serving a variety of clients over an extended period of time, and continuing to develop, manage, and directly participate in consulting projects.

Does your firm provide for on-site day care? If not, do you provide compensation for day care? Is flextime possible?

KSA does not provide on-site day care. We have established a Flexible Spending Account program, which enables employees to pay for child day care expenses with pretax dollars.

KSA does not have a formal flextime policy because our consultants' work hours are driven by the needs of their clients and projects. However, where appropriate, consultants and their management have worked out mutually acceptable flexible schedules to accommodate specific needs.

Hay Group, Inc.

100 Penn Square East
Philadelphia, PA 19107
(215) 861-2000
Web site: www.haygroup.com

MBA Recruiting Contact(s):
Marcia O'Connor, National Recruiting Manager

Locations of Offices:
14 U.S. field offices, international locations in 33 countries, 60 international offices

Total Number of Professionals (U.S. and worldwide):
2,200

Ownership Structure of the Firm:
Wholly owned subsidiary

Company Description

Describe your firm by type of consulting work performed and by types of clients served. What changes are planned in the next few years in terms of services, clients, or locations of offices?

Hay is known primarily for its leadership in human resources management consulting, but over the last ten years the organization has diversified its services. Within the human resources function, Hay's pioneering work in the fields of compensation and job evaluation/analysis has been supplemented by the development of successful practices in employee surveying, business culture studies, employee benefit plan design, actuarial services, and human resources planning and development. Other practice areas include strategic management, communications, and technology integration.

With more than 7,000 worldwide clients, Hay's client base transcends industry type and size. The company consults to manufacturing firms in many industries, including aerospace, electronics, and pharmaceuticals. Clients in the service sector include banks, insurance companies, and transportation firms. Nationally, Hay has worked with various units of local, state, and federal governments, as well as government-run industries around the world.

Hay will continue to solidify special practice areas in human resources as our clients discover critical needs. The company will continue to open new offices in the United States and internationally in strategic locations.

Who are your competitors, and how does your approach to consulting differ from theirs?

Competition is generally fragmented and practice-specific. There are no comprehensive competitors. Hay has many established long-term client relationships that account for a significant portion of our business. Other consulting projects come from referrals from established clients. In competitive situations, the company's reputation for progressive, state-of-the-art consulting services is augmented by highly professional and knowledgeable project teams.

Hay's approach differs from others because it emphasizes implementation. Specific recommendations for action rather than "academic" results build a pragmatic client and consultant partnership.

Summarize your growth in terms of revenues (both domestic and international) and professional staff over the past year; over the past five years.

Hay has maintained a steady growth rate during the last five years. Professional staff has grown at approximately the same rate during that time.

Consultant's Job Description

Describe the career path and corresponding responsibilities for an MBA at your firm.

The new associate's first task is to learn the scope of the firm's core services and use his or her background to develop skills in one or more of those services. Training takes place through both formal and informal means, including project involvement with more experienced consultants. To be successful, an associate must be quickly accepted by other consultants as a useful contributor. As experience grows, associates are given increasing accountability for projects and may take over smaller client relationships. Career progression depends on criteria such as value and dependability as a project team member, acceptance by clients, understanding and interpretation of Hay processes, and verbal and written articulation. Movement through consulting management ranks is based exclusively on merit issues.

How big is a typical case team? How many cases does a consultant work on simultaneously?

The average project team consists of three to five consultants but varies depending on the complexity of the project. In some divisions, it would not be unusual for a consultant to be involved in five projects simultaneously.

Discuss the lifestyle aspects of a career with your firm; i.e., average hours per week, amount of travel, flexibility to change offices.

Success in consulting demands a great deal of professional commitment. It is not uncommon for consultants to work 60- to 70-hour weeks. Amount of travel varies but can be as much as 12 to 15 days per month. Transfer to other offices generally occurs only in cases of promotion; however, the company has been flexible and allowed lateral transfers of consultants who have become distinguished contributors and wish to relocate.

What is your firm's turnover rate for professionals? What careers do your ex-consultants typically pursue after leaving?

Hay's professional turnover is very low when compared with that of other large consulting firms. Consultants who do leave pursue such diverse career options as teaching at the university level, starting their own business ventures, entering corporate general management, or following literary and publishing interests.

The Recruiting Process

Describe your recruiting process and the criteria by which you select candidates.

Campus interviews are followed by invitations to interview in one or more field offices. Hiring decisions are made jointly by the general managers and other consultants who aid in the recruitment process. Generally, the company selects candidates based on a variety of criteria, including energy level, enthusiasm, articulation, academic performance and accomplishments, commitment to consulting, and professional experience.

From which schools do you actively recruit? Do you consider applicants from other schools?

The company has an active college relations program and recruits from several of the top graduate business schools. Applicants from other institutions are also considered through our Human Resources Department.

Human Resources Practices

What benefits does your company provide for maternity, paternity, or adoption leave?

We offer a salary continuation plan for medical disabilities. In addition, employees may be eligible to take an unpaid leave of absence for up to 12 weeks in a 12-month period in accordance with The Family and Medical Leave Act of 1993.

Please describe any initial training programs or ongoing professional development programs for young professionals.

Our consultants receive technical and professional skills training as necessary or desirable throughout their consulting careers.

Health Advances, Inc.

40 Grove Street
Wellesley, MA 02482
(781) 235-6626
Web site: www.healthadvances.com

MBA Recruiting Contact(s):
Recruiting Coordinator
E-mail: rec@healthadvances.com

Company Description

Describe your firm by type of consulting work performed and by types of clients served. What changes are planned in the next few years in terms of services, clients, or locations of offices?

Health Advances is an entrepreneurial consulting firm focused exclusively on the health care industry. Our clients include suppliers (biotech, pharmaceutical, medical device, and diagnostic companies), for-profit and not-for-profit providers, and the organizations and individuals who invest in those companies. Much of our work revolves around issues central to the development and commercialization of new products and services, often as an element in helping address a broader question of business planning, mergers and acquisitions, or company valuation. In addition to large, well-established organizations, Health Advances clients include very early-stage start-up companies. Each year Health Advances undertakes a number of projects where at least a portion of its compensation is in the form of equity or success fees.

This last opportunity gets to the heart of Health Advances' entrepreneurial spirit. We proactively seek out emerging opportunities in health care that lend themselves to the formation of unique business concepts. When we find those opportunities we are quick to invest our talented staff in defining the strategy and assembling the infrastructure for a new venture. Not only does it offer attractive upside potential for Health Advances, but also different learning experiences for our staff. All of our clients directly benefit from the hands-on, practical knowledge we gain from working in a start-up environment.

Over the next five years, we expect our growth to be at least 20% on a compound annual basis. This growth will come from maintaining our strong track record of repeat engagements, as well as work with new clients across the United States and internationally.

Who are your competitors, and how does your approach to consulting differ from theirs?

Three features differentiate Health Advances from its competitors: our commitment to health care, our entrepreneurial philosophy, and our dedication to a participative, supportive culture. Our work is characterized by rigorous quantitative analysis conducted by professionals that work in the health care industry every day. When you have the opportunity to apply a particular methodology or analytical technique repeatedly in this highly regulated industry you learn the subtleties of risk and return that underlie the most difficult decisions faced by managers. The accumulated expertise of hundreds of cases in health care combined with our willingness to align our goals with those of our clients when we accept equity compensation, places our teams at the cutting edge of industry developments.

Consulting is unusual in the range of learning experiences it offers and the pace at which one can move up the learning curve. Based on their own experiences, the partners at Health Advances understand that new consultants learn most quickly from a combination of structured training and formal, on-the-job mentoring. They also appreciate the need to achieve a balance between commitments to work, family, and outside activities. Our staff, our company, and our clients all benefit from this unique, progressive consulting environment.

Health Advances is a unique consulting organization. In our larger strategy assignments we compete against the leading management consulting firms and with smaller clients we compete against one- and two-person organizations. Our senior professionals have years of experience in large consulting companies and have been directly involved in founding venture backed companies. Health Advances' expertise, health care focus, and flexibility enable it to compete successfully across the health care spectrum.

Summarize your growth in terms of revenues (both domestic and international) and professional staff over the past year; over the past five years.

Health Advances was founded in 1992 by two former partners at Bain & Company. Today we have over 20 professionals and a third partner with extensive health care consulting experience from Arthur D. Little, Inc. Over the last five years, the firm's revenues have grown at more than 20%.

Consultant's Job Description

Describe the career path and corresponding responsibilities for an MBA at your firm.

Our professional staff includes managing directors, managers, associates, and analysts. Entry-level MBAs, whom we call associates, direct major parts of the case. Responsibilities include designing the core analytical elements of projects, thinking through client issues and potential solutions, assembling data and compelling analyses that will lead clients to the appropriate action steps, as well as interacting with and presenting to clients.

Over the course of the next few years, associates will take on broader responsibilities for casework and be considered for promotion to manager. Generally, two to three years of experience are required to develop the experience base necessary to be an effective manager.

At the manager level the consultant will be more involved in the selling process, participate in case staffing decisions, be directly involved in setting broad strategy for the project, and work closely with senior level clients. Managers also participate in various aspects of managing the consulting organization.

As an MBA advances through the firm, how much is he or she required to specialize by level?

Health Advances believes that a consultant must possess the experience to assist clients with a range of issues that they might face in their business, and we attempt to manage the career track of a consultant to develop that exposure. There is no formal requirement to specialize, except for the concentration in health care. However, it is quite common that, driven by personal interest and the normal evolution of case experiences, consultants will have the opportunity to develop areas of deeper expertise such as reimbursement, drug discovery, novel service-delivery models, mergers and acquisitions, or business plan preparation.

How big is a typical case team? How many cases does a consultant work on simultaneously?

Four levels of professionals contribute to the work of a typical consulting team. One of our three partners is involved in each assignment. Unlike many other consulting firms, our partners also become involved in the project work and take seriously their responsibility to mentor others in the techniques, methods, and craft that is management consulting. Managers and associates are responsible for conducting and overseeing critical pieces of

analysis, managing project workplans, synthesizing and incorporating team data, and managing client relationships. One or more of Health Advances' analysts are also assigned to case teams to conduct analysis, coordinate client and expert interviews, gather data, and assist in presentation preparation.

Each consultant is involved in an average of two cases at a time. With the typical case lasting approximately eight weeks, consultants are exposed to a wide range of projects over the course of a year at Health Advances, thus enhancing the learning process.

Discuss the lifestyle aspects of a career with your firm; i.e., average hours per week, amount of travel, flexibility to change offices.

Health Advances is very dedicated to its employees' personal lives. Our practice is centered in the New England area, eliminating excessive travel and long hours. With the rich concentration of biotechnology in the Northeast, diverse and enticing projects are plentiful. Our average workweek consists of 50 hours, with weekends free.

What is your firm's turnover rate for professionals? What careers do your ex-consultants typically pursue after leaving?

Health Advances provides exposure to a wide variety of industry experience. Consultants are not only exposed to executive level management in some of the nation's largest biotech and pharmaceutical companies, but also to entrepreneurs and scientists on a smaller level. Our consultants are able to make educated career decisions based on a wealth of experience within the health care community.

In addition, the entrepreneurial framework of Health Advances has helped generate many successful start-ups in which case team members are given the opportunity to continue management. In the event that they wish to return to consulting, they are welcome to return to Health Advances at that time.

The Recruiting Process

Describe your recruiting process and the criteria by which you select candidates.

Health Advances has a formalized recruiting process in which senior consultants review candidate resumes and conduct face-to-face interviews. We look for candidates at leading business schools, possessing prior consulting experience and, ideally, a strong background in the life sciences or significant industry experience.

From which schools do you actively recruit? Do you consider applicants from other schools?

Health Advances actively recruits at a select group of the nation's leading business schools where we have been successful at finding candidates working to complete their MBAs, while possessing a background in consulting and the life sciences. Other applicants are certainly encouraged.

How many full-time consultants do you expect to hire in the coming year?

We anticipate that the majority of our growth in personnel in the next few years will come directly from our MBA recruiting efforts. We do not set a specific number per year. It is entirely dependent on the quality of the candidates we see. We are fortunate that the growth potential in our segment of the industry allows us the flexibility to hire truly exceptional candidates when such an opportunity presents itself.

Human Resources Practices

Describe your firm's performance appraisal system for consultants. Are there explicit criteria against which an MBA is evaluated before being promoted? How many times a year is there a performance appraisal and hence an opportunity for promotion? Is there an upward evaluation process too?

Consultants are evaluated twice per year, one of those times occurring promptly on their anniversary date. Each consultant has an individual skill plan that is developed with the mentor he or she has chosen. While specific job descriptions exist for what is expected of consultants at different levels of tenure, we appreciate that individuals develop skill sets at different rates.

Each manager and director is also expected to offer guidance by debriefing at the end of a case. This provides an opportunity for open, constructive communication among case team members. Mentoring is an integral element of the culture at Health Advances.

Senior staff are evaluated on an annual basis by means of upward feedback.

Please describe any initial training programs or ongoing professional development programs for young professionals.

When a consultant joins Health Advances, approximately 50 percent of his or her time over the first three weeks will be spent in a formal training program with the remaining 50 percent allocated to a client project. Including everything from industry overview material to time-tested analytic techniques to operating procedures, the training program instills a basic set of skills and familiarizes the consultant with various Health Advances practices. At the conclusion of training, the consultant, often paired with another consultant, will undertake a case-like project on a contemporary industry issue of broad interest in the firm. The intent is to enable the consultant to become a valuable contributor to project teams as soon as possible.

Health Advances also offers on-site training programs including computer software, time management, etc., to anyone who may be interested. Off-site seminars are offered based on individuals' interests.

I•F Consulting, Inc.

101 Federal Street
19th Floor
Boston, MA 02110
(617) 342-7053
Fax: (617) 342-7370
E-mail: i-fchannels@i-f.com

MBA Recruiting Contact(s):
Gino Morelli

Locations of Offices:
Boston, London, Melbourne, São Paulo

Total Number of Professionals (U.S. and worldwide):
30–35

Company Description

Describe your firm by type of consulting work performed and by types of clients served. What changes are planned in the next few years in terms of services, clients, or locations of offices?

I•F Consulting is an international management consulting firm specializing in marketing channel strategy. I•F was founded in 1969 and since then it has been advising some of the world's largest organizations on how to restructure their marketing channels or create new channels. We focus on increasing our clients' return on their investments in distribution by reducing distribution costs and enhancing marketing channel performance.

In a global competitive environment characterized by reduced product differentiation, fierce price competition, and rapid productivity improvements, marketing channels often represent the critical differentiating factor that can allow an organization to continue sustaining a dominant market position or acquire one. For this reason, we expect our field to grow and we foresee the opening of two more U.S. offices within the next year, thus allowing us to better service our clients.

Describe your organizational structure. Is the firm geographically structured or based around practices? If you have practices, please list them.

I•F is a fairly flat organization and doesn't have specialist practices. Although each office is managed independently and has responsibility for a geographical territory,

consultants from different offices will at times work together in teams on a specific assignment depending on their individual skills and the assignment requirements.

Who are your competitors, and how does your approach to consulting differ from theirs?

Depending on the nature of the assignment, we compete with both leading international strategy consulting companies and smaller local generalist and/or marketing consulting firms.

Our differentiation is based on the following:

- Functional specialization that has enabled us to develop specific methodologies and analytical tools unique to our consulting process

- Ability to cross-fertilize marketing channel ideas and concepts from other companies and industries on an international basis

- Implementation and hands-on experience at how to introduce marketing channel changes.

Summarize your growth in terms of revenues (both domestic and international) and professional staff over the past year; over the past five years.

The revenue and staff growth over the past five years has been steady and in line with our growth plans.

Consultant's Job Description

Describe the career path and corresponding responsibilities for an MBA at your firm.

An MBA's career path is exclusively determined by his/her abilities. Typically, an MBA joins I•F as a consultant and we expect him/her to progress to senior consultant within one year. The next step would be that of engagement manager, a position that involves both project supervision and client management. Again, the speed of progression is entirely based on performance.

As an MBA advances through the firm, how much is he or she required to specialize by level?

As an MBA progresses through I•F, we actually expect him/her to become less of a specialist and more of a generalist with the ability to work across industries and to deal with different types of marketing channel strategy and implementation issues. To achieve this, we ensure that newly recruited MBAs gain the exposure and the experience that will enable them to develop their career, and expertise.

How big is a typical case team? How many cases does a consultant work on simultaneously?

Although each project is different, two to four consultants can be working on each assignment. Our approach is to dedicate consultants fully to one project at a time in order to provide maximum client focus and satisfaction.

Discuss the lifestyle aspects of a career with your firm; i.e., average hours per week, amount of travel, flexibility to change offices.

All our assignments are carried out at the client's premises. This involves a lot of traveling and spending extended periods of time away from home. Average hours per week are in the high 50s. We have made and continue to make a real effort at leveraging our 30-year consulting experience to identify and implement working practices, methodologies, and processes that, while maximizing the value delivered to our clients, also allow our people to maintain balanced lifestyles. We are also quite flexible in evaluating alternative working arrangements to accommodate our people's specific circumstances.

What is your firm's turnover rate for professionals? What careers do your ex-consultants typically pursue after leaving?

Our turnover rate is in line with the industry. Our ex-consultants will typically pursue careers at other consulting firms or major companies.

The Recruitment Process

Describe your recruitment process and the criteria by which you select candidates.

The recruitment process starts with an initial resume screening followed by three to five face-to-face interviews involving case studies. Sometimes, written case studies may be used also. We believe it's equally important that the candidate gets to know as much as possible about us and our business during the recruitment process. For this reason, interviews are conducted both by the head of the office where the candidate is applying and by several consultants. In addition to the criteria common to most consulting organizations (e.g., analytical skills, commercial awareness, quantitative skills, and communication abilities), we also seek people who, by virtue of their backgrounds, can enrich our clients and us. More specifically, while we look primarily for people with a

marketing and/or commercial background in a large, preferably multinational, organization, we also consider people with a more diverse and unusual background.

From which schools do you actively recruit? Do you consider applicants from other schools?

We recruit from all major business schools in North America and Europe.

How many full-time consultants do you expect to hire in the coming year?

Up to 10.

How many summer interns do you expect to hire? If you have a formal summer program, please describe it. Please be sure to indicate whether the program is in place for all offices or just some.

We don't offer a formal summer intern program. Our summer internship program is based on the specific requirements we may have at the time.

Human Resources Practices

Describe your firm's performance appraisal system for consultants. Are there specific criteria against which an MBA is evaluated before being promoted? How many times a year is there a performance appraisal and hence an opportunity for promotion? Is there an upward evaluation process too?

Our appraisal system is based on three sets of reviews:

- Yearly peers' review. Every 12 months, each consultant chooses three peers that will evaluate his/her performance. Clear guidelines and criteria are provided to evaluate the consultant. The review's objective is to provide the consultant with action points to continue improving his/her performance.

- End of project review. This is performed by the engagement manager and/or the senior consultant at the end of each assignment. Again, clear guidelines and criteria are in place.

- Yearly performance appraisal. The head of each office carries out a performance appraisal of all the people working in his/her office. This appraisal is also based on pre-established criteria.

What benefits does your company provide for maternity, paternity, or adoption leave?

Each office's benefits are tailored to the country's specific legislation and regulations.

Please describe any initial training programs or ongoing professional development programs for young professionals.

All our newly hired employees go through our comprehensive initial training program covering both consulting methodologies and marketing channel strategy. Ongoing professional development programs are based on the specific requirements emerging from the reviews described above.

Describe your firm's outplacement services.

We rarely fire people, so we have none. In 30 years we have never laid off a professional for lack of work.

Does your firm provide for on-site day care? If not, do you provide compensation for day care? Is flextime possible?

On-site day care is not available. Compensation for day care is by negotiation. Flextime is possible.

Integral, Inc.

104 Mount Auburn Street, Floor 3R
Cambridge, MA 02138-5019
(617) 349-0600
Fax: (617) 864-3862
Web site: www.integral-inc.com

MBA Recruiting Contact(s):
Valerie Paric
E-mail: recruiting@integral-inc.com

Locations of Offices:
Cambridge, MA; Menlo Park, CA; Cambridge, England

Total Number of Professionals (U.S. and worldwide):
65

Company Description

Describe your firm by type of consulting work performed and by types of clients served. What changes are planned in the next few years in terms of services, clients, or locations of offices?

Integral, Inc. is an international consulting firm that specializes in creating growth strategies for disruptive markets. We consult to and venture-partner with clients, helping them to identify and create new areas of wealth within companies and industries. Integral helps organizations—from current market leaders to new breakthrough enterprises—to enhance innovation efforts in current product and service areas and to identify new market opportunities. Our work is composed of four practice areas: Innovation and Growth Management, Disruptive Technology Strategies, Innovative Supply Chain Management, and Customer Value Strategies.

Since our founding in 1998 by distinguished professors Kim Clark, Ph.D., and Steven Wheelwright, Ph.D., of Harvard Business School, and economist Bruce Stangle, Ph.D., Integral has maintained close relationships with a network of well-respected affiliates at preeminent universities and research institutions. We collaboratively define leading solutions to emerging business challenges. Our value lies in integrating our breadth and depth of experience with unparalleled thought leadership to bring our clients unique, workable solutions and demonstrated, measurable results.

Consultant's Job Description

Describe the career path and corresponding responsibilities for an MBA at your firm.

Integral's approach to professional development is based on meritocracy and individuality. Career progression is based on demonstrated ability to create value for the client and for the firm, which is determined by the individual's background, natural aptitudes, and rate of learning. MBAs enter at the consultant level and are expected to play an active role in all aspects of case management including research, analysis, development of recommendations, client relations, presentations, and further business development. Case teams range widely in size depending on the scope and intensity of assignments but they typically involve consultants, supported by associates, with a case manager responsible for day-to-day operations, and a principal responsible for ensuring the identification and fulfillment of client needs. The successful Integral consultant will value and display integrity, intellectual rigor, sense of humor, dedication to client best interest, and team dedication.

The Recruiting Process

Describe your recruiting process and the criteria by which you select candidates.

Integral's recruiting process is based on a continuous assessment of business development plans, market environment, and skill base needs. Prospective candidates are initially selected on the basis of demonstrated achievement in addition to background experience and education. Two rounds of case interviews explore critical thinking, interpersonal skills, creativity, team orientation, and a general affinity for our work and environment. Integral draws candidates from a broad base, including leading business schools, industry, and other academic disciplines, with the primary criteria being the ability to add extraordinary value to client and firm. Our recruiting cycle follows the academic calendar but we actively seek non-campus inquiries throughout the year. Integral also offers a summer intern program for MBA candidates between their first and second years.

Human Resources Practices

Please describe any initial training programs or ongoing professional development programs for young professionals.

Professional growth is supported by formal training, one-to-one counseling, and semiannual 360° performance review—the overall process of which is tailored and coordinated for the individual by an assigned "sponsor." Training and company meetings feature sessions delivered by our faculty affiliates as well as social events to foster strong working relationships. Integral encourages migration of staff across offices to maintain the one-firm culture as well as accommodate individual need.

John Barry & Associates

3020 Newport Boulevard
Newport Beach, CA 92663
(949) 675-3551

MBA Recruiting Contact(s):
Bob Barry, President

Location of Offices:
Newport Beach

Total Number of Professionals (U.S. and worldwide):
10

Ownership Structure of Firm:
Equity positions available

Company Description

Describe your firm by type of consulting work performed and by types of clients served. What changes are planned in the next few years in terms of services, clients, or locations of offices?

Our firm works with the following principal industries: manufacturing, service, restaurants, industrial laundry/dry cleaning, and office operations.

The following major functional areas of consulting are our specialties:

- General management consulting

- Strategic consulting

- Organizational consulting

- Operations consulting

- Information technology

We assist our clients with facility planning, workstation design, work measurement, financial analysis, and marketing consulting.

Who are your competitors, and how does your approach to consulting differ from theirs?

Our major competitors are major accounting firms and other engineering consulting firms. Due to our size and to the expertise of our teams, we have a more hands-on orientation than do our competitors.

Summarize your growth in terms of revenues (both domestic and international) and professional staff over the past year; over the past five years.

We did approximately $1 million in volume over the past year, with 95% of that domestic and 5% international—primarily in Australia, England, and Canada.

Consultant's Job Description

Describe the career path and corresponding responsibilities for an MBA at your firm.

Due to our aggressive bonus plan, the career path for an MBA is directly related to the consultant's expertise and strengths.

The progression of titles in our firm is as follows: consultant, senior consultant, vice president, and president. Requirements can be waived under some conditions.

How big is a typical case team? How many cases does a consultant work on simultaneously?

A typical case team consists of one to three consultants. A consultant typically works on two to five cases.

Discuss the lifestyle aspects of a career with your firm; i.e., average hours per week, amount of travel, flexibility to change offices.

The average workweek at our firm is 50 hours, and most consultants travel two to six days per month.

What is your firm's turnover rate for professionals? What careers do your ex-consultants typically pursue after leaving?

Our turnover rate is very low and not planned. Ex-consultants often pursue general management of medium to large firms or sometimes enter the industrial engineering departments of large firms.

The Recruiting Process

Describe your recruiting process and the criteria by which you select candidates.

We conduct MBA interviews at Harvard, Stanford, and UCLA. We hire using the following criteria: education, experience, and predicted client sensitivity.

How many full-time consultants do you expect to hire in the coming year?

We expect to hire three to five consultants this year.

How many summer interns do you expect to hire? If you have a formal summer program, please describe it. Please be sure to indicate whether the program is in place for all offices or just some.

We expect to hire two to three summer interns at our Newport office. The summer intern is involved in active jobs with a senior consultant as a manager and mentor.

Human Resources Practices

What benefits does your company provide for maternity, paternity, or adoption leave?

We provide standard insurance benefits.

Please describe any initial training programs or ongoing professional development programs for young professionals.

We involve our professional staff in continuous education courses in the areas of management, marketing, JIT, and other technical fields.

KPMG, LLC
Consulting Practice

Three Chestnut Ridge Road
Montvale, NJ 07645
Web site: www.kpmgconsulting.com

MBA Recruiting Contact(s):
Sean Huurman, (214) 754-2000
Mary E. Sullivan, Director of Human Resources
(201) 307-7000

Locations of Offices:
157 offices worldwide; 130 offices in the United States

Total Number of Professionals (U.S. and worldwide):
Over 26,000 partners and staff in the U.S. serving our
Tax, Assurance, and Consulting Practices. Over 6,500
partners and staff in the Consulting Practice in the
United States.

Company Description

*Describe your firm by type of consulting work performed
and by types of clients served. What changes are planned
in the next few years in terms of services, clients, or locations of offices?*

KPMG, LLC is one of the Big Five consulting firms in
the United States with revenues in excess of $3.5 billion.

Our consultants possess both technical and industry
specific knowledge and experience. Consulting is organized to provide technology management consulting services to key lines of businesses including:

- Financial Services

- Public Sector

- Health Care and Life Sciences

- High Tech

- Communications & Content

- Consumer & Industrial Markets

Our services include

- Strategy

- Operations

- Package Implementation

- Solution Integration

- Application Outsourcing

Our solutions include

- Customer Management

- Supply Chain Management

- Knowledge Management

- World Class Finance

- World Class Human Resources

*Who are your competitors and how does your approach
to consulting differ from theirs?*

Competition comes from technology integrators as well
as consulting arms of public accounting firms.

KPMG's consulting practice is structured to provide industry specific services that meet the needs of our clients.
Teams of cross-functional and industry professionals are
organized to deliver added value to clients. In our professional recruits we look for the ability to work with
teams, creativity, problem-solving skills, leadership, and
a strong commitment to serving clients by providing the
highest level of leadership.

*Approximately how many professionals do you have at
each level, i.e., how wide is your pyramid?*

Our Consulting Practice is made up of approximately 365
partners, 2,550 management members, and 3,560 professional staff members.

Consultant's Job Description

*Describe the career path and corresponding responsibili-
ties for an MBA at your firm.*

MBAs beginning their career at KPMG usually enter as
consultants or senior consultants, depending on prior experience or expertise. We look for people who have the

134

mastery of both technical and industry skills in specific areas. Progression to managing director through the senior consultant, manager, and senior manager positions is based on performance and business needs. The firm emphasizes professional development and provides extensive training opportunities to develop professional skills, as well as industry and functional expertise.

How big is a typical case team? How many cases does a consultant work on simultaneously?

The size of engagement teams will vary. KPMG offers its consultants the opportunity to participate in a wide variety of projects. This provides a broad base of experience and gives consultants exposure to a wide variety of client issues. Our emphasis is on team planning, and partner involvement contributes to ongoing professional development.

Discuss the lifestyle aspects of a career with your firm; i.e., average hours per week, amount of travel, flexibility to change offices.

Individual travel varies with the line of business and a consultant's area of specialization. Consultants can expect to travel extensively. Whenever possible, engagement teams are selected based on proximity to the client. However, knowledge and technical skills are the primary selection guidelines. When on assignment within the continental United States, our consultants are able to return home on weekends.

What is your firm's turnover rate for professionals? What careers do your ex-consultants typically pursue after leaving?

Turnover this past year has been approximately 20%, which we consider to be healthy. Our alumni have developed excellent careers in industry, government, and the not-for-profit sector. The firm has an active alumni relations program.

The Recruiting Process

Describe your recruiting process and the criteria by which you select candidates.

Our highly diversified management consulting practice requires a wide range of skills. Each practice unit analyzes its future needs and provides campus recruiters with up-to-date information on job requirements. We are looking for individuals who can respond with creativity, energy, maturity, and leadership to highly competitive situations. The following abilities are most important:

- Two to five years' work experience in a functional or an industry practice area

- Ability to focus on critical areas of concern

- Ability to respond quickly to highly complex issues

- Ability to establish client rapport and credibility in a general business sense as well as in specific technical areas

- Strong problem-solving and communication skills

Following on-campus interviews, selected candidates are invited to meet with partners, managers, and consultants at one of our offices.

From which schools do you actively recruit? Do you consider applicants from other schools?

The firm recruits from major business schools throughout the country. Superior candidates who are interested in a geographic location other than the one where they are interviewing are referred through KPMG's firmwide referral network to its consulting departments in other cities.

How many full-time consultants do you expect to hire in the coming year?

With the strong growth of the consulting practices we plan to hire a significant number of new consultants.

How many summer interns do you expect to hire? If you have a formal summer program, please describe it. Please be sure to indicate whether the program is in place for all offices or just some.

We do not have a formal internship program for the Consulting Practice.

Human Resources Practices

Describe your firm's performance appraisal system for consultants. Are there explicit criteria against which an MBA is evaluated before being promoted? How many times a year is there a performance appraisal and hence an opportunity for promotion? Is there an upward evaluation process too?

Consulting professional staff receive a performance review at the end of each engagement. In addition, there is an annual review for all employees in the spring of each year, when promotion, salary, and bonus decisions are made. There are basic criteria against which all professionals are measured depending on whether one is staff or management. However, each industry area has specific core criteria. KPMG has an upward feedback process in place whereby staff and management give feedback to partners.

What benefits does your company provide for maternity, paternity, or adoption leave?

Employees can take up to 12 weeks of unpaid leave for the birth or adoption of a child or to care for a sick child, spouse, or parent.

Please describe any initial training programs or ongoing professional development programs for young professionals.

The consulting training curriculum includes core courses in the development of communication and consulting skills. In addition, the firm, through its Center for Leadership Development, offers a full array of technical and industry-specific programs.

Does your firm provide for on-site day care? If not, do you provide compensation for day care? Is flextime possible?

On-site day care is offered at certain locations for emergency and backup purposes.

Kurt Salmon Associates
Retail and Consumer Products Division

1355 Peachtree Street, NE, Suite 900
Atlanta, GA 30309
(404) 892-0321
Fax: (404) 253-0388
Web site: www.kurtsalmon.com

MBA Recruiting Contact(s):
Marian N. Crandall, Principal, Director of Recruiting

Locations of Offices:
North America: Headquarters in Atlanta; other offices in Greensboro, Chicago, Los Angeles, Miami, Minneapolis, New York, Princeton, San Francisco, and Mexico City

Europe: Altrincham, Great Britain; Barcelona, Spain; Düsseldorf, Germany; London, Great Britain; Milan, Italy; Paris, France; Zug, Switzerland

Asia/Pacific: Kowloon, Hong Kong; New Delhi, India; Tokyo, Japan

Total Number of Professionals (U.S. and worldwide):
Over 350 professionals in the North American Division, over 600 in all areas worldwide.

Company Description

Describe your firm by type of consulting work performed and by types of clients served. What changes are planned in the next few years in terms of services, clients, or locations of offices?

KSA serves retailing and manufacturing clients across the full spectrum of consumer products from apparel to food, and from sporting goods to home improvement. Our clients range from mid-sized ($100M wholesale, $200M retail), entrepreneurial organizations to multibillion dollar global corporations.

KSA's expertise throughout the related segments of the supply chain—from consumer to retailer, wholesale/distributor, product marketer, and raw materials supplier—adds significant value for clients and thus has become an increasingly important factor in the firm's growth. Our clients operate in rapidly changing competitive environments where a global perspective, speed-to-market sensi-

tivity, and consumer marketing know-how are critical to their success.

Describe your organizational structure. Is the firm geographically structured or based around practices? If you have practices, please list them.

The firm's organizational structure is designed to provide quality service to the client. Because of the integrated nature of so many of the problems and solutions with which we deal, our organization must remain flexible and responsive. We are organized around industry and functional lines, and frequently assemble international intergroup teams to meet an individual client's unique challenges.

KSA's Retail and Consumer Products Division is composed of the following practices:

eStrategy

Corporate/Divisional Strategy
Revenue Acceleration Strategy
Functional Strategy
eCommerce Strategy

Operations

Operations Audit
Sourcing Strategy
Performance Improvement
New Manufacturing Capacity Development
Manufacturing Inventory Effectiveness
Custom Interactive Training

Merchandising

Product Development
Sourcing
Category Management
Inventory Effectiveness
Store Operations and Customer Service
Business Transformation

Information Technology

IT Strategy
Business Process Design
Systems Architecture and Design
Package Selection and Implementation
Custom-Built Systems
System Testing, Deployment and Operations
Millennium Management® Services
Integrated Enterprise Wide Systems Implementation

Logistics

Strategy
Facilities Planning
Distribution Systems
Implementation Assistance
Performance Improvement

Corporate Finance

Sell-side
Buy-side
Financing

Client service teams include Retail Direct Marketing, Soft Goods, and Food, Drug, and Grocery.

Geographically, KSA's practice is 65% North America, 25% Europe, and 10% other areas of the world. The major North American offices for our Retail and Consumer Products Division are in Atlanta, New York, Princeton, Miami, Greensboro, Los Angeles, San Francisco, and Chicago.

Who are your competitors, and how does your approach to consulting differ from theirs?

KSA occupies a dominant position in its chosen industries. Our competitors are the top strategy consulting firms (including McKinsey & Company, Inc., Booz•Allen & Hamilton, and A.T. Kearney), the larger generalist consulting firms (including the consulting divisions of the Big Five accounting firms), and much smaller industry/financial specialists. We believe KSA's approach to consulting is unique in two ways. First, we specialize exclusively in retailing and consumer products industries; and second, KSA is an implementation consulting firm. After developing the strategic direction for the client, KSA consultants work alongside client personnel to implement lasting change.

While the firm is always developing new relationships, approximately 80% of KSA's projects are for former clients. Because of our high profile in our chosen industries and our long-standing client relationships, few of KSA's proposals involve competitive proposals from other consulting firms.

An essential component of our approach to consulting is the combination of active involvement of senior consultants and full participation by staff consultants in client engagements. Senior consultants, who have a wealth of experience to contribute, regularly participate in client interviews, brainstorming and decision-making sessions, strategic and implementation planning meetings, and boardroom presentations. KSA's staff consultants are involved in all aspects of an engagement from research and analysis to on-site client presentations at the boardroom level. New consultants have frequent interaction with clients.

Our approach to consulting begins with our hiring philosophy. KSA's hiring philosophy may be considered quite different from other firms in the industry: We hire future principals. The firm invests in the long-term development of its people because of the desire to see consultants grow with their experiences. Immediately upon joining KSA, consultants play an integral role within a project team. New consultants will have significant exposure and develop close working relationships with highly experienced consultants. Someone familiar with KSA, a former senior manager of a top strategy consulting firm, may have stated the view of our firm the best. She remarked, "You can have a great consulting experience at my former firm, or you can join KSA and have a great consulting career."

Summarize your growth in terms of revenues (both domestic and international) and professional staff over the past year; over the past five years.

Kurt Salmon Associates has sustained an average annual growth rate of 21% over the last five years.

Consultant's Job Description

Describe the career path and corresponding responsibilities for an MBA at your firm.

MBAs are typically hired into Corporate Finance, eStrategy, or Merchandising. MBAs are generally hired to work in such areas as strategic planning, marketing, corporate finance, and business process re-engineering. Depending on the group, these positions are based in Atlanta, New York, or San Francisco. Consulting engagement teams include an account executive (usually an officer or a principal) with an ongoing relationship with a client, a project manager (usually a principal or a manager), and one or more consultants assigned to the project. Because of the multi-faceted nature of the issues with which we deal, KSA's structure encourages integration of the other service groups' expertise in providing solutions.

The career path runs from consultant to manager to principal. An unusual aspect of working at KSA is the consultant's rapid development and assumption of responsibility. Consultants with as little as one or two years of experience often find themselves working directly with senior managers or CEOs of client firms. The typical challenge is to translate recently learned principles of business management into practical solutions for demanding, sophisticated clients.

After three to five years with the firm, the consultant progresses to manager, assuming greater responsibilities in the management of individual client engagements. Specific responsibilities include managing multidisciplinary projects and further developing a functional or industry specialization. Proactive business development efforts also become more important.

After six or more years with the firm, the manager may be promoted to principal with an ownership stake in the firm. (The firm is solely owned by its active principals.) The primary responsibilities of principals are business development and relationship management. Principals may also be asked to manage a functional, industry, or geographic portion of the practice. These assignments rotate periodically.

How big is a typical case team? How many cases does a consultant work on simultaneously?

A typical project team consists of three to six consultants, including the project manager. New consultants, therefore, have significant opportunities for interaction with senior client management and to make a major contribution to the project's success.

New consultants typically work on one project at a time, with some overlap at the beginning and end of projects. As consultants assume more supervisory responsibility and develop continuing client relationships, they are likely to be involved in two or more projects at a time.

Discuss the lifestyle aspects of a career with your firm; i.e., average hours per week, amount of travel, flexibility to change offices.

Consulting is a challenging but rewarding career. KSA consultants typically work 50 hours or more per week, averaging two to three nights away from home. Increasingly, our engagements involve full-time on-site consulting, requiring five days per week of travel to the same client site. Interoffice transfers may be arranged where they are consistent with the development of the individual and the practice.

What is your firm's turnover rate for professionals? What careers do your ex-consultants typically pursue after leaving?

As a result of careful selection and the nature of the firm and the practice, KSA's annual turnover rate is quite low for a consulting firm, averaging 17% annually. We believe this reflects our healthy balance between the intense demands of consulting and the equally important demands of family and personal commitments. KSA consultants have left to pursue a wide variety of opportunities from management positions in client companies to their own enterprises.

The Recruiting Process

Describe your recruiting process and the criteria by which you select candidates.

KSA is very selective in its recruiting process. We seek special people who respond eagerly to professionalism and independence in an environment encouraging participation. We expect low turnover and target recruiting efforts accordingly. Our goal is to select and develop satisfied, contributing, productive consultants who have the potential to become principals of the firm. To do so, we conduct in-depth interviews at a select group of campuses and with other sources.

Hiring for the European and Far East practices is handled independently by those regions. For the North American-based practice, candidates who are not U.S. citizens must have the right to work in the United States on an unlimited basis. Candidates interested in our Latin American practice, KSA Americas, can be interviewed in the United States.

Business school candidates usually have at least three years of relevant experience prior to obtaining their MBAs. They tend to be in the top 10% of their classes. Many are fluent in a second language. In addition to intelligence, drive, tact, and judgement, candidates must have solid analytical, creative, and communication skills. Also important is a strong interest in management consulting and rapid professional development.

From which schools do you actively recruit? Do you consider applicants from other schools?

In recent years, KSA has recruited at the following schools for our Retail and Consumer Products Division: the Columbia Business School at Columbia University, the School of Management at Georgia Tech, the Kelley School of Business at Indiana University, the Wharton School at the University of Pennsylvania, the Goizueta Business School at Emory University, and the Leonard N. Stern School of Business at New York University. We encourage candidates from other graduate programs, who have an interest in management consulting, to send their resumes to our director of recruiting for employment consideration.

How many full-time consultants do you expect to hire in the coming year?

Our recruiting needs vary from year to year. We plan to add 100 new consultants to the firm overall in 2000, including 10–12 MBAs in the Retail and Consumer Products Division.

How many summer interns do you expect to hire? If you have a formal summer program, please describe it. Please be sure to indicate whether the program is in place for all offices or just some.

The number of interns hired each summer varies from year to year. When we hire interns, we do so based on a specific need, offering an opportunity for a meaningful and rewarding summer experience. Interns function as members of project teams, assuming significant amounts of project responsibility.

Human Resources Practices

Describe your firm's performance appraisal system for consultants. Are there explicit criteria against which an MBA is evaluated before being promoted? How many times a year is there a performance appraisal and hence an opportunity for promotion? Is there an upward evaluation process too?

Performance is the sole basis for success at KSA. At every level, our consultants continually develop their skills to provide the best service to our clients. Performance is reviewed against published criteria for promotion to the next level and against individually established development objectives. Formal performance reviews are sched-uled at the end of each project. In addition, service group directors also conduct year-end and career reviews to assess each consultant's readiness for promotion. During these reviews, new goals are established for future development and progress is monitored and discussed with the consultant on a periodic basis.

Please describe any initial training programs or ongoing professional development programs for young professionals.

Within their first year, new KSA consultants participate in a one-week company orientation program, and receive additional training covering their particular service group. Professional development for KSA is a career-long commitment made mutually by the firm and each consultant and monitored annually. Consultants devote at least 60 hours per year to professional development activities. Throughout the career of a consultant, emphasis is placed on the broad and deep professional development required to be an effective account executive, serving a variety of clients over an extended period of time, and continuing to develop, manage, and directly participate in consulting projects.

Does your firm provide on-site day care? If not, do you provide compensation for day care? Is flextime possible?

KSA does not provide on-site day care. We have established a Flexible Spending Account program that enables employees to pay for child day care expenses with pretax dollars.

KSA does not have a formal flextime policy because our consultants' work hours are driven by the needs of their clients and projects. However, where appropriate, consultants and their management have worked out mutually acceptable flexible schedules to accommodate specific needs.

L.E.K. Consulting LLC

28 State Street, 16th Floor
Boston, MA 02109
Web site: www.lek.com

MBA Recruiting Contact(s):
Catherine Dupuis, Recruiting Coordinator (United States and Australia)
Sheila North, Recruiting Coordinator (London and all European offices)

Locations of Offices:
Auckland, Bangkok, Boston, Chicago, London, Los Angeles, Melbourne, Milan, Munich, Paris, Sydney

Total Number of Professionals (U.S. and worldwide):
350 worldwide

Company Description

Describe your firm by types of consulting work performed and by types of clients served. What changes are planned in the next few years in terms of services, clients, or locations of offices?

L.E.K. Consulting is a leading strategy consulting firm. We work in a variety of industries for a broad spectrum of clients, from the largest multinationals to small, new ventures. The mission of L.E.K. Consulting is to assist the world's leading companies in achieving superior returns for shareholders. To this end, we work collaboratively with senior management to make well-informed decisions based on externally validated facts and compelling analysis.

L.E.K. offers a comprehensive range of consulting services and executive education programs to support clients in making decisions involving critical strategic and financial issues. Our consulting services include Business Strategy, Shareholder Value, and Mergers and Acquisitions. The common theme across all of our services is helping our clients achieve superior shareholder returns.

Our business strategy practice delivers pragmatic solutions to organizations confronting complex strategic challenges amidst dynamic change within their industries. We advise executives on building, exploiting, and maintaining a competitive advantage in their company's core markets.

Our distinctive approach combines factual, objective analysis with seasoned judgement to help our clients achieve superior results. Our services include market assessment, customer segmentation and analysis, competitive positioning, strategic development, and strategic planning.

L.E.K. assists CEOs, senior management, and boards on critical issues such as new product introductions, assessments of new technologies and markets, pricing analyses, and turnarounds of troubled business units.

L.E.K.'s shareholder value practice originates from Al Rapport's pioneering work and is dedicated to helping clients manage for superior total returns to shareholders. Founded on the principle that cash flow drives value, we have developed a holistic approach for using shareholder value principles to understand investor expectations, to develop business unit strategies, to allocate capital, and to both measure and reward performance. Because our approach is data-driven, we provide practical solutions based on objective facts. L.E.K.'s areas of expertise include market signals analysis, value driver identification, value-based compensation, asset allocation process improvement, and executive education on shareholder value.

L.E.K. Consulting is the leading strategic advisor on mergers and acquisitions. Over the past five years, L.E.K. has advised on 300 transactions valued at over $200 billion. On the buy side, our services include M&A strategy development, target screening and selection, strategic due-diligence, target valuation, synergy identification, negotiation strategy, and post acquisition planning. On the sell side, we work with clients to divest non-core businesses for maximum price.

Our hallmark is providing timely, independent, and rigorous evaluations to ensure value-creating transactions.

Over the next five years, we expect our growth to be at least 15% on a compounded annual basis. However, our profit growth may be higher. To accommodate this growth, L.E.K. will continue to open additional offices in continental Europe, North America, and the Asia-Pacific region.

Describe your organizational structure. Is the firm geographically structured or based around practices? If you have practices, please list them.

L.E.K. is organized based on geography, which typically means that the office serves clients closest to them regardless of the industry or nature of the assignment.

However, the firm has developed considerable expertise in a number of specific industry segments, including financial services, biotechnology, emerging-growth companies, telecommunications, consumer goods, media and entertainment, agribusiness, and environmental businesses. These practices are generally headed by multiple partners across several international offices. Consultants are not assigned to specific industry practices and are encouraged to develop a broad range of experiences among several industries and strategic issues.

Who are your competitors, and how does your approach to consulting differ from theirs?

L.E.K.'s focus is on business results—specifically, on creating shareholder value. We believe that this focus requires a commitment from senior management. That being said, it is our policy to work at the CEO or board level.

L.E.K. is distinctive in the degree of analytic rigor and depth of supporting evidence we provide to our client. We strongly believe that recommendations should be based on a careful understanding of objective facts to minimize uncertainty. We develop practical solutions that can be implemented effectively. Our recommendations are action oriented and focused on ways to improve bottom-line performance.

L.E.K. is also distinguished by its entrepreneurial flavor. A very successful part of our practice targets emerging-growth companies where we will work (in whole or in part) for equity. Many of the senior professionals in the firm have small company or venture capital backgrounds. A number of our clients are successful entrepreneurs themselves and find this orientation particularly valuable. This diversity of backgrounds enhances both the learning experiences within the firm and the quality of work delivered to our clients.

Another unique feature of L.E.K. is the degree to which consultants are staffed on cross-office and international assignments. The partnership structure encourages cross sharing of resources among L.E.K. offices, and this usually presents considerable opportunities for consultants who desire to work in more than one office.

We regard the main international strategy consulting companies as our main competitors.

Summarize your growth in terms of revenues (both domestic and international) and professional staff over the past year; over the past five years.

Three former partners of Bain & Company established L.E.K. Consulting in 1983. By the end of 1985 we had 30 professionals located primarily in London. In 1987, we opened our first North American office in Boston with seven professionals. Today we have over 350 professionals worldwide, with 120 in the U.S. Over the last five years, the firm's revenues have grown at 16%, with the U.S. outpacing overall growth.

Consultant's Job Description

Describe the career path and corresponding responsibilities for an MBA at your firm.

Our professional staff includes partners, managers, consultants, and associates. The entry-level position for MBAs is consultant, however, this position differs considerably from the equivalent at our competitors. Our organizational structure is such that we hire two undergraduates for every one consultant; therefore, an L.E.K. consultant has the opportunity to shoulder greater management responsibility. Our consultants structure analysis, work directly with client management, and manage a team of several associates. Promotion to manager generally takes three years, with an additional two to three years before election to partner.

As an MBA advances through the firm, how much is he or she required to specialize by level?

Professionals are not required to specialize at L.E.K. by industry or function. All new consultants receive a wide variation in case assignments. However, as managers begin to progress toward the partner level, often a particular industry emerges as an area of expertise or professional interest. Therefore, many partners spend a significant portion of their time in two or three particular industries.

How big is a typical case team? How many cases does a consultant work on simultaneously?

A typical case team numbers five professionals, led by a partner of the firm. A manager is responsible for day-to-day management of the case, supported by a consultant who directs specific aspects of the case. The consultant is responsible for managing the activities of at least two associates.

L.E.K. professionals typically work on two cases simultaneously, which maximizes the consultant's learning through exposure to different industries, clients, and analytical concepts. However, in certain instances, a consultant may have only one case assignment because of travel requirements or other circumstances.

Discuss the lifestyle aspects of a career with your firm; i.e., average hours per week, amount of travel, flexibility to change offices.

Approximately one-third of L.E.K. projects involve an international component, which allows consultants to work on international case teams or, if they choose, to relocate to international offices on either a temporary or full-time basis. Relocation within the U.S. is also an option, usually based on the needs of the professional as well as the needs of the firm. This flexibility is particularly attractive to dual career couples.

Travel tends to be of short duration, with a consultant typically being away from home on average one night per week. In very rare cases, a consultant will work on-site at a client, requiring him or her to be away from home three to four nights a week. On average, our consultants expect to work approximately 55–60 hours per week.

What is your firm's turnover rate for professionals? What careers do your ex-consultants typically pursue after leaving?

Professional turnover is comparable with that of major strategy consulting firms. Most consultants voluntarily leave the firm for attractive opportunities with other business organizations.

There is no typical career path after L.E.K. In recent years, consultants have accepted positions in a wide variety of industries and firms ranging in size from the Fortune 500 to venture capital start-ups.

The Recruiting Process

Describe your recruiting process and the criteria by which you select candidates.

The search for outstanding candidates is a three-step process that includes campus presentations and events, a rigorous screening of resumes, and selective interviews. Throughout the recruiting process, candidates will have the opportunity to meet members of our firm to discuss our business and learn more about L.E.K. Consulting.

While we do not have a strict set of standards, we do look for the following attributes: academic excellence, robust work experience, and a proven track record of leadership roles and management experience.

From which schools do you actively recruit? Do you consider applicants from other schools?

L.E.K. actively recruits from leading business schools worldwide and encourages applicants from those schools where we are not active on campus. In addition, the firm considers applicants from other post-graduate programs as well as those from industry.

How many summer interns do you expect to hire? If you have a summer program, please describe it. Please be sure to indicate whether the program is in place for all offices or just some.

The summer program is an important link in the process of mutual evaluation and acquaintance. It has always been an integral part of our search for full-time employees. In the U.S., Boston is the only office that currently offers a formal summer program, although there can be opportunities in Chicago and Los Angeles, depending on need. For international offices, London and Sydney have formal summer programs, with occasional opportunities in other offices for outstanding candidates.

Summer consultants assume the full range of consultants' responsibilities with the support of more experienced members of the firm. Our needs for summer consultants vary from year to year, but we typically hire 15–20 worldwide. Generally the program is 12 weeks in duration.

Human Resources Practices

Describe your firm's performance appraisal system for consultants. Are there explicit criteria against which an MBA is evaluated before being promoted? How many times a year is there a performance appraisal and hence an opportunity for promotion? Is there an upward evaluation process too?

Consultants receive a formal evaluation after each case is completed; they receive honest and direct feedback on their performance. Additionally, they receive a consensus review every six months. The most important component of L.E.K.'s evaluation process is the design of a specific development plan to address development needs and leverage strengths. Professionals are promoted commensurate with their capabilities and contribution.

What benefits does your company provide for maternity, paternity, or adoption leave?

L.E.K. offers eight weeks of paid maternity leave as well as eight weeks of unpaid disability leave. For those employees not covered under the Family and Medical Leave Act, we offer two weeks of unpaid leave for fathers of newborns and parents of adopted children. In addition, the firm considers requests for part-time employment or additional leave on a case-by-case basis.

Please describe any initial training programs or ongoing professional development programs for young professionals.

L.E.K. has an extensive professional development program for all levels in the firm, which is an integral part of our consultants' professional experience. New consultants attend an initial one-week orientation program to familiarize them with the firm, our strategy and valuation techniques, and other areas relevant to basic consultant skills. In addition, consultants attend biweekly training sessions throughout the year on varied topics such as presentation skills, new strategy concepts, etc.

Marakon Associates

300 Atlantic Street
Stamford, CT 06901
(800) 695-4428
Fax: (203) 961-1460
Web site: www.marakon.com

MBA Recruiting Contact(s):
Denise Le Van, Senior MBA Recruiting Coordinator

Locations of Offices:
Chicago; London; New York; San Francisco; Stamford, CT

Total Number of Professionals (U.S. and worldwide):
280 (approximately)

Company Description

Describe your firm by type of consulting work performed and by types of clients served. What changes are planned in the next few years in terms of services, clients, or locations of offices?

Marakon Associates provides consulting services in corporate strategy, business strategy, organization, and management process to CEOs and senior management of major corporations around the world. The firm was founded in 1978 with the ambitious goal of helping the world's largest and most complex companies build the capabilities to achieve consistently superior returns for shareholders.

Our practice is singularly focused on this objective, and reaches across all dimensions of strategy, finance, organization, and change management. Many concepts and ideas we originated are changing the way businesses think about managing for value, and we are the leading implementer of systematic programs for sustaining superior shareholder returns.

Our clients are a diverse group of complex, multibusiness, multinational companies headquartered in North America and Europe. They are typically Fortune 100 companies or their international equivalents. They compete in a wide spectrum of industries, including consumer products, pharmaceuticals, financial services, chemicals, technology, forest products, automotive manufacturing, and retailing.

Describe your organizational structure. Is the firm geographically structured or based around practices? If you have practices, please list them.

Marakon is managed as one firm, with branch offices cooperating on multinational engagements and consultant development. The firm is not structured around specific industry or functional practices. Consultants are encouraged to build experience across industries and develop the full range of strategic, financial, and organizational capabilities, along with the client skills needed to interact effectively with CEOs and senior management. This gives us the flexibility to best serve client needs and provides a rich environment for our people to develop a broad set of general management skills.

Who are your competitors, and how does your approach to consulting differ from theirs?

Marakon competes with other major consulting firms. In a broad sense, what sets us apart is our shared commitment to help the world's largest companies bring about fundamental change and create superior shareholder value, while expanding a highly respected firm into an excellent worldwide consultancy.

In more concrete terms, we differ from other consulting firms in three additional ways:

1. Our engagements are broad-scale, CEO-led programs resulting in overall transformation of companies—not incremental studies of issues or functions. We know how to help clients organize and manage what can be a multiyear effort reaching across the organization into every business and function. We have dealt successfully with the many barriers that can arise when management redirects a company's energy to improve shareholder value. Our consultants gain multiple experiences in planning and executing broad-scale organizational change, solving a diversity of real life strategic issues and generating tangible results. They also enjoy the excitement and privilege of recrafting the direction of some of the world's largest companies.

2. Marakon has built a proprietary understanding of how shareholder value is created and destroyed. We continue to invest heavily in developing insight into how strategy, organization, and management process interact to drive value creation, and in applying these concepts to create sustainable improvements in company performance. Every member of our firm benefits from, and is challenged to build on, the firm's commitment to innovation.

3. Each member of our consulting staff is a generalist with in-depth knowledge of strategy, finance, organization, and change management. Building on previous experience and graduate education through extensive in-house training and focused career development, our people acquire a powerful and broadly applicable set of lifetime skills and practical experiences.

Since 1980, we have tracked the performance of the common stocks of our clients and are proud to have helped them produce returns that have exceeded market returns by 25 percent. For all clients, our focus is always on delivering tangible results. The results that count most are the sustainable improvements in competitive position and organizational capabilities that drive superior performance in the capital and product markets.

Summarize your growth in terms of revenues (both domestic and international) and professional staff over the past year; over the past five years.

Marakon follows a conscious policy of managed growth. Since 1987, the firm has grown at a 25 percent compound rate. This growth has been fueled by both an increasing demand for management consulting in general and an increase in our share of the consulting market. Plans are in place to establish additional offices in Europe to continue meeting the needs of our clients.

Looking forward, we believe that the demand for high value-added consulting services will continue its double-digit pace throughout the 1990s. In particular, increasing emphasis on shareholder value improvement as the key management objective is driving the demand for integrated, organization-wide solutions. Given the complexity of the task, along with de-layering and downsizing of most corporate staff functions, a large proportion of this demand will need to be met by the handful of firms specializing in strategy and organizational consulting.

We believe that Marakon will continue to increase its share of this market. Our investment and practice development has enabled us to continue to advance the state-of-the-art in systematically managing for shareholder value. In addition, our capabilities to provide an integrated set of services throughout an organization and facilitate fundamental change in the way large companies are managed are new capabilities that are unique to our firm.

Our success to date is due to the commitment we have made to concept innovation, consultant development, and the needs of our clients. This commitment remains the cornerstone of our practice and will be the key to our success in the future.

Approximately how many professionals do you have at each level, i.e., how wide is your pyramid?

Marakon worldwide is currently staffed approximately as follows:

Partners	31
Managers	36
Associates	135
Analysts	78

Consultant's Job Description

Describe the career path and corresponding responsibilities for an MBA at your firm.

Marakon basically has four professional levels: analyst, associate, manager, and partner. MBAs join the firm as associates and contribute to all phases of client engagements including strategic, financial, and organizational analysis; development and evaluation of recommendations; and implementation of solutions. Associates play a major role in enabling change in client organizations and are exposed to all levels of client personnel through working sessions, presentations, and top management discussions.

Associates take on greater and more independent responsibility for structuring and leading the work of the team and managing its relationship with the client as they build their skills and experience. Associates who demonstrate excellent intellectual, client, and team leadership advance to manager and take on increasingly broad responsibility. Promotion to manager typically occurs within two to three years of joining the firm. Once a manager has demonstrated consistently superior skills, he/she may be elected a partner (and shareholder) of the firm.

Consultants at all levels also participate formally in firm development and decision making, and are given the opportunity to take leadership roles and have an impact in a variety of internal firm activities.

As an MBA advances through the firm, how much is he or she required to specialize by level?

Since Marakon's practice cuts across all dimensions of strategy, finance, organization, and change management, our consultants are generalists who build in-depth capabilities in each of these areas. The specialized knowledge they develop is the simultaneous application of these functional skills to large, integrated corporate change efforts.

How big is a typical case team? How many cases does a consultant work on simultaneously?

A typical Marakon case team consists of four to six consultants, and often includes client representatives. Teams are structured to provide associates with the opportunity to work closely with senior consultants as well as to demonstrate independent initiative and leadership.

Consultants are generally assigned to one case at a time. Our experience shows that consultants achieve faster professional growth and deliver more substantial impact when they are immersed in a single client's strategic, financial, and organizational issues.

Discuss the lifestyle aspects of a career with your firm; i.e., average hours per week, amount of travel, flexibility to change offices.

Our mission of bringing about broad-scale change in large organizations and building an excellent worldwide consultancy results in a demanding lifestyle, consistent with industry norms. While the rewards—solving complex problems, achieving lasting impact, and working with talented and interesting people—are great, we strongly believe that the long-term satisfaction and development of our people is crucial to our mission.

Therefore, we are firmly committed to balancing our business needs and the personal needs of our employees, and have implemented approaches to case team assignments, performance measurement, project management, and upward feedback to further this goal. We have also instituted policies for managing workload with the goal of limiting average hours to 60 per week. Since consultants spend an average of two to three nights per week away from the office, we have also implemented guidelines for managing the impact of travel along with programs to maintain a cohesive firm culture.

What is your firm's turnover rate for professionals? What careers do your ex-consultants typically pursue after leaving?

Marakon's turnover rate is comparable to the industry average. The lifetime skill set our consultants gain through solving strategic, financial, and organizational issues and by helping CEOs and senior management implement broad-scale change prepares them well for subsequent leadership positions in business. Our alumni have distinguished themselves pursuing careers in a variety of line management, corporate staff, investment banking, venture capital, entrepreneurial, and other positions.

The Recruiting Process

Describe your recruiting process and the criteria by which you select candidates.

Marakon seeks associates with the initiative and intellectual capabilities to develop into outstanding client and team leaders. All candidates meet with several partners, managers, and associates during the recruiting process. Successful candidates typically possess superior academic credentials, a track record of increasing responsibility prior to graduate school, and the entrepreneurial desire to help build an excellent worldwide consultancy.

From which schools do you actively recruit? Do you consider applicants from other schools?

We actively recruit MBAs on-campus at top business schools including Harvard, Wharton, Kellogg, Chicago, MIT-Sloan, Stanford, Tuck, Yale SOM, INSEAD, and London Business School. We also consider applicants from other graduate schools, Ph.D. programs, and from industry.

How many full-time consultants do you intend to hire in the coming year?

We continue to seek superior candidates to keep pace with our growth. For 2000, we expect to hire approximately 50 associates and 40 analysts worldwide. Typically, we extend offers to all candidates who meet our hiring criteria.

How many summer interns do you expect to hire? If you have a formal summer program, please describe it. Please be sure to indicate whether the program is in place for all offices or just some.

Our summer program is a key component of our search for full-time associates, and is designed to provide an in-depth experience as a consultant at Marakon. Each summer associate functions as a full member of a case team, with responsibilities and expectations similar to those of new full-time associates. For the summer of 2001, we expect to hire 29 summer interns worldwide for our 10-week program, 10 interns for our U.S.-based two-week program, and 12 students for our one-week master classes held in the UK office.

During the summer, we combine formal and informal in-house training, on-the-job case team experience, and social events to provide summer associates the opportunity to learn about our practice, get to know a broad cross section of our people, and demonstrate their capabilities and potential for long-term success at Marakon.

Human Resources Practices

Describe your firm's performance appraisal system for consultants. Are there explicit criteria against which an MBA is evaluated before being promoted? How many times a year is there a performance appraisal and hence an opportunity for promotion? Is there an upward evaluation process too?

Marakon has a formal performance appraisal program. Consultants' progress in developing and demonstrating leadership and key consulting skills is reviewed semiannually against extensive written guidelines. A key output of the review is a specific action plan for furthering development. These development plans are an explicit part of subsequent case team assignment decisions. Since managers and partners provide active coaching and informal feedback, consultants are continually challenged and supported in building their skills and capabilities.

Marakon also has implemented a formal upward feedback and evaluation process that takes place twice a year. Case team members provide confidential feedback to managers and partners along specific leadership dimensions. Managers and partners are expected to develop the skills and knowledge of the consultants on their case teams, and this feedback is a key element of their performance reviews.

Marakon offers a formal mentoring program to all consultants. Junior consultants are matched with more experienced managers and partners in a long-term, one-on-one mentoring relationship. The program is designed to enhance the career development and progression of consultants by providing ongoing feedback and coaching in confidential discussions with their mentor. Both the mentor and consultant receive training to increase the effectiveness of the mentoring relationship.

Everyone benefits from an effective professional development program—our consultants in the form of greater personal growth and career satisfaction; our clients in the form of consistent, high-quality work; and the firm overall, with growth supported by capable people.

What benefits does your company provide for maternity, paternity, or adoption leave?

As part of our commitment to strike a good balance between our business needs and the personal needs of our employees, we provide very competitive paid maternity and paternity leave policies. In addition, the firm provides the option of part-time employment or unpaid leave of absence to attend to important family matters.

Please describe any initial training programs or ongoing professional development programs for young professionals.

Our practice requires in-depth knowledge of and practical experience applying most of the concepts that students have been exposed to in business school. We provide extensive formal and on-the-job training at the start of and throughout a consultant's career in order to help each of our consultants build the strategy, finance, organization, and change management skills and experience needed to advise CEOs and senior management.

Associates participate in a comprehensive two-week training program upon joining the firm. Training is designed to build on the concepts introduced in business school, focusing on integrating various functional disciplines and developing a sophisticated set of lifetime skills.

Describe your firm's outplacement services.

Marakon offers a formal career transition program to provide assistance to consultants who decide to pursue new opportunities outside the firm. The program is managed by a senior executive with extensive industry experience and includes guidance and assistance throughout all phases of the transition process. In addition, the firm recently launched an Alums Relations program to maintain strong ties with Marakon alumni.

Mars & Co

Mars Plaza
124 Mason Street
Greenwich, CT 06830
(203) 629-9292
Web site: www.marsandco.com

MBA Recruiting Contact(s):
Francine Even, Director of Administration

Locations of Offices:
Greenwich, London, Paris, San Francisco, Tokyo

Total Number of Professionals (U.S. and worldwide):
300 worldwide

Ownership Structure of the Firm:
Private

Company Description

Describe your firm by type of consulting work performed and by types of clients served. What changes are planned in the next few years in terms of services, clients, or locations of offices?

Mars & Co is an international consulting firm dedicated to helping clients achieve superior financial returns by gaining leverage over competitors. We serve a limited number of clients—all Fortune 100 or their European equivalents—to which we give exclusivity of our services and pride ourselves on the long-term partnerships we build with them.

Who are your competitors, and how does your approach to consulting differ from theirs?

Our primary competitors are McKinsey and BCG. Other general consulting firms that have diversified into strategy consulting can also be competitors from time to time (e.g., Booz•Allen & Hamilton).

Although we obviously share some common traits with our competitors, we believe our approach to the practice of strategy consulting and our organizational structure set us apart. The foundation of Mars & Co's strategic recommendations rests on our unique capacity to integrate an analysis of market structure and demand with a quantified assessment of a client's competitive position by basic economic activity. Our analytical techniques allow us to identify and, more important, quantify in great detail the leverage points our clients can use to improve their competitive position. In short, we are in the business of reducing the uncertainty inherent in the process of allocating resources among competing claims on our clients' capital.

Our style is to develop a comprehensive fact base that will illuminate key issues in a way that allows top management to exploit their overall functional and industry savvy. We find distasteful an overreliance on forcing strategic hypotheses in advance of the facts. In our view, the types of clients we target do not require additional industry expertise. They have that capacity in-house.

We do not work for competing clients. This policy is of increasing importance to clients since they know from the outset that we are totally committed to their security as well as to their economic success.

Mars & Co's five offices are run as an integrated whole rather than as autonomous units. Thus, for any client we can draw upon our worldwide expertise and staff. A very important part of our work is transnational and is performed by teams staffed out of two or more offices.

Summarize your growth in terms of revenues (both domestic and international) and professional staff over the past year; over the past five years.

On a headcount basis, our compound annual growth rate over the period has been approximately 20%.

Consultant's Job Description

Describe the career path and corresponding responsibilities for an MBA at your firm.

Consultant is the entry-level position at Mars & Co for MBAs. As a matter of policy, Mars & Co promotes only from within. Thus, the successful consultant can be rapidly promoted to more senior positions. Below the chairman and the president, there are six professional levels at Mars & Co: vice president, project manager, senior consultant, consultant, and, for non-MBAs, senior associate consultant and associate consultant.

- A consultant is responsible for the rigorous, timely, and imaginative execution of analytic tasks leading to practical solutions of complex business problems.

- A senior consultant must be able to design and manage a module of a project so that it is intellectually coherent and useful to the client. This requires excellence in the application of analysis and the capacity to work with both junior and senior colleagues.

- A project manager must be able to train other professionals, provide intellectual leadership in the application of analysis to value-creating solutions for a client, and manage an entire project that meets Mars & Co's quality standards.

- A vice president must possess perfected project management skills plus the ability to contribute to marketing, client acquisition, and concept development.

How big is a typical case team? How many cases does a consultant work on simultaneously?

In addition to the project manager, a typical team will consist of three to ten other professionals.

Contrary to some of our competitors, we do not have a "free market" system within the firm; rather, we assign consultants to teams in a centralized fashion in order to maximize the professional experience of our consultants. The norm is that any professional at Mars & Co works on two projects at a time; there are, however, periods when work is restricted to a single assignment.

Discuss the lifestyle aspects of a career with your firm; i.e., average hours per week, amount of travel, flexibility to change offices.

Mars & Co's practice requires considerable analysis of client and industry data at our offices. Most consultants work at least a 60-hour week. We generally do not have an "office" at the client's location.

Given the transnational nature of a significant percentage of our assignments, consultants can be posted to another office for periods ranging up to a few months.

What is your firm's turnover rate for professionals? What careers do your ex-consultants typically pursue after leaving?

Since its founding, Mars & Co has experienced approximately a 10% turnover rate for professionals. Ex-consultants have followed careers in industry, securities research, homemaking, and consulting.

The Recruiting Process

Describe your recruiting process and the criteria by which you select candidates.

Mars & Co devotes considerable time to the interview process so that each interviewee speaks with at least three senior members of the professional staff, as well as the chairman, the president, or both.

From our viewpoint, we want to assess whether otherwise-brilliant analysts can become catalysts for change in major organizations. We are attracted to balanced individuals who thrive on teamwork. Mars & Co does not specialize by function or industry. Thus, we require individuals who, as generalists, can develop practical strategic recommendations from detailed analyses of clients' competitors and market environments. A consultant at Mars & Co must have strong quantitative skills in addition to energy, maturity, creativity, and common sense.

From which schools do you actively recruit? Do you consider applicants from other schools?

We recruit actively at five top business schools in the United States and their equivalents in Europe.

McKinsey & Company, Inc.

75 Park Plaza, 3rd Floor
Boston, MA 02116
(617) 753-2001
Fax: (617) 753-2099
Web site: www.mckinsey.com

MBA Recruiting Contact(s):
Leslie Holley, Recruiting Administrator

Locations of Offices:
77 cities in 40 countries

Total Number of Professionals (U.S. and worldwide):
5,000

Company Description

Describe your firm by type of consulting work performed and by types of clients served. What changes are planned in the next few years in terms of services, clients, or locations of offices?

McKinsey & Company is a professional service firm that advises senior management on issues of strategy, operations, and organization. The firm's clients are many of the world's leading organizations. McKinsey also serves an increasing number of middle market companies and small entrepreneurial clients in high growth industries. In addition, McKinsey has a long-standing tradition of providing pro bono consulting services to educational, social, medical, environmental, and cultural organizations in the communities where we operate.

Describe your organizational structure. Is the firm geographically structured or based around practices? If you have practices, please list them.

McKinsey is managed by a "one-firm" philosophy. We do not serve clients solely from locations that are close in proximity to the client. Rather we bring our expertise to bear in all situations from around the world. New employees are generally hired into an office to be generalists. Recently, we have started to hire more people directly into our practices. These people bring a deep expertise of an industry or functional specialty and focus their work in that area.

Consultant's Job Description

Describe the career path and corresponding responsibilities for an MBA at your firm.

Each assignment requires the staffing of an engagement team usually consisting of three to six consultants, often drawn from different offices. Assignments generally last from four to six months. Team members work closely with the leaders and decision makers of the client organization and spend considerable time at client offices and facilities. On-the-job training is supported by ongoing coaching and feedback from more experienced colleagues on the team and in the office.

The Recruiting Process

Describe your recruiting process and the criteria by which you select candidates.

McKinsey's more than 5,000 consultants come from a variety of backgrounds—business, law, economics, science, engineering, and the like. In recruiting associates, McKinsey looks for individuals with strong achievement who also have the capacity for continuous development. Equally important is the ability to motivate others, to communicate complex ideas clearly, to win the respect of clients and colleagues, and to work collaboratively.

Human Resources Practices

Please describe any initial training programs or ongoing professional development programs for young professionals.

McKinsey consultants take part in an extensive formal development program that covers subjects from basic consulting skills to leadership. Consultants also further their development by getting involved in practice work, participating in recruiting efforts, conducting client workshops, leading training sessions, presenting at worldwide conferences, and transferring to other McKinsey offices on either a short- or long-term basis.

Mercer Management Consulting, Inc.

1166 Avenue of the Americas
New York, NY 10036
(212) 345-3400
Web site: www.mercermc.com

MBA Recruiting Contact(s):
North America: Dana Grube, (202) 778-7560
Worldwide Recruiting: Cathy Baker, (202) 778-7181
2300 N Street NW, Suite 800
Washington, DC 20037

Locations of Offices:
Beijing, Boston, Bueños Aires, Chicago, Cleveland,
Hong Kong, Lisbon, London, Madrid, Mexico,
Montreal, Munich, New York, Paris, Pittsburgh, San
Francisco, Toronto, Washington, DC, Zurich

Total Number of Professionals (U.S. and worldwide):
1,200

Company Description

Describe your firm by type of consulting work performed and by types of clients served. What changes are planned in the next few years in terms of services, clients, or locations of offices?

One of the leading international management consulting firms, Mercer Management Consulting is the first in consulting to focus its practice on the link between profitable growth and shareholder value creation. We work in partnership with our clients to help them design and align their businesses around changing customer priorities, economics, and environments, thereby enabling them to create sustainable shareholder value growth in an increasingly discontinuous world. Our capabilities—an unparalleled knowledge of customer behavior, a detailed understanding of customer profitability, and sophisticated market research tools—along with value-driven business designs, value migration patterns, and high-value profit models allow us to offer clients an unprecedented single integrated source of profitable growth solutions.

While our assignments cover the full range of general management disciplines—strategy, organization, finance, marketing, operations—our goal is always to help clients design and execute customer-driven, profitable growth strategies that create exceptional shareholder value for their companies.

Mercer Management Consulting was formed in 1990 through the merger of Temple, Barker & Sloane and Strategic Planning Associates. TBS and SPA were two of the most innovative and fastest growing strategy consulting firms over the past two decades, and Mercer is building aggressively on that legacy. Most recently, we have enhanced our presence in Europe, the Pacific Rim, and Canada and plan to aggressively continue our expansion worldwide over the next five years. In 1997, Mercer merged with Corporate Decisions, Inc., a Boston-based consulting firm focused on value-driven growth strategies. This merger combines leading-edge intellectual capital and consulting assets that will solidify Mercer's position as the industry leader on issues of stockholder value creation through profitable growth.

Describe your organizational structure. Is the firm geographically structured or based around practices? If you have practices, please list them.

Mercer Management Consulting is organized around eleven groups:

- Core Consulting Group

- Mercer Digital

- Communication, Information, and Entertainment

- Private Equity

- CI Fund

- Finance Institutions and Risk Enterprise

- Energy and Process Industries

- Manufacturing

- Transportation

- Strategic Capabilities Group

- Retail, Consumer, and Healthcare

Associates join the firm as part of the Core Consulting Group (CCG), which gives them the opportunity to work on a variety of issues, functional areas, and industries across any or all of our practices. Mercer staffs all domestic projects from across North America, keeping two imperatives in mind: what provides the best service for the client and what provides the best training for our people.

As the individual progresses toward partner level, she/he will select an area on which to focus. As individuals then progress to the VP level and beyond, they might again broaden their horizons.

Who are your competitors, and how does your approach to consulting differ from theirs?

Mercer Management Consulting competes primarily with other leading international strategy consultancies. While we share many qualities in common with these firms, four key characteristics set us apart:

1. A commitment to helping clients grow. We believe that profitable growth is the only route to lasting business success. There are times when a company may need to downsize, but to thrive over the long term it needs to grow. For four years we have been studying the experience of the world's most successful growth companies, and on the basis of our research we have developed the Mercer Value Growth Framework, which is being used by many of our clients as the basis for their long-term strategic positioning.

2. A view of change as opportunity. Change is the fundamental fact of business today. Unlike some other consulting firms, which view change as a problem to be solved, we see change as an opportunity to be seized. We have developed an array of sophisticated analytical tools and models that allow clients to see how the market will react to changes they instigate in product portfolio, product features, service levels, pricing, positioning, and so forth. By firmly basing our solutions on facts, we enable clients to drive change rather than simply adapt to it.

3. Focused expertise. We believe that in today's complex marketplace, successful management consulting demands both the perspective of a generalist and the skills of a specialist. For this reason, we have built a firm that offers career paths for both those who conceptualize solutions across industries and functions and those who develop a depth of knowledge and experience in a focused practice area. By designing our client teams to include the mix of expertise best suited to the client's needs, we ensure efficiency in our work, creativity in our thinking, and practicality in the solutions we develop and help to execute.

4. A sense of excitement. Because we focus on critical issues and approach them in innovative ways, our consultants and our clients share a sense of excitement in

our work. What we contribute to a client organization is something both new and meaningful. We see no conflict between producing significant results and having fun. In fact, our experience shows that the more fully a consultant is engaged in an assignment, the better are the results produced.

Consultant's Job Description

Describe the career path and corresponding responsibilities for an MBA at your firm.

From a career perspective, Mercer Management Consulting encourages its consultants to assume project leadership and client responsibilities as rapidly as their skill development allows. The firm's career development process is designed to support a wide range of career paths and features an advisor system, regular case performance feedback, and formal, semiannual career reviews. Our objective is to provide an exciting and rewarding career through a combination of challenging client opportunities, supportive feedback, and performance-driven compensation.

As an MBA advances through the firm, how much is he or she required to specialize by level?

We seek to encourage our professional staff to develop to their highest potential. Recognizing that each of our consultants has a unique set of skills, we have structured ourselves internally to support a wide range of career paths. While most associates will join us as generalists, we have opportunities for those interested in focusing on a particular area. Thereafter, as individuals' careers develop, they will often concentrate in an area of expertise they see as exciting and rewarding and in which they can make a significant contribution to our clients, but they may also choose to remain a generalist.

How big is a typical case team? How many cases does a consultant work on simultaneously?

While a case team will typically consist of a vice president, a principal and/or senior associate, one or two associates, and one or two research analysts, its composition will vary according to the nature and demands of the client study.

Within the case team, roles are flexible depending on individuals' talents and motivation. Typically the vice president is responsible for the overall relationship with the client; the principal and/or senior associate is responsible for the day-to-day management of the case; the associate, for structuring, producing, and presenting analyses for the study. Mercer Management Consulting encourages its consultants to assume project leadership and client responsibilities as rapidly as they can.

Discuss the lifestyle aspects of a career with your firm; i.e., average hours per week, amount of travel, flexibility to change offices.

Although management consulting is of necessity a demanding profession requiring hard work and long hours, at Mercer Management Consulting we do not equate sacrifice with good consulting. We appreciate dedication, but we also advocate a manageable lifestyle. Consultants spend the appropriate time at the client site gathering data, working with client management to develop solutions, and helping to implement recommendations, while carrying out much of the analysis at their home office. Our goal is to balance the needs of the consultant with the imperative to deliver superior quality work to our clients.

What is your firm's turnover rate for professionals? What careers do your ex-consultants typically pursue after leaving?

Turnover at Mercer Management Consulting is on par with the industry average. Those who leave enter a variety of fields, typically in senior positions.

The Recruiting Process

Describe your recruiting process and the criteria by which you select candidates.

Mercer Management Consulting interviews and hires candidates primarily from leading graduate schools in North America and Europe. Although the firm hires many individuals directly from graduate school, virtually all of them have had from three to ten years of full-time work experience. In selecting new consultants, we look for a blend of academic achievement, intellectual curiosity, and interpersonal skills—the ability to structure problems logically, to develop innovative yet practical solutions, to work effectively as a member of a team, and to communicate clearly with both colleagues and clients.

From which schools do you actively recruit? Do you consider applicants from other schools?

We have formal recruiting programs at a number of top MBA schools. In the United States, these include Harvard, Kellogg, Michigan, Sloan, Stanford, Tuck, and Wharton. We also actively consider résumés of candidates from other schools and from industry.

How many full-time consultants do you expect to hire in the coming year?

In a normal year, Mercer Management Consulting hires more than 50 graduates from leading business schools. The total hired in any given year depends on the needs of our business and the availability of qualified individuals.

How many summer interns do you expect to hire? If you have a formal summer program, please describe it. Please be sure to indicate whether the program is in place for all offices or just some.

Mercer Management Consulting offers a highly selective summer program to individuals who meet the aforementioned selection criteria. The firm provides 35 to 45 summer associates with an opportunity to experience consulting at Mercer as fully functioning members of the case team. The summer internship is in place for all our offices, and includes casework, substantial training, and exposure to all of Mercer's practices.

Human Resources Practices

Describe your firm's performance appraisal system for consultants. Are there explicit criteria against which an MBA is evaluated before being promoted? How many times a year is there a performance appraisal and hence an opportunity for promotion? Is there an upward evaluation process too?

Our commitment to building both the skill base and the careers of our consultants can be seen in our extensive performance appraisal system.

We highly value feedback to consultants and provide it formally and informally, both orally and in writing. Our standard is to provide a project performance review every three months and then to put that feedback in a career context every six months. In both forums, the feedback is balanced and offers an assessment of the consultant's strengths and development objectives. As a final outcome of the six-month career review, we benchmark each consultant relative to an absolute set of performance standards and, using those standards, consider candidates for promotion. The significant investment of senior staff time to developing this feedback is necessary to meet our objective of growing careers through supportive feedback linked to growth opportunities and performance-driven compensation.

We also value the opportunity for nonpartner consulting professionals to offer constructive criticism on the performance of the case managers and officers through an upward feedback system. At the conclusion of a case, the nonpartner members of the case team fill out a feedback form evaluating case management's performance. The team then meets with the case leaders for a candid discussion of the strengths and weaknesses of their performance. The feedback is then integrated into the partner career review.

What benefits does your company provide for maternity, paternity, or adoption leave?

We offer a competitive benefit program designed to support our staff as they build families. This includes family leave of absence and financial support for both medical and adoption expenses.

Please describe any initial training programs or ongoing professional development programs for young professionals.

Mercer is committed to the continuing professional development of our consultants and has established a comprehensive training curriculum consisting of three components: core programs, JIT programs, and informal tutorials.

The core programs are linked to key development points in a Mercer consulting career. For example, when individ-

uals join our firm, they attend an orientation to the firm and their own office, as well as an in-depth five-day skills training program. Both the programs are designed to provide new consultants with some of the key tools they will use and to expose them to the many practice areas within the firm. Three to four months later, all new consultants participate in a five-day case simulation training to help them further develop their consulting skills. This training is supplemented by other formal training programs designed to build higher-level consulting skills throughout our consultants' careers.

JIT programs are case-driven and are intended to deliver the industry information necessary to make a team case-ready. CRG professionals are also encouraged to customize their own training path and career development through the use of informal tutorials.

Does your firm provide for on-site day care? If not, do you provide compensation for day care? Is flextime possible?

We do not have on-site day care, but we do offer an extensive referral system for qualified day care providers and a tax-advantaged savings plan for child care expenses. We always try to be as flexible as possible in accommodating the personal needs of each employee.

Monitor Group

2 Canal Park
Cambridge, MA 02141
(617) 252-2000

MBA Recruiting Contact(s):
Rachel Dardinski
(617) 252-2523

Locations of Offices:
Amsterdam, Athens, Cambridge, Frankfurt, Hong Kong, Istanbul, Johannesburg, London, Los Angeles, Madrid, Manila, Milan, Moscow, Munich, New Delhi, New York, Paris, São Paulo, Seoul, Singapore, Stockholm, Tel Aviv, Tokyo, Toronto, Zurich

Total Number of Professionals (U.S. and worldwide):
850

Company Description

Describe your firm by type of consulting work performed and by types of clients served. What changes are planned in the next few years in terms of services, clients, or locations of offices?

Monitor Group is a family of competitive service firms linked by shared ownership, management philosophy, and interrelated assets. Each entity in the Group is dedicated to providing products and services that fundamentally enhance the competitiveness of our clients. We aspire to operate as an "intelligent switch" in a closely-lined global network of expertise and experience, not merely as a narrowly defined consulting firm, a research company, or a merchant bank. We are dedicated to creating innovative, winning, action-oriented solutions by deploying our human, knowledge, and social assets in unique combinations dictated by each *client's* unique circumstances—consulting interventions, capital infusions, deal structuring, management development programs, customized software, cutting-edge market research, and so on as appropriate.

Monitor Group is organized into three major operating units:

- Monitor Action Group, which consults to top management to help resolve their most important and intractable competitive problems;

- The Monitor Merchant Banking Group, which marries capital investment with advisory services to enhance company competitiveness;

- The Intelligent Products Group, which provides customized data and software products to support competitive decision making.

Our client base consists of Fortune 500 companies and their international and private equivalents in a wide range of industries. These clients are typically leaders of their respective fields, including consumer products, retailing, electronics, telecommunications, industrial manufacturing, natural resources, professional services, financial services, and a variety of other service industries. We also work with governments and not-for-profit institutions.

Describe your organizational structure. Is the firm geographically structured or based around practices? If you have practices, please list them.

Monitor is a globally integrated firm. Offices and regions are viewed as resources, rather than profit centers, to avoid barriers to cross-regional cooperation and to maximize our ability to service our global clients. The firm is not divided into distinct practice areas. Instead, its consulting operations are surrounded by a number of affiliated entities that provide cutting-edge expertise in areas such as market research, software-based decision-support tools, operations and asset configuration, corporate finance, and e-commerce. In addition, Monitor has established a group of related businesses that include a not-for-profit institute, an executive education practice, and a merchant banking/investment operation.

Monitor recognizes that strategic answers are only a means to an end. We believe that we create value not so much by helping our clients make incremental improvements in their performance, but by helping them win—that is, by helping them make discontinuous, step-function leaps in their ability to compete. To create this change, we build long-term, collaborate relationships with our clients, characterized by an intensive, participative process. The kind of client participation we embrace is more than a perfunctory concession to helping clients feel included. We create a fully integrated process, whereby case teams consisting of client and Monitor personnel create not just strategic recommendations but comprehensive plans for change.

In support of this process, Monitor Group makes a substantial ongoing investment in the development of strategic techniques and concepts. The investment allows us to provide our clients with innovative, state-of-the-art tools as we develop strategies together and give our consultants the opportunity to advance current thinking about business strategy.

Summarize your growth in terms of revenues (both domestic and international) and professional staff over the past year; over the past five years.

Monitor Group was founded in 1983 and has sustained a rapid growth rate ever since. We have established a new international office virtually every year and continue to expand the consulting staff accordingly. We plan to maintain an aggressive but healthy growth pattern.

Approximately how many professionals do you have at each level, i.e. how wide is your pyramid?

Monitor hires actively at undergraduate institutions as well as graduate schools. As a result, we have a deep and wide "pyramid." The only relevant hierarchy at the firm is based on demonstrative skill. The only title at Monitor below director is that of consultant.

Consultant's Job Description

Describe the career path and corresponding responsibilities for an MBA at your firm.

Monitor Group focuses on the primacy of the individual. Responsibility and rewards are based on achievement, and progress within the firm is limited only by one's ability to learn.

How big is a typical case team? How many cases does a consultant work on simultaneously?

Case teams vary widely in size. Generally, a case team consists of a global account manager, a case team leader, and a number of Monitor consultants and client personnel. Usually, a consultant works on two cases at a time. However, in deference to travel requirements or specific developmental needs, a consultant may at times have only one case assignment.

Discuss the lifestyle aspects of a career with your firm; i.e., average hours per week, amount of travel, flexibility to change offices.

Monitor is committed to ensuring that its staff members can have a successful consulting career while maintaining a healthy life outside work. The nature of strategy consulting requires each consultant to make a substantial time investment in the firm and its clients, typically spending two to three days each week at client sites. However, consultants are encouraged to (and generally do) structure their own work commitments to allow for adequate personal time away from the demands of client work.

Monitor offers the opportunity to transfer offices, dependant on the needs of the offices in question. Many of our consultants have chosen to work in foreign offices for extended periods, thus expanding their global perspective and their understanding of international markets. Every effort is made to accommodate the location preferences of consultants.

What is your firm's turnover rate for professionals? What careers do your ex-consultants typically pursue after leaving?

Monitor's turnover rate is significantly lower than the industry average. Increasingly, those who do choose to leave start their own businesses or join entrepreneurial firms in the high-tech sector rather than, as was more common in the past, assume top corporate staff positions or line management positions in large companies.

The Recruiting Process

Describe your recruiting process and the criteria by which you select candidates.

The recruiting process consists of a resume screening, a series of interviews with members of the firm, a case analysis, a group problem-solving exercise, and a role-play exercise. The effect here is to give each individual an innovative and robust opportunity to demonstrate the full range of his or her talents and abilities. We are much less interested in formal grade point averages than in how a candidate actually thinks, interacts with others, explores complex problems, and deals with incomplete data. Successful applicants will demonstrate a keen intellect, outstanding interpersonal and communication skills, a genuine interest in competitive strategy and the change process, and a commitment to the core values of Monitor Group.

From which schools do you actively recruit? Do you consider applicants from other schools?

Monitor Group recruits outstanding candidates from the world's top graduate schools, including—but not limited to—business schools.

How many full-time consultants do you expect to hire in the coming year?

Monitor will hire more than 40 MBA candidates this year.

How many summer interns do you expect to hire? If you have a formal summer program, please describe it. Please be sure to indicate whether the program is in place for all offices or just some.

The Summer Consultant Program will consist of 10 to 15 individuals. The program is designed to develop and support summer consultants while giving them significant case responsibilities. The program strives to provide a realistic view of the role of a Monitor Group consultant. The summer program is focused in Cambridge, New York, and Toronto, but we try to be flexible to strong personal needs.

Human Resources Practices

Describe your firm's performance appraisal system for consultants. Are there explicit criteria against which an MBA is evaluated before being promoted? How many times a year is there a performance appraisal and hence an opportunity for promotion? Is there an upward evaluation process too?

Monitor has invested heavily in defining the skills that its consultants must demonstrate to create value for clients and advance within the firm. These skill definitions provide a road map for consultant development as well as criteria for advancement. As these new levels of performance and contribution are achieved, salary increases accordingly. Performance and salary changes are evaluated annually. Upward evaluations are critical for learning and are included in compensation evaluation as well.

Navigant Consulting/Strategic Decisions Group

2440 Sand Hill Road
Menlo Park, CA 94025-6900
(650) 854-9000

MBA Recruiting Contact(s):
Menlo Park and Houston: Terri Tippets and Sydney Higa
Boston and New York: Kim McDonald
London: Caroline Craig

Locations of Offices:
Boston, Houston, London, Menlo Park, and New York

Total Number of Professionals (U.S. and worldwide):
185 in the Strategic Consulting Practice

Company Description

Describe your firm by type of consulting work performed and by types of clients served. What changes are planned in the next few years in terms of services, clients, or locations of offices?

The company formerly known as Strategic Decisions Group (SDG) now forms the Strategic Consulting practice of Navigant Consulting, Inc. (NCI). NCI is an international professional services company that works with clients to create, deliver, and protect value in the face of uncertainty and change. NCI specializes in providing full-service support for mergers, acquisitions, and divestitures; developing and implementing e-commerce strategies; extracting additional value from business and asset portfolios; helping regulated companies manage the transition to competition; providing litigation support; valuing and managing intellectual property and other tangible and intangible assets; and identifying and delivering new business strategies and operating models that maximize shareholder value creation.

Our Strategic Consulting practice helps clients identify and deliver superior shareholder returns through strategic change. We specialize in helping clients develop and implement creative strategies for growth, embrace and profit from risk, and transform their organizations to become stronger and more capable. Our areas of expertise are corporate and business strategy development; implementation and change management; comprehensive risk man-

agement; R&D, marketing, technology, and e-commerce strategy; asset portfolio optimization; supply chain optimization; and process improvement.

Most of our clients are Fortune 100 industrial and service companies worldwide. About 20% of our business is from clients outside the United States, and our work for U.S. clients frequently entails worldwide strategy development.

In the past year, in response to client needs, we have enhanced our service offerings in comprehensive risk management and in implementing broad programs to help our clients achieve superior shareholder return. Geographically, we expect to expand our capabilities and senior staff in Europe during the next year.

Describe your organizational structure. Is the firm geographically structured or based around practices? If you have practices, please list them.

The Strategic Consulting practice is organized by vertical industry practice areas rather than by geography. Our consulting is based on specific, unique competencies—strategy development and implementation; R&D strategy and portfolio management; real options; marketing, channel, and e-commerce strategy—and on industries where we hold a knowledge advantage—pharmaceuticals, oil and gas, utilities, high tech, telecom, and most manufacturing industries.

Who are your competitors, and how does your approach to consulting differ from theirs?

Our competitors are the top-tier strategy consulting firms and certain niche competitors in specific segments, such as R&D or e-commerce. Among these competitors, clients often select us for our unique approach and for our ability to facilitate alignment in environments of diverse values. Our process to achieve this is unique; we work with clients to develop strategic options and clarify the potential consequences of each so they can choose and act with confidence. The use of joint consultant-client teams develops the management buy-in and commitment necessary for successful implementation of the selected strategy. In addition, our clients tell us that our consultants are fun and easy to work with, and that we leave their organizations better equipped to meet future challenges.

Summarize your growth in terms of revenues (both domestic and international) and professional staff over the past year; over the past five years.

Successful long-term client engagements have fueled the successful growth of the Strategic Consulting practice in the years before we became part of Navigant Consulting and continue to generate more than 80% of our revenue. Navigant Consulting does not release the growth rates of its subpractices. Overall, Navigant Consulting is a rapidly growing professional services firm, achieving record levels of growth among all consulting firms through acquisition.

Consultant's Job Description

Describe the career path and corresponding responsibilities for an MBA at your firm.

The Strategic Consulting practice hires MBAs, Ph.D.s, MSs, and MAs. New hires typically join the practice as consultants. Over the years, they progress to senior consultant, senior engagement manager, principal, and then director. Strategic Consulting is a meritocracy, and we hire people we believe will progress to partner.

Consultants participate in all aspects of a project—problem definition, information gathering and analysis, generating strategic alternatives, using models and other tools to evaluate strategies, facilitating meetings, and making presentations to client management. In the strategy implementation phase of a project, consultants align key client players with the change program, define change requirements, negotiate detailed implementation plans, design congruent changes, use models and other tools to evaluate design options, facilitate meetings, gain commitment to results, and make presentations to client management.

Senior consultants and senior engagement managers lead the day-to-day activities of the project team, which is composed of both Strategic Consulting and client personnel. As senior consultants and senior engagement managers advance, they take on greater responsibility for client relationship management and business development.

Partners supervise project work, manage client relationships, and lead practice and business development activities.

Our analyst program offers bachelor's degree holders opportunities to participate in Strategic Consulting projects for three to four years before seeking graduate degrees. Analysts are fully integrated project team members, depended upon to produce reliable and meaningful information and analysis. After initial business assessment and analysis, they participate in synthesizing and integrating their insights into the decision-making process for important client business issues. This program offers outstanding growth opportunities and preparation for graduate school or a career in industry.

As an MBA advances through the firm, how much is he or she required to specialize by level?

The Strategic Consulting practice encourages new consultants to gain experience in a wide range of industries and practice areas. As they advance toward partner, they generally tend to develop expertise in either a practice area or an industry. Yet, consultants have considerable latitude in defining their career path in Strategic Consulting. Our partners are diverse—some are experts in a particular industry group; others are generalists, with a broad management and strategy development perspective.

How big is a typical case team? How many cases does a consultant work on simultaneously?

Project teams vary in size but typically have two to four consultants, including the partner supervising the project. New consultants quickly assume responsibility for leading major tasks and guiding client team members. Work on one project at a time is the norm.

Discuss the lifestyle aspects of a career with your firm; i.e., average hours per week, amount of travel, flexibility to change offices.

A career in consulting is challenging, both intellectually and physically. Delivering superior consulting services often requires extensive travel and long hours. The amount of travel and hours varies depending on the project and the client's location, but consultants average 55 hours per week and can expect to be away from home three to four nights a week.

We believe that careers must be balanced with other interests to ensure personal satisfaction and professional growth. Thus, we are committed to providing the flexibility our consultants need to have a satisfying life while enjoying a rewarding career.

What is your firm's turnover rate for professionals? What careers do your ex-consultants typically pursue after leaving?

The turnover in Strategic Consulting averages 12–15% annually—much lower than that of most consulting firms. Consultants who leave Strategic Consulting pursue a range of different opportunities, including senior management positions in start-ups or major corporations. In addition, some of our consultants take leaves of absence to pursue line experience in industry and then return to the firm.

The Recruiting Process

Describe your recruiting process and the criteria by which you select candidates.

In recruiting consultants, Strategic Consulting is looking for future partners. Most candidates have three to five years of prior work experience and outstanding academic records. We evaluate candidates on the basis of alignment with the company's values; outstanding intellectual capability; superior business, analytic, and problem-solving skills; strong interpersonal skills; creativity; maturity; and good judgment. We are seeking professionals who have a passion for helping clients solve problems, are committed to a consulting career, and want to create lasting value for the company and our clients.

The recruiting process generally begins with an interview on campus with one of our consultants, very often a partner. Second- and third-round interviews are mostly held at our offices. Candidates who receive offers typically have had about seven interviews.

From which schools do you actively recruit? Do you consider applicants from other schools?

We actively recruit consultants from the top graduate schools in the United States and Europe. We accept applications from all universities.

How many full-time consultants do you expect to hire in the coming year?

We expect to hire 25–30 full-time consultants worldwide.

How many summer interns do you expect to hire? If you have a formal summer program, please describe it. Please be sure to indicate whether the program is in place for all offices or just some.

We expect to hire six summer interns. Strategic Consulting provides summer interns with an experience rewarding to the intern, our clients, and the firm. We strive to provide an experience indicative of a full-time consulting position. Summer interns experience face-to-face time with clients as well as learn many new skills and techniques. We provide the appropriate training to set summer interns up for success on their client engagements. Summer internships are available for MBA candidates; six-month to one-year internships are available for MA/MS/Ph.D. candidates.

Human Resources Practices

Describe your firm's performance appraisal system for consultants. Are there explicit criteria against which an MBA is evaluated before being promoted? How many times a year is there a performance appraisal and hence an opportunity for promotion? Is there an upward evaluation process too?

Our performance appraisal system is designed to support our meritocracy and to attract and retain excellent, motivated, and committed consultants. We have explicit criteria for promotion, and the performance appraisal process and evaluation criteria are shared with all consultants to ensure that the promotion and compensation processes are understood. Compensation and promotion decisions are made annually. During and on conclusion of client projects, the team members give each other project performance evaluations—upward and downward.

What benefits does your company provide for maternity, paternity, or adoption leave?

Pregnant staff members are granted 12 weeks of maternity leave with pay, and fathers are granted five days of paternity leave with pay after the birth of a child. Adoption leaves are considered case by case because each situation is unique. Balancing family and work is essential, and we strive for flexibility in all types of leaves.

Please describe any initial training programs or ongoing professional development programs for young professionals.

New consultants (at all levels) from all Strategic Consulting offices attend a three-week training and orientation program at our Menlo Park office. This program includes a two-week case study that takes the consultants through a "typical" project from problem definition, to a final presentation for a mock client review board consisting of several of our partners. Immediately after the initial training, new consultants are staffed on projects, where they receive regular feedback and coaching from senior consultants and senior engagement managers. Perhaps the most important component of professional development is the interaction of consultants on projects. Each project team member is concerned about the professional development of the other, so all work together to attain professional development goals.

In addition to on-the-job training, we offer experienced consultants periodic professional training throughout the year, including Staff Development Forums, courses (e.g., on presentation skills and project leadership), and learning fairs (where consultants share their latest thinking and innovations).

All newly hired consultants are also assigned a development coach. Development coaches are generally partners who draw on their experience and organizational knowledge to help consultants clarify their development needs and avenues for meeting them. Coaches meet with consultants at least twice a year to assist with development planning. In addition, coaches are available throughout the year for guidance and counseling.

New consultants are also assigned a mentor—a colleague with one or two years of experience who is available to answer questions and help make the transition to the company and consulting life easier.

Does your firm provide for on-site day care? If not, do you provide compensation for day care? Is flextime possible?

Navigant Consulting offers a flexible benefits account program that allows employees to pay for child day care expenses with pretax dollars. Flextime is available and is evaluated case by case.

Nextera Enterprises, Inc.

One Cranberry Hill
Lexington, MA 02421
(781) 862-3200
Fax: (781) 674-1300
Web site: www.nextera.com

MBA Recruiting Contact(s):
David Rigali, Director Nextera Recruiting

Locations of Offices:
Chicago, IL; Los Angeles, CA; New York, NY;
Princeton, NJ; Raleigh, NC; Rochester, NY; San
Francisco, CA; London; Toronto

Total Number of Professionals (U.S. and worldwide):
450

Company Description

Describe your firm by type of consulting work performed and by types of clients served. What changes are planned in the next few years in terms of services, clients, or locations of offices?

Nextera is an international consulting firm that helps businesses meet the challenges of global, Web-based competition. Our multidisciplinary teams help clients act on market shifts, formulate and implement strategies, transform business processes, build and leverage human capital, and creatively apply emerging technologies to support new strategic approaches.

Describe your organizational structure. Is the firm geographically structured or based around practices? If you have practices, please list them.

Nextera, based in Lexington, MA, was formed in February, 1997. Nextera believes in the value of human capital and we have applied those beliefs to ourselves. Our industry experience, technical competence, and innovative and progressive thought enable Nextera to provide our clients with the insights, strategies, implementation plans, and technology that lead to outstanding business results. We do this through the selective acquisition and ongoing internal development of innovative companies. Nextera's practice areas include: strategy and research, process transformation, information technology, and human capital. Our multidisciplined approach uniquely positions us

to assist clients to take full advantage of e-business and other emerging opportunities.

Nextera is a subsidiary of Knowledge Universe, an exciting new firm whose mission is to help improve and enrich "human capital" from birth to post-retirement, to provide life-long learning opportunities for individuals and businesses, and to help businesses better utilize the power of their human capital.

Who are your competitors, and how does your approach to consulting differ from theirs?

Our Approach—The Nextera Difference

We believe that today's complex business issues, and the competitive situations that spawn them, can be mastered by an integrated and comprehensive approach to problem solving—this requires a combination of expertise. The Nextera Approach is our process for delivering innovation, value, and results. It is a technique that provides a clear-cut path for all phases of an engagement, detailing areas such as:

- Project proposals and work planning

- Skills assessment and matching

- Project management

- Quality control

- Client feedback

This approach helps Nextera to address complex client issues with greater ability, flexibility, and focus on results. It also helps us rapidly assemble multidisciplinary client service teams by drawing from experts in four equally important but distinct practice areas.

Consultant's Job Description

Describe the career path and corresponding responsibilities for an MBA at your firm.

Our career paths vary by operating unit within Nextera. There are common aspects of career paths that are generic in each unit's culture. We believe that every individual should be challenged and developed at an exciting pace. This pace takes into consideration each individual's personality, capabilities, and background to obtain a balanced level of experience and development. Responsibility levels can vary from leadership roles to team participant on larger engagements. Career movement on the various tracks within each operating unit presents multiple opportunities for classic growth through the ranks or significant specialization.

As an MBA advances through the firm, how much is he or she required to specialize by level?

Specializing in practices, technology, industry, and functional aspects of our client service is a natural by-product of acquiring experience. We recognize many individuals have prior interests and experience and we make every attempt to accommodate their future portfolio of experience as their career progresses. It is commonly expected that individuals will have several areas of expertise with varying degrees of breadth and depth.

How big is a typical case team? How many cases does a consultant work on simultaneously?

Our case team sizes vary significantly by type of engagement. Often, there can be one-on-one experiences with a principal or senior consultant, or a team situation on larger engagements. The demands of our client service are very situational and we attempt to create a combined work and development experience on each assignment. Our consultants often have multiple case responsibilities.

Discuss the lifestyle aspects of a career with your firm; i.e., average hours per week, amount of travel, flexibility to change offices.

Lifestyle issues are often a reality in the consulting business. Nextera, with its seasoned consultant teams, makes every effort to improve work/life issues for our consultants. Oftentimes there is very little opportunity to minimize the realities of deadlines, long weeks, travel, etc. But wherever possible we work to accommodate the equally important realities of life. We've been successful at steadily improving our ability to telecommute, do client work in the office, economize on travel, use teleconferencing, etc. Each operating unit is also flexible concerning work schedules.

What is your firm's turnover rate for professionals? What careers do your ex-consultants typically pursue after leaving?

Our retention rate to date has been well below industry experience. People who have decided to leave Nextera have usually left the consulting business for corporate or industry positions.

The Recruiting Process

Describe your recruiting process and the criteria by which you select candidates.

Each operating unit of Nextera manages their own recruiting process customized to the culture and management style of their group. The criteria for candidate selection, while relative to each operating unit, has common themes. We place heavy emphasis on the following candidate characteristics:

- Leadership

- Imagination and Creativity

- Intelligence

- Personality and Interpersonal Skills

- Business Common Sense

- Team Work

- Commitment and Enthusiasm

From which schools do you actively recruit? Do you consider applicants from other schools?

Our national recruiting program participates in many of the top campuses throughout the U.S. and Europe.

How many full-time consultants do you expect to hire in the coming year?

A successful recruiting year for us will involve hiring 190 new consultants; 70+ of these individuals will come from the campus.

How many summer interns do you expect to hire? If you have a formal summer program, please describe it. Please be sure to indicate whether the program is in place for all offices or just some.

Currently we consider summer interns on a case-by-case basis. If an internship is granted, programs are customized to maximize the experience for each individual.

Human Resources Practices

Describe your firm's performance appraisal system for consultants. Are there explicit criteria against which an MBA is evaluated before being promoted? How many times a year is there a performance appraisal and hence an opportunity for promotion? Is there an upward evaluation process too?

Each operating unit within Nextera has its own performance appraisal system for all personnel. Typically people are evaluated twice each year. The process is comprehensive and focuses on counseling for development and performance improvement.

Promotion and compensation adjustments are typically done once each year according to each operating unit's particular schedule.

What benefits does your company provide for maternity, paternity, or adoption leave?

From its inception, Nextera's strategy regarding benefits for its employees has been to simply provide the best quality program, cost structure, and ease of use for all employees. We fully recognize the challenges of today's competitive environment and strive to accommodate the multiple issues facing our employees and their families.

Please describe any initial training programs or ongoing professional development programs for young professionals.

Each Operating Unit of Nextera manages an orientation program and appropriate development opportunities for the themes of their businesses. In accordance with our appraisal processes individuals are ensured the proper training experience to provide a balanced professional growth.

Describe your firm's outplacement services.

On a very selective basis we have provided individuals with the appropriate professional outplacement services to assist our alumni with their future beyond Nextera.

Does your firm provide for on-site day care? If not, do you provide compensation for day care? Is flextime possible?

Flextime is an operational reality for all employees of Nextera. To date we have not made arrangements for on-site day care but do provide the opportunity to set aside pretax dollars for privately arranged day care.

Oliver, Wyman & Company, LLC

666 Fifth Avenue, 16th Floor
New York, NY 10103
(212) 541-8100
Fax: (212) 541-8957

MBA Recruiting Contact(s):
Ronna Hermann, Global Head of Recruiting

Locations of Offices:
Frankfurt, London, Madrid, New York, Paris,
Singapore, Toronto

Total Number of Professionals (U.S. and worldwide):
Approximately 250

Company Description

Describe your firm by type of consulting work performed and by types of clients served. What changes are planned in the next few years in terms of services, clients, or locations of offices?

Oliver, Wyman & Company, LLC was formed in July 1984 by a group of five senior consultants with experience at Booz•Allen & Hamilton and the Boston Consulting Group. The firm focuses on strategy in its broadest sense, covering corporate and business strategies and the organization, processes, management information, and infrastructure necessary to support these strategies. The firm's goal is to be the consultant of choice for the top management of financial institutions. Our experience covers the full spectrum of the financial services industry. Our client list includes prominent institutions worldwide, such as New York money center banks, first- and second-tier investment banks, regional banks, large insurance companies, major European banks, and specialized financial companies.

Who are your competitors, and how does your approach to consulting differ from theirs?

Few of our projects are attained through competitive proposals. When they are, we generally compete with the major strategy consulting firms.

Our approach responds to the fact that consulting firms are generally overleveraged—those individuals with the greatest experience are stretched too far to supervise the management of each project, assimilate and synthesize their teams' input, and bring their knowledge and judgment to bear. Our projects typically benefit from the perspectives of at least two directors, one of whom is responsible for the day-to-day management of our work, with the other playing a significant role in initial interviewing and foundation setting.

Similarly, most consulting firms are superficial in their approach to industry specialization. They often assign entry-level consultants to a generalist pool from which assignments are staffed based on availability, not on relevant personal experience. We take enormous care in our project staffing to draw on the full depth of our collective experience. We also find that entry-level consultants gain relevant experience much more rapidly in our specialized firm than they do at our generalist competitors. With 250 professionals, we are one of the financial services industry's largest dedicated consulting resources.

The major consulting firms are fundamentally similar—as these write-ups invariably demonstrate. Generally consulting takes curious, intelligent people and puts them to work as a team on a project that addresses significant client issues. Surface differences among firms lie in the types of consulting services they offer, the industries they serve, and—above all—in how they package themselves.

The real distinctions among firms—those that should drive your choice—are much more subtle. These exist in the attitudes a firm holds toward its members, its clients, and consulting as an endeavor. These are elements of a firm's culture, and it is precisely these factors that will determine whether you are successful and happy at a particular firm.

At Oliver, Wyman & Company, we view consulting as a career—not merely as a springboard to a position in industry. We hire people who have what it takes to become a director in our firm, and we realistically have the expectation that a significant number of our consultants will do so (of our 42 directors, 22 were hired from undergraduate or graduate schools). We aggressively create opportunities for people to take on additional responsibilities and to develop new skills. We look for people who will not be penned in by an idea of their role but who will contribute to all aspects of consulting at every point in their careers—from the execution of client work to the development of new insights and practice areas; from marketing our services to clients to building a supportive and exciting culture within our firm.

The essence of successful consulting is delivering the appropriate service to your client and making sure it is of exceptional quality. This is rewarding for both the client and the consultant. Specializing as we do in the financial services industry, our business offers tremendous opportunities for our consultants to develop their abilities, and we are positioned to deliver a leading-edge product to our clients.

We are dedicated to providing our consultants with an invigorating, positive, and respectful environment. Each of us is responsible for creating this atmosphere within our firm and in our relationships with our clients.

Consequently, we are very choosy when it comes to adding members to our firm—as you should be when choosing a firm. Rather than make claims about our people and our values, we invite you to explore this through the extensive interviewing that we offer to appealing candidates.

Summarize your growth in terms of revenues (both domestic and international) and professional staff over the past year; over the past five years.

Our consulting opportunities continue to exceed our growth rate in personnel, and we expect a staff growth rate of approximately 15% worldwide per year for the foreseeable future.

Consultant's Job Description

Describe the career path and corresponding responsibilities for an MBA at your firm.

Our client staff organization has only three levels—director, manager, and associate. Directors share the responsibilities for setting the firm's strategy and managing the business, for setting the approach and ensuring the quality of each assignment, and for maintaining client relations. Managers have the responsibility for leading individual assignment teams and directing associates. Associates collect and analyze data, develop conclusions, and formulate recommendations.

We believe that new members of our staff should be capable of rapid growth in their energy and enthusiasm and in their intellectual capability. We commit significant amounts of time each month to a training program for all staff. We also hold team managers accountable for the growth of team members.

We have defined explicitly the standards of performance we expect at each level. A significant amount of time is spent with individuals to help them understand these standards and how they have performed against them. As a

result, individuals compete against themselves, not against each other.

We believe that our rapid growth and our policy of hiring prospective directors and then teaching them to consult will lead to faster promotion cycles than occurs at other firms.

How big is a typical case team? How many cases does a consultant work on simultaneously?

The number of consultants on a project varies from two or three on a smaller assignment to seven or eight on larger projects. A consultant initially works on one project at a time, expanding to a second project over the next 12 to 24 months.

Discuss the lifestyle aspects of a career with your firm; i.e., average hours per week, amount of travel, flexibility to change offices.

The average week is about 50 to 60 hours. We rarely require work on the weekends.

The amount of travel varies widely by assignment; however, since much of the domestic financial service industry is located on the East Coast, the amount of overnight travel is less than in consulting to other industries.

Relocation to a different office is an option for consultants who wish to move. Generally, relocation is contingent upon the consultant's having fluency in the appropriate language. Some legal limitations apply, which are usually overcome as the consultant becomes experienced.

What is your firm's turnover rate for professionals? What careers do your ex-consultants typically pursue after leaving?

Oliver, Wyman & Company is a young firm that has experienced little turnover. Our alumni have gone on to positions of significant responsibility in investment banking, finance, and general management.

The Recruiting Process

Describe your recruiting process and the criteria by which you select candidates.

We are seeking personable individuals with a track record of achievement and academic distinction. Relevant work experience in consulting and/or financial services is an appreciated advantage. Successful candidates for our European offices have fluency in one or more languages in addition to English.

Overall compensation is very competitive. Our base compensation is in line with that offered by the other first-rate consulting firms. We offer a significant profit-sharing bonus based on the firm's performance.

Further, we believe we beat the competition on growth and equitability of distribution. We believe that superior individuals develop at a rapid rate and should be so rewarded. Rewards are, therefore, related to current year's contribution rather than to the contributions of prior years.

From which schools do you actively recruit? Do you consider applicants from other schools?

We seek candidates from leading U.S. business schools and undergraduate institutions. In Europe, we recruit from a few of the leading undergraduate and graduate institutions in the United Kingdom, France, Spain, Switzerland, and Germany.

How many full-time consultants do you expect to hire in the coming year?

We intend to hire 60 consultants worldwide.

How many summer interns do you expect to hire? If you have a formal summer program, please describe it. Please be sure to indicate whether the program is in place for all offices or just some.

We do not expect to hire any summer interns at the graduate level.

The Parthenon Group

200 State Street
Boston, MA 02109
(617) 478-2550
Fax: (617) 478-2555
Web site: www.parthenon.com

MBA Recruiting Contact(s):
Eileen McBride, Recruiting Coordinator

Locations of Offices:
Boston, MA; London, England

Total Number of Professionals (U.S. and worldwide):
75

Company Description

Describe your firm by type of consulting work performed and by types of clients served. What changes are planned in the next few years in terms of services, clients, or locations of offices?

The Parthenon Group is an entrepreneurial firm engaged in strategy consulting and principal investing. Our mission is to partner with CEOs and senior executives who have high ambition for their companies, have the ability to make strategic change, and are willing to address the fundamentals of their competitiveness. We work with these business leaders on their most important challenges to create breakthrough financial results and long-term growth in market value.

Parthenon provides strategic advice to the senior management and corporate boards of numerous public and private companies. We undertake consulting assignments in a broad range of industries, such as publishing, financial services, consumer products, technology and information services, and healthcare. Our clients range from Fortune 500 companies to high potential start-ups.

Describe your organizational structure. Is the firm geographically structured or based around practices? If you have practices, please list them.

As generalists serving clients from our Boston and London offices, we are not structured according to practice areas. Consultants have the opportunity to work on a broad range of management issues in a number of different industries.

Who are your competitors, and how does your approach to consulting differ from theirs?

In those instances when we compete for client services, frequently it is against other leading management consulting firms, such as McKinsey, BCG, or Bain. More often, the value we create and individual support we provide has led to many long-term relationships and opportunities to continue to advise our clients.

As strategic advisors, three principles provide the foundation for The Parthenon Group's strategy consulting business:

Client Partners: As providers of strategic advice, we believe success lies in our ability to partner with our clients, as individuals, and to build lasting relationships. We recognize the profound impact our advice can have and that successful client relationships are built on mutual trust and respect.

Results Orientation: Parthenon is deeply committed to impacting our clients' financial performance in an extraordinary way. Our focus is on our clients' most leveraged issues. We view the quality of our work not by how reasonable our advice is, but by whether it truly enhances the value of our clients' companies.

Performance Consulting: Ultimately, our clients' success is measured by the increased economic value of their companies. In some situations, we seek to link our success with that of our clients' by aligning our fees, usually in stock or options, with their companies' actual performance. Performance consulting facilitates the right attitude and alignment with our clients—we succeed or fail together.

Summarize your growth in terms of revenues (both domestic and international) and professional staff over the past year; over the past five years.

Since its founding in Boston in 1991, The Parthenon Group has experienced rapid growth. Our revenues and staff have been growing at an average rate in excess of 15% per year. The growing mix of clients has enabled the firm to build a blue-chip client base while providing a stable foundation for future growth.

Approximately how many professionals do you have at each level, i.e., how wide is your pyramid?

In addition to the two founding partners, there are eight managing directors. The balance of the professional staff is comprised of principals and associate consultants.

Consultant's Job Description

Describe the career path and corresponding responsibilities for an MBA at your firm.

MBA graduates join Parthenon as principals and work on a variety of client issues. The range of assignments will be broad, such as assisting with the acquisition and integration of companies, developing new marketing channel strategies, turning around underperforming business units, reducing operating and purchasing costs, or evaluating new business ventures. Focusing on these types of issues allows principals to work with clients at all levels of the organization.

The pace of a new principal's progression is set by his/her demonstrated ability to handle greater levels of responsibilities. When a principal has gained experience at successfully managing project teams and developing client relations he or she will be considered for promotion to managing director. Managing directors have a more active role in managing the development of the firm in addition to nurturing senior client relationships.

As an MBA advances through the firm, how much is he or she required to specialize by level?

There is no requirement to specialize in order to advance at Parthenon. However, individuals may choose to focus in particular industries or develop expertise in certain practice areas.

How big is a typical case team? How many cases does a consultant work on simultaneously?

Usually a case team will consist of three to six consultants and is comprised of a managing director, principals, and associates. But due to the variability of engagements, case team size and structure vary greatly. Principals generally work on two cases at a time so that they may gain greater exposure to and experience from client situations. In some cases, depending on the nature of the work, a principal may only be assigned to a single case.

Discuss the lifestyle aspects of a career with your firm; i.e., average hours per week, amount of travel, flexibility to change offices.

A career at Parthenon in many aspects has similar characteristics to other leading consulting firms with regard to lifestyle. Principals work about 60 hours per week and often travel two to three days a week to work with clients at their offices.

What is your firm's turnover rate for professionals? What careers do your ex-consultants typically pursue after leaving?

Historically, Parthenon's turnover rate has been much lower than that of other leading management consulting firms. Principals who have left the firm have gone on to become CEOs and presidents of companies, or to join start-up ventures.

The Recruiting Process

Describe your recruiting process and the criteria by which you select candidates.

Parthenon seeks individuals with superior intellectual and interpersonal skills who have ambition to succeed in a team-oriented entrepreneurial environment. Candidates should have an inclination toward innovation and risk taking, such as receiving a portion of their compensation in equity or options, while assuming responsibility for the effectiveness of their advice. Most important, we look for individuals who have a desire to help shape a dynamic and growing firm, such as by opening new offices or developing practice areas, and to create a work environment that is fun and exciting.

From which schools do you actively recruit? Do you consider applicants from other schools?

Parthenon focuses its recruiting at a select number of top graduate business schools. We do consider applications from other leading business schools where we are unable to participate in the on-campus recruiting process.

How many full-time consultants do you expect to hire in the coming year?

The number of full-time consultants we hire each year varies according to the number of highly qualified candidates we interview and the needs of our business.

How many summer interns do you expect to hire? If you have a formal summer program, please describe it. Please be sure to indicate whether the program is in place for all offices or just some.

We expect to hire between six and ten exceptional individuals for our summer principal program. This program is designed to provide an opportunity for individuals interested in a consulting career to work on real client issues. Summer principals receive extensive training at the start of the program and are assigned mentors who they can turn to and learn from over the course of the summer.

Although limited in duration, summer principals become full team members, work directly with clients, and make significant contributions to help create client value.

Human Resources Practices

Describe your firm's performance appraisal system for consultants. Are there explicit criteria against which an MBA is evaluated before being promoted? How many times a year is there a performance appraisal and hence an opportunity for promotion? Is there an upward evaluation process too?

Principals receive feedback on their performance on a systematic basis. In addition to an annual review by senior members of the firm, case team managers provide feedback to principals at the end of every project. A principal's promotion is entirely based on his/her demonstrated ability to successfully create client value and manage client relationships while making significant contributions to the development of the firm.

What benefits does your company provide for maternity, paternity, or adoption leave?

Parthenon offers a paid benefit for maternity leave. In addition, we are flexible and willing to work with firm members to help them manage their situations.

Please describe any initial training programs or ongoing professional development programs for young professionals.

Parthenon promotes continuous development for its professionals. New principals receive extensive formal training to help them develop basic analytical tools and client skills. Training is on-the-job, where principals are coached by senior members of the firm on the various elements of creating value, developing workplans, managing project teams, building client relationships, and developing new business. For individuals who have a proven performance record prior to joining Parthenon, we encourage their immediate involvement in taking lead roles on project teams and working with senior firm members to develop new clients and practice areas.

Describe your firm's outplacement services.

Because there is low turnover at Parthenon, there has been no need to provide formal outplacement services. Parthenon will help individuals in any way it can if they seek opportunities outside the firm.

Does your firm provide for on-site day care? If not, do you provide compensation for day care? Is flextime possible?

We will always work with individuals to accommodate their needs and provide support. Our benefits program allows individuals to make pretax contributions toward child support costs.

PHB Hagler Bailly, Inc.

1776 Eye Street, NW
Suite 500
Washington, DC 20006
Fax: (202) 785-4052

MBA Recruiting Contact(s):
Consulting Recruiting Coordinator
Fax: (202) 785-4052

Locations of Offices:
Domestic
Arlington, VA (Hagler Bailly, Inc. headquarters);
Boulder, CO; Cambridge, MA; Houston, TX; Los
Angeles, CA; Madison, WI; New York, NY; Palo Alto,
CA; Washington, DC

International
Auckland, New Zealand; London, United Kingdom;
Melbourne, Australia; Paris, France; Rugby, United
Kingdom; Sydney, Australia; Toronto, Canada;
Wellington, New Zealand

Company Description

*Describe your firm by type of consulting work performed
and by types of clients served. What changes are planned
in the next few years in terms of services, clients, or locations of offices?*

PHB Hagler Bailly, a subsidiary of Hagler Bailly, Inc., is
an international management and economic consulting firm committed to assisting clients through the application of economic concepts and sophisticated analytical methods and tools. The firm is a leading provider
of economic and financial analysis for commercial and
environmental litigation, regulated industries, and the
energy industry. Its diverse consulting staff includes
economists, MBAs, MPPs, CPAs, engineers, and other
technical experts. PHB Hagler Bailly serves clients worldwide through its international network of
offices.

*Describe your organizational structure. Is the firm geo-
graphically structured or based around practices? If you
have practices, please list them.*

Energy and Network Industries

PHB Hagler Bailly aids clients in regulated industries,
such as electric and gas utilities and telecommunications,
with the development of successful strategies for dealing
with increased competition, regulatory reform, and deregulation. The company has extensive experience in
guiding utility executives through deregulation. PHB
Hagler Bailly has been a key advisor on major utility restructuring and privatization efforts in many areas around
the world. PHB Hagler Bailly also assists clients with a
variety of regulatory issues, ranging from rate cases and
strategic planning to mergers and acquisitions. The firm
has worked with most of the major utilities in the United
States, as well as independent power producers, to execute sound economic strategies in a variety of contexts.

PHB Hagler Bailly's energy practice builds on the firm's
extensive experience in economic analysis for clients in
the oil, gas, and coal industries. On behalf of these and
other clients, PHB Hagler Bailly assesses the unique
challenges and opportunities presented by energy issues,
ranging from litigation and regulatory proceedings to the
development of new investment or market opportunities.

Litigation and Environment

PHB Hagler Bailly is a leader in the provision of economic and financial analysis of liability and damages issues arising in business and environmental litigation. In
its commercial litigation work, PHB Hagler Bailly provides expert counsel in antitrust litigation, intellectual
property rights disputes, securities fraud litigation, mergers and acquisitions, and contract disputes. PHB Hagler
Bailly's environmental litigation practice offers clients
comprehensive services in litigation and settlement negotiation support, which include environmental liability assessment as well as regulatory and legislative analysis. A
growing segment of PHB Hagler Bailly's environmental
work involves business strategy and the development of
cost-saving responses to environmental concerns.

Increasingly, the successful resolution of complex litigation matters requires a combination of financial, statistical, and economic analytical techniques as well as public
policy expertise. The firm provides a full range of services to meet the needs of both large and small projects,
including preparation of expert reports, critiques of reports filed by opposing experts, development of direct
and cross-examination testimony, assistance in deposi-
tions, and consultation on litigation strategy.

Consultant's Job Description

Describe the career path and corresponding responsibilities for an MBA at your firm.

Consultants at PHB Hagler Bailly provide economic and management consulting services to our clients in cooperation with the directors and principals of our firm. Consultants are involved in all phases of a project, from coordination of research to implementation of project-related analyses and research plans, design and operation of quantitative models, and client interaction. Entry-level staff begin to make analytical contributions to our work immediately and progress to increasing levels of project conceptualization, management, and client relationships.

The Recruiting Process

Describe your recruiting process and the criteria by which you select candidates.

A strong consultant candidate will have:

- An advanced professional degree in business, economics, law, or public policy from a leading institution, with course work in economics, finance, and statistics

- High academic credentials, with academic rank in the upper portion of one's class

- Strong analytical and quantitative skills, and significant experience with computers

- Demonstrated ability to communicate effectively in both written and oral forms

- High degree of self-motivation and creativity

- Ability to handle multiple projects while working both as a team player and as a delegator

Interested individuals should mail or fax a resume, transcript, and cover letter (indicating geographic preference, if any) to the Consulting Recruiting Coordinator.

PHB Hagler Bailly is committed to extending opportunities for employment and advancement to qualified applicants on an equal basis, regardless of an individual's age, race, color, gender, sexual orientation, religion, national origin, marital status, disability, or veteran status.

Hagler Bailly is a worldwide provider of consulting, research, and other professional services to corporations and governments on energy, telecommunication, transportation, and the environment. To learn more, visit Hagler Bailly's Web site at www.haglerbailly.com.

Human Resources Practices

Describe your firm's performance appraisal system for consultants. Are there explicit criteria against which an MBA is evaluated before being promoted? How many times a year is there a performance appraisal and hence an opportunity for promotion? Is there an upward evaluation process too?

The performance evaluations for consultants are conducted twice a year; one covering the period October through March and the other covering the period April through September. Project directors complete Project Performance Reports for each client engagement on which a consultant has billed a minimum of 40 hours during the review period. Performance evaluation results form the basis for employment decisions, salary increases, and discretionary bonus awards. The process offers an opportunity for two-way feedback. Employees learn not only how they performed on individual projects, but more importantly how the firm perceives their overall performance. The firm's evaluation goes beyond the project performance report of any one project director; it involves comparisons of individual performance, plus an evaluation of individual performance as compared to target performance for employees at the same level. The process identifies strengths, weaknesses, and goals for improvement. The performance evaluation process also affords the firm the opportunity to learn how employees perceive their own performance and professional development.

Salaries paid to consultants are generally reviewed annually in January. If employment commences on or before 1 August 2000, a consultant's first salary review will occur in January 2001. If employment commences after 1 August 2000, the first salary review will occur in January 2002.

What benefits does your company provide for maternity, paternity, or adoption leave?

Paid leave and salary continuance are available for medically required absences due to pregnancy and childbirth. Depending upon the circumstances, paternity leave, adoption, or illness in an employee's immediate family, among other circumstances, may be covered under provisions of the Family and Medical Leave Act of 1993, or the laws of the applicable state in which a particular employee is employed.

Leave(s) of Absence: Requests for unpaid leaves of absence, not already covered under the Family and Medical Leave Act of 1993, or applicable state law, and temporary reductions in work hours, will be considered on a case-by-case basis, at the discretion of management.

Please describe any initial training programs or ongoing professional development programs for young professionals.

In the fall of each year, the firm conducts an orientation program for all new consultants. The program not only acquaints staff with the firm and its practice areas, but also affords them the opportunity to meet senior staff and peers from across the firm. In addition to the orientation program, various office-specific programs are run during the course of the year.

Describe your firm's outplacement services.

The firm does not provide any formal outplacement services.

Does your firm provide for on-site day care? If not, do you provide compensation for day care? Is flextime possible?

Employees may set up flexible spending accounts for health and/or dependent care. The maximum annual contribution is $5,000 per year for dependent care. Contributions are on a pretax basis and are taken via payroll deduction.

Pittiglio Rabin Todd & McGrath

1050 Winter Street
Waltham, MA 02451-1297
(781) 647-2800

1503 Grant Rd., Suite 200
Mountain View, CA 94040
(650) 967-2900

25 The Quadrant
Abingdon Science Park
Abingdon, Oxford OX14 3YS
England
+44(0)1235-555500

Web site: www.prtm.com

MBA Recruiting Contact(s):
Kathleen Ferris (kferris@prtm.com), Recruiting
Coordinator, Eastern Region
Jane Jacobson (jjacobson@prtm.com), Recruiting
Coordinator, Western Region, Asia

Please contact only the coordinator in the region of
your primary interest. If you are open to multiple
locations, please specify on your correspondence.

Locations of Offices:
United States:
Atlantic Region: Waltham, MA; Stamford, CT;
Rosemont, IL; Washington, DC; Detroit, MI
Western Region: Mountain View, CA; Costa Mesa, CA;
Dallas, TX
Europe: Oxford (England), Paris, Frankfurt, Glasgow
Asia: Hong Kong, Tokyo

Total Number of Professionals (U.S. and worldwide):
350 U.S.; 450 worldwide

Company Description

*Describe your firm by type of consulting work performed
and by types of clients served. What changes are planned
in the next few years in terms of services, clients, or locations of offices?*

Founded in 1976, Pittiglio Rabin Todd & McGrath has
now grown to 400 consultants in 14 offices worldwide.

We're a market of one in offering implementation consulting to technology-based companies, currently serving
10 industry sectors. Our areas of expertise are:

- Product Development Strategy and Development using
  PRTM's Product And Cycle-time Excellence®
  (PACE®) Framework

- Operations Excellence (including implementation of
  the Supply Chain Operations Reference-model developed by PRTM and Advanced Manufacturing Research
  and adopted by the Supply Chain Council)

- Customer Service and Support

- Marketing and Sales

Our knowledge base is the result of extensive experience,
educational backgrounds in technological fields, continual tracking of industry best practices through
benchmarking studies, and industry contacts. It has
helped us set new benchmarks for best practices, develop
new concepts, and lead in the application of these concepts in industry's strategic planning, product development, manufacturing processes, and integrated supply-
chain management.

We work for top management at today's leading-edge
technology-based companies. They are aggressively pursuing new market opportunities, faster product development, high-performance manufacturing, and new ways of
integrating their supply-chain management. We focus on
the following industry segments:

- Aerospace and Defense

- Automotive and Industrial Products

- Chemicals and Advanced Materials

- Computers

- Electronic Equipment

- Medical Devices

- Pharmaceuticals

- Semiconductor

- Software

- Telecommunications

Describe your organizational structure. Is the firm geographically structured or based around practices? If you have practices, please list them.

We are organized to be as flat as possible and still meet the needs of our clients and our consultants. As a global firm, we have offices in two operating regions, within which consultants can expect to travel widely. These are:

- Atlantic Region, including offices in Waltham, Massachusetts; Stamford, Connecticut; Chicago, Illinois; Washington, D.C.; and Detroit, Michigan

- Western Region, including offices in Mountain View and Costa Mesa, California; and Dallas, Texas

- European Region, including offices in Oxford, England; Glasgow, Scotland; Paris, France; Frankfurt, Germany

- Asia: Hong Kong, Tokyo

Although we have regional affiliations, we operate as one firm, communicating with each other using the same applications and systems worldwide.

Who are your competitors, and how does your approach to consulting differ from theirs?

PRTM offers expertise in technology-related issues, solid experience in the effective management of all core business areas of a company, and a demonstrated track record in the implementation of solutions to client problems. This combination of an industry and functional focus uniquely positions PRTM within the consulting industry. PRTM competes with almost all general management consulting firms, and many strategy and specialty consulting firms that provide limited support to high-tech companies.

In addition, we satisfy some of our clients' needs for ongoing assistance in a management capacity by providing temporary senior-level management through a unique program of interim management. Such assignments are on either a part-time or a full-time basis for periods of 6–18 months. In the past, PRTM professionals have held positions such as president, chief operating officer, vice president of operations, director of logistics systems, MIS manager, vice president of finance, and materials manager. These engagements usually occur in turnaround or start-up situations. Interim management engagements ensure that we retain an understanding of the demands of line management, and these experiences greatly enhance the skills our staff brings to subsequent engagements.

PRTM is an exciting opportunity for the MBA interested in a career in management consulting. We do things differently from most consulting firms.

- *We implement our ideas.* You will not only get experience at conceptualizing, but you will also experience the rewards and frustrations of making change happen in line management. Your role will be that of an active participant, not a passive bystander.

- *We work to enhance our clients' success.* Most of our clients are successful and changing rapidly. You will be working for the top management of aggressive companies, and what you do will have a meaningful impact.

- *We get the client involved.* PRTM actively involves the client rather than working independently. Experience has shown such interdependence to be critical to a project's success.

- *We lead through innovation.* Today's rapidly changing and competitive environment calls for the constant monitoring and development of new, more effective approaches and techniques to meet the challenges facing management. Working closely with clients, PRTM addresses these concerns with imagination and intelligence.

- *We are general managers, not technocrats.* PRTM is the established leader in its field because our consultants have a general management perspective in a variety of disciplines. Often, well-intentioned specialists will fail to act effectively because they only address part of a larger and more complex problem.

- *We believe in our people.* PRTM consultants are given significantly greater responsibilities than are their counterparts at some larger firms. These greater responsibilities offer significant opportunities for personal and professional growth.

Summarize your growth in terms of revenues (both domestic and international) and professional staff over the past year; over the past five years.

Founded in 1976, the firm has become established as the world's leading management consulting firm to technology-based companies. Over the past ten years, PRTM has achieved revenue growth of 30% per annum.

Approximately how many professionals do you have at each level, i.e., how wide is your pyramid?

This is another area of significant differentiation between PRTM and other consulting firms. At PRTM, the ratio of consulting staff to directors is 4:1, not 10:1 or 15:1. Our current pyramid at PRTM is far flatter than any other consulting firm, with 20% directors, 15% principals, 25% managers, and 40% associates. This means that you will have greater access to the directors, who remain highly chargeable as consulting resources, not just administrators, salespeople, or overhead. It also means that we have a greater need for a continuing stream of new directors, which translates into greater opportunity for advancement and a more sincere interest on the part of the firm in sustaining a consultant's career development.

Consultant's Job Description

Describe the career path and corresponding responsibilities for an MBA at your firm.

Our philosophy from the beginning has been to create value by remaining highly active as consultants throughout our careers at PRTM. One of the ramifications of this philosophy is that we have a need for a continuing stream of directors, a need which, in turn, translates into greater opportunity and encouragement for advancement within the firm.

We maintain an exceptionally low consultant to director ratio (4:1), further ensuring that all projects have senior expertise and that all consultants have the benefit of senior experience. Another program that accomplishes this goal is our mentoring program: Consultants have responsible directors who mentor them for 12- to 18-month periods. The director-buddies shift frequently so consultants will be exposed to a variety of personalities and specializations at PRTM.

As one of our consultants explains it, "Growth in our business is driven by two things: Good ideas and hard work. Just as in other small companies, at PRTM everyone is expected to pitch in to help build the business. We realize that if we have good ideas and work hard at making them happen, good things will happen."

PRTM has four levels of job responsibility for MBA graduates:

- **Associate**—Conducts client projects, manages client personnel, participates in marketing activities

- **Manager**—Manages and conducts projects, has some administrative responsibilities, participates in focused new business development

- **Principal**—Manages and conducts projects, manages ongoing client relationships, leads marketing activities

- **Director**—Manages ongoing client relationships, responsible for practice and staff development, ensures quality and effectiveness, leads in client consulting.

PRTM also hires interns from MBA programs.

Because everyone feels ownership of the firm in terms of his or her own added value, all levels of consultants share special responsibilities for the firm's management and growth, participating on internal project teams for recruiting, professional development, new business development, and publishing, for instance.

How big is a typical case team? How many cases does a consultant work on simultaneously?

Our experience has demonstrated that to properly leverage our skills, PRTM should keep project teams small and work with client personnel to execute project tasks. In general, a project team consists of two to five staff members working in conjunction with a director. On occasion, more significant engagements require the efforts of more professionals. An associate is typically involved in one or two engagements at any point in time.

Discuss the lifestyle aspects of a career with your firm; i.e., average hours per week, amount of travel, flexibility to change offices.

PRTM strives to produce a work environment that is challenging, yet pleasant—one that does not lead to employee burnout. This commitment is reflected in our travel and workload requirements. Our original offices were located in the midst of our immediate client base, and subsequent expansion has been triggered by a desire to be located close to growth areas for the firm. Demand for our services has grown faster than our geographic expansion, so travel requirements have grown as well. These requirements vary from region to region, but offices that require heavy travel have accompanying policies that attempt to mitigate the difficulties associated with such travel. We strive to maintain a reasonable workload for all members of the staff, especially relative to other consulting firms. A 40-hour week is rare, to be sure, but so is a 70-hour week.

What is your firm's turnover rate for professionals? What careers do your ex-consultants typically pursue after leaving?

Turnover is highly variable, but has been running between 10 to 12 percent for the last few years. Generally, our turnover rate is low in comparison with that of other consulting firms. Typically, our consultants leave to rejoin industry in a senior line-management position.

The Recruiting Process

Describe your recruiting process and the criteria by which you select candidates.

In a time of increasing competition, companies who turn to us for expertise are faced with some of the most complex management challenges ever in industry. They rely on expertise they can trust, expertise that brings results for both the short term and the long term.

To deliver these results, we recruit consultants with unique qualifications. They're intelligent and pragmatic. They're able to succeed in complex environments with minimal direction. They're good communicators. And they're committed to being consultants for the long term.

Additionally, they have:

- First-rate technical educations and advanced degrees in business management

- Significant industry and management experience

- Strong interpersonal skills and the ability to lead others

- A determination to be successful

The unique focus and expectations of PRTM's practice make our hiring process highly selective. Minimum qualifications for consideration are:

- Graduate education at a top MBA program

- Undergraduate education in one of the technological fields that supports work in the 10 high-tech industry sectors of our focus. Typically, our consultants have bachelor of science or bachelor of engineering degrees in chemical engineering, electrical engineering, or mechanical engineering, or in the life sciences, computer sciences, telecommunications, etc.

- Significant, relevant work experience in either a high-technology or a consulting environment.

From which schools do you actively recruit? Do you consider applicants from other schools?

PRTM actively recruits from 25 of the leading business schools in the United States and Europe. However, we welcome the opportunity to review the résumé of any individual who fits our candidate profile.

How many full-time consultants do you expect to hire in the coming year?

We are constantly seeking to identify qualified individuals to join the firm. Ideally, we would like to find 150 qualified professionals across the various offices. This is dependent on our ability to find people with the proper blend of skills and experience.

How many summer interns do you expect to hire? If you have a formal summer program, please describe it. Please be sure to indicate whether the program is in place for all offices or just some.

It is our policy to hire summer interns only if we have identified meaningful projects on which the interns could assist our firm. This ensures that the summer experience will be a true representation of full-time employment with PRTM. In addition, our size does not permit us to support an internship program that does not contribute to specific consulting projects. In 2000 we expect to hire 40–50 summer interns.

Human Resources Practices

Describe your firm's performance appraisal system for consultants. Are there explicit criteria against which an MBA is evaluated before being promoted? How many times a year is there a performance appraisal and hence an opportunity for promotion? Is there an upward evaluation process too?

Each employee within PRTM is formally appraised semi-annually against an agreed-upon set of expectations and objectives as part of the Professional Development Program (PDP). All expectations and objectives are clearly communicated to the employee at the time of each review session.

Please describe any initial training programs or ongoing professional development programs for young professionals.

Although all consultants at PRTM are expected to make professional contributions from the outset, there is a Director Mentoring and Professional Development Planning program at the firm. We have also established Industry Days and Practice Days devoted to sharing our experiences and learning at client projects.

PRTM has historically conducted technology industry benchmark studies that allow us to be cognizant of industry best practices and continuous improvement tools and techniques. In fact benchmarking has become such an important part of our consulting that PRTM has established a spin-off company. This knowledge base is augmented by on-the-job experience and by other supplementary information provided by PRTM.

Our consultants are selected because of their pragmatic application of business and technological expertise. Every attempt is made within the firm to match individuals' interests, skills, and career objectives with client opportunities in order to promote true growth, learning, and leveraging of all of our intellectual property.

Describe your firm's outplacement services.

Our extensive network of industry contacts forms the basis of our assistance with outplacement.

Does your firm provide for on-site day care? If not, do you provide compensation for day care? Is flextime possible?

PRTM has no on-site day care. We do, however, provide a child-care expense reimbursement plan that allows employees to use pretax earnings toward child care.

PricewaterhouseCoopers Management Consulting Services

11 Madison Avenue, 18th Floor
New York, NY 10010
Web site: www.pwcglobal.com

MBA Recruiting Contact(s):
Karen Kantor, Recruiting Manager
(212) 591-4866
E-mail: karen.kantor@us.pwcglobal.com

Locations of Offices:
Numerous offices in all major cities throughout the
United States and in over 150 countries.

Total Number of Professionals (U.S. and worldwide):
Over 13,000 in North America
Over 24,000 worldwide

Company Description

*Describe your firm by type of consulting work performed
and by types of clients served. What changes are planned
in the next few years in terms of services, clients, or locations of offices?*

PricewaterhouseCoopers is a global consulting firm providing integrated services from strategy through implementation and serving the largest and most respected
businesses around the globe. Our job is channeling
knowledge and value through six lines of service and major industries, including energy, media, financial services,
healthcare, and consumer products.

The essence of the Management Consulting Services
(MCS) strategy is to add value to each client engagement
by seamlessly bringing together in-depth service skills
with industry expertise. Our industries are the primary
means through which we "go to market." The industries
we serve are grouped into five clusters: Consumer and Industrial Products, Energy and Mining, Financial Services,
Service Industries, and Technology Info-Com and Entertainment. Our services our divided into Strategic Change,
Process Improvement, and Technology Solutions.

The PricewaterhouseCoopers Strategic Change Group
works with clients to develop value-creating enterprise-

wide business & market strategies in a number of ways.
Consultants within Strategic Change address where and
how companies should compete and also work to build
competencies and potential sources of advantage. The
disciplines within Strategic Change are:

- Corporate Strategy

- Operations Strategy

- IT Strategy

- Organization Strategy

- Change Strategy

Process Improvement combines technical skills and industry experience to implement pragmatic situation-
specific strategy solutions and find innovative ways to
align existing capabilities and resources to improve an organization's processes. Process Improvement is comprised of the following disciplines:

- Market & Customer Management

- Supply Chain Management

- Financial & Cost Management

- Human Resource Management

- Information Technology Management

- Industry-Specific Process Improvement

Technology Solutions provides integrated cross-
functional software and world-class technology solutions
to tackle the challenges that our clients face every
day. The Technology Solutions Service line is comprised of:

- Enterprise Resource Planning Systems

- Information Technology/Systems Integration

Consultant's Job Description

*Describe the career path and corresponding responsibili-
ties for an MBA at your firm.*

On a day-to-day basis, new MBA hires can expect to participate in the preparation of proposals, research client issues and industry trends, analyze client market opportuni-

ties and their operations, develop organizational and systems requirements, collaborate in developing integrated solutions, and present findings and recommendations to clients.

PricewaterhouseCoopers' career approach allows consultants the freedom to pursue those areas that are of special interest to them while supporting the firm's business goals. New MBA hires have many options to choose from within the firm. They may choose to be part of a national cross-industry strategy practice or regional industry focused strategy practice. Career planning is flexible, responsive, and personal. The progressive career model is not "up or out"; to the contrary, promotion and progression are based on demonstrated capabilities and skills, not tenure.

How big is a typical case team? How many cases does a consultant work on simultaneously?

Consultants typically work on one project at a time. Due to the variation in size and duration of client engagements there is no typical engagement team size. Regardless of the team's size, each team's leadership will seek to provide new MBA hires with a balance of independent latitude and directional guidance to meet overall engagement objectives and to appropriately develop their consulting skills.

Discuss the lifestyle aspects of a career with your firm; i.e., average hours per week, amount of travel, flexibility to change offices.

PricewaterhouseCoopers strives to make consulting a viable long-term career by emphasizing work-life balance and is responding to consultants needs with the implementation of programs such as "More Nights at Home." The program provides incentive and impetus for the overall firm and individual project leadership: to strive to operate globally, yet staff engagements regionally, or even locally, if possible. The program focuses on structuring our projects so more work can be performed away from the client site. The framework offers alternative work arrangements to support our project leaders in addressing travel-related issues.

Other firm initiatives for worklife quality include:

• Adoption Financial Assistance

• Maternity and adoption leave

• New Mom's Corporate lactation program

• Emergency Childcare Backup Services

• Community Outreach programs

• Generous Vacation Policy based on length of service and job level

• "For Your Convenience" personal errand service

The Recruiting Process

Describe your recruiting process and the criteria by which you select candidates. From which schools do you actively recruit? Do you consider applicants from other schools?

PricewaterhouseCoopers has a formalized professional recruiting program at the world's top-tier business schools. There are two rounds of interviews conducted on campus followed by local office visits. The interview format is comprised of a combination of industry/functional cases and behavioral/competency type interviews.

Typically, PricewaterhouseCoopers consultants have at least three years of industry or management consulting experience. While our consultants have diverse backgrounds, we look for students with strong records of achievement, both in school and in business. Also required are excellent oral and written communication skills, the ability to think creatively and analytically in a problem-solving environment, the ability to be self-directed, and the capacity to work effectively as part of a diverse team.

How many full-time consultants do you expect to hire in the coming year? How many summer interns do you expect to hire? If you have a formal summer program, please describe it. Please be sure to indicate whether the program is in place for all offices or just some.

PricewaterhouseCoopers Management Consulting recruits MBAs for both full-time and summer internship positions. Both programs are national and support all practice areas. There are plans to hire close to 300 full-time MBAs this coming year with locations in most major cities. The formalized summer internship program, on the other hand, is a smaller program with the majority of positions limited to the major cities on each coast (New York, Chicago, Washington, D.C., San Francisco, and Los Angeles). The tentative hiring goal for summer interns is approximately 70.

The duration of the summer internship program is generally ten weeks with an option of staying longer if the client needs exist. Summer interns function as members of engagement teams, performing all the functions of MBA hires in their first year. The program includes a national and practice-specific orientation, as well as various social and team-building events throughout the summer.

Quantum Associates, Inc.

43 Water Street
Beverly, MA 01915
(978) 232-3450
Fax: (978) 232-3499

MBA Recruiting Contact(s):
Sue Golden, Recruiting Coordinator

Locations of Offices:
Boston, Johannesburg, London, Paris

Total Number of Professionals (U.S. and worldwide):
85

Company Description

Describe your firm by type of consulting work performed and by types of clients served. What changes are planned in the next few years in terms of services, clients, or locations of offices?

Quantum Associates is an international strategy and operations consulting firm. Our clients are primarily Fortune 500–type companies based in the United States and overseas. We also have a number of mid-sized clients and work with small companies and start-ups.

Our mission is to help our clients become the best-managed companies in their industries. Our client contacts are typically chief executives or divisional presidents, for whom we often work in multiyear relationships.

Our work covers a range of topics within the areas of strategy, operations, and infrastructure (e.g., cultural change, organization structure).

Our practice has a strong international flavor. During the past year we have completed assignments in the United States, Europe, South America, Asia, and Africa. In part this reflects the global character of our clients' businesses; we also have a number of offshore-based clients.

Describe your organizational structure. Is the firm geographically structured or based around practices? If you have practices, please list them.

Each office is largely self-contained and maintains the capability to serve its own client base. Staff are sometimes assigned to other offices, and project teams may be configured with members from more than one office. We do not maintain rigid practice specialties; individuals are encouraged to develop a mix of skills and experiences that suits their interests.

Who are your competitors, and how does your approach to consulting differ from theirs?

While relatively little of our business involves competitive bids, Quantum does compete in the same client markets as other leading general management consulting firms. From a client's perspective, what differentiates us is a client-driven problem-solving approach that results in better implementation and client skill-building. The difference can be measured in tangibles: clients are often project team leaders, they take responsibility for analytical modules, and they make presentations to senior management. This collaborative approach strengthens the organization and results in better solutions at lower cost. It also affords our consultants an experienced view of the industry and company they are working in.

Quantum's work product can be characterized by frame-breaking creativity, analytical and quantitative rigor, and pragmatism.

Consultant's Job Description

Describe the career path and corresponding responsibilities for an MBA at your firm.

In terms of formal structure, our firm is like many others: MBAs progress from consultant to manager to vice president (effectively, partner). In practice, we are more flexible than most firms due to our smaller size and unique way of working with clients. These same factors mean that MBAs typically assume greater levels of responsibility faster at Quantum than might occur in a larger firm. MBAs can expect more extensive client exposure, greater project authority, and opportunities for project management and business development earlier in their careers. Advancement within the firm has more to do with demonstrated performance of the individual than with seniority. As a result, Quantum is an excellent place for highly motivated, self-starting individuals.

As an MBA advances through the firm, how much is he or she required to specialize by level?

As noted above, there is no requirement at any level for staff specialization. Individuals may, however, choose to develop one or more areas of expertise and serve as an informal practice leader in the firm. Such specialization can occur at any point in one's career. Most consultants pursue a mix of industry and functional interests.

How big is a typical case team? How many cases does a consultant work on simultaneously?

Generally, consultants are dedicated full-time to an assignment. Team size varies as a function of client needs and may range from just one consultant to as many as six or more consultants. In addition to Quantum staff, there may be as many as 20 client staff involved in an assignment.

Discuss the lifestyle aspects of a career with your firm; i.e., average hours per week, amount of travel, flexibility to change offices.

Our small size and entrepreneurial orientation give us greater flexibility than most larger firms to accommodate personal lifestyle needs. In some cases, this has involved time spent in overseas offices or at overseas client sites. In others, it has involved time off to start a new business or to pursue civic interests.

The philosophy of the firm is to build a group of talented professionals who work hard, play hard, and have fun in the firm. During an assignment, typical workweeks average 55–65 hours. Between assignments, we encourage professionals to take it easy. Firm social events have included ski trips, off-site training retreats, visits to animal game parks, golf days, and a variety of other activities.

Travel depends upon the assignment. Domestic assignments may require as little as one or two trips a month, while some international work involves extended overseas stays. Staffing decisions, especially those involving long-term travel obligations, seek to balance individual and firm needs.

The Recruiting Process

Describe your recruiting process and the criteria by which you select candidates.

In recent years, we have not conducted on-campus interviews. Our recruiting needs are modest and we find that interested individuals will seek us out. To ensure high staff utilization, we increase staff only in line with increases in the business base. We hire individuals both directly out of leading business schools and from industrial positions. For specific assignments, we also hire individuals with consulting experience on a short-term or flextime basis.

From which schools do you actively recruit? Do you consider applicants from other schools?

We do not actively recruit on-campus but will consider top prospects from leading business schools. Past hires have included MBAs from Harvard, Sloan (MIT), Tuck, Wharton, Darden, INSEAD, and Chicago, among others.

How many full-time consultants do you expect to hire in the coming year?

We have no specific hiring target for the coming year. Instead, we will hire as necessary based on long-term business needs.

How many summer interns do you expect to hire? If you have a formal summer program, please describe it. Please be sure to indicate whether the program is in place for all offices or just some.

We do not conduct a formal summer program but instead hire summer interns against specific assignments. This approach ensures that summer interns will have a meaningful real-world experience well-suited to their skills and interests. As a result, we tend to hire interns relatively late in the spring, when our needs become clear.

Human Resources Practices

Describe your firm's performance appraisal system for consultants. Are there explicit criteria against which an MBA is evaluated before being promoted? How many times a year is there a performance appraisal and hence an opportunity for promotion? Is there an upward evaluation process too?

The small size of the firm and constant exposure to senior staff allows for immediate and ongoing feedback and evaluation. Formal performance reviews are conducted twice annually and include upward feedback. The pace of advancement is determined largely by the achievements of the individual; there is no set schedule for professional development or promotion.

Please describe any initial training programs or ongoing professional development programs for young professionals.

We have developed an extensive training program covering tools and techniques, consulting skills, and managing the Quantum approach. Many of these modules have been packaged to deliver to client teams as part of our ongoing work. In addition, we believe that training is best absorbed on the job, and we seek to structure assignments to properly balance learning and substantive performance.

What benefits does your company provide for maternity, paternity, or adoption leave? Describe your firm's outplacement services. Does your firm provide for on-site day care? If not, do you provide compensation for day care? Is flextime possible?

We provide three weeks paid and unlimited unpaid leave for maternity, paternity, and adoption, but we are too small to provide on-site day care or formal outplacement services. However, Quantum is an extremely flexible organization that strives to accommodate the personal lifestyles of accomplished professionals. Individual programs can be arranged, and we continually evaluate company policies in light of newly emerging needs.

Roland Berger & Partners

350 Park Avenue
27th Floor
New York, NY 10022
(212) 651-9660

MBA Recruiting Contact(s):
Tara Barry, Director of U.S. Recruiting

Locations of Offices:
36 offices worldwide

Total Number of Professionals (U.S. and worldwide):
900 consultants worldwide

Company Description

Describe your firm by type of consulting work performed and by types of clients served. What changes are planned in the next few years in terms of services, clients, or locations of offices?

Roland Berger & Partners is the leading management consultancy of European origin with global capability. Services focus on essential questions relating to a company's future—its strategy, organization, and operations. Clients include large multinationals as well as medium-sized companies, which often are the leaders in their field. In addition, during the last few years Roland Berger & Partners has been increasingly involved in the privatization and restructuring of industries on behalf of governments in the East and West. Our most recent area of growth has been in the practice that consults to the e-commerce and telecom industries.

Describe your organizational structure. Is the firm geographically structured or based around practices? If you have practices, please list them.

As a partnership, the company is internationally organized along functional (strategy, organization, operations, ecology, etc.) and industry competence centers. The different areas of expertise of these competence centers are drawn together into project teams according to the specific needs of the client on a global basis.

Who are your competitors, and how does your approach to consulting differ from theirs?

The company's main competitors are a small number of other management consultancies operating on a global basis, mainly of U.S. origin. Roland Berger & Partners is differentiated by its client-specific approach and its focus on readily implementable solutions based on thorough quantitative analysis. Given its European background, the company appreciates the need to respect different cultures and to take an integrated perspective in the solutions it proposes.

Summarize your growth in terms of revenues (both domestic and international) and professional staff over the past year; over the past five years.

Established in 1967, Roland Berger & Partners has experienced an average annual growth rate of approximately 20% over the last decade. After expanding into other West European countries, South America, and Japan, new offices have also been opened over the last three years in Eastern Europe, Asia, and North America.

Consultant's Job Description

Describe the career path and corresponding responsibilities for an MBA at your firm.

Typically an MBA graduate joins Roland Berger & Partners as a senior consultant. Project manager, principal, and partner are the next steps in a successful career.

A senior consultant is responsible for well-defined modules within a project, under the supervision of the project manager. Nevertheless, he or she will be confronted with the integrated perspective of the problem and have direct client exposure. Simultaneously, consultants receive intensive training covering the growing needs of a successful career in the firm; this takes the form of a combination of hands-on and in-house training, as well as external seminars and courses.

As an MBA advances through the firm, how much is he or she required to specialize by level?

Having gained a broad experience through assignments in a variety of industries and functional problems, our professionals tend to specialize in one or two competence centers. With increasing seniority, consultants are encouraged to develop new fields of experience for the firm.

How big is a typical case team? How many cases does a consultant work on simultaneously?

The typical duration of a client assignment varies between three and six months. According to the scope of the problem, Roland Berger & Partners normally operates in a number of different modules under the supervision of at least one partner. This modularized approach to problem solving exposes junior consultants to all the aspects of business problem solving under senior guidance. Close and informal contact with project leaders and business managers is viewed as an important contribution to the development of professional skills.

Discuss the lifestyle aspects of a career with your firm; i.e., average hours per week, amount of travel, flexibility to change offices.

The emphasis on assisting clients with their most complex business issues certainly requires a higher degree of involvement and a more flexible professional approach to business than other careers. Roland Berger & Partners is keen to develop staff on both a personal and professional basis. Professionals are encouraged to participate in an international staff exchange program as well as in one-off assignments abroad. Because the case teams predominantly work on the client's premises, consultants may be required to travel up to four to five days a week.

What is your firm's turnover rate for professionals? What careers do your ex-consultants typically pursue after leaving?

Staff turnover is low compared to industry standards. The career is strictly performance driven, and there is no set schedule for promotion. Professionals typically leave for senior line management positions with clients or set up their own businesses.

The Recruiting Process

Describe your recruiting process and the criteria by which you select candidates.

Roland Berger & Partners' interactive approach to consulting requires professionals with strong interpersonal and communication skills. A successful candidate will combine intellectual brilliance with an ability to formulate solutions that result in a tangible change in the client's corporation and a substantial and lasting contribution to the client's business.

After qualifying in on-campus interviews, successful candidates will be assessed and interviewed in one of our offices.

From which schools do you actively recruit? Do you consider applicants from other schools?

Roland Berger & Partners recruits outstanding individuals from many leading business schools in the world. Our recruiting policy aims to attract top graduates and well-seasoned industrialists with relevant experience.

How many full-time consultants do you expect to hire in the coming year?

Given Roland Berger & Partners' past and foreseeable growth, positions are offered to all candidates meeting the selection criteria.

How many summer interns do you expect to hire? If you have a formal summer program, please describe it. Please be sure to indicate whether the program is in place for all offices or just some.

Roland Berger & Partners invites candidates to apply for positions as summer interns in most offices. A summer associate will be a full team member, with responsibilities and exposures. A summer associate is expected to make a tangible contribution to the case team effort. In return, Roland Berger & Partners offers insight into their clients' problems and a hands-on approach to solving them.

San Francisco Consulting Group
A Division of KPMG Peat Marwick

Suite 1700
3 Embarcadero
San Francisco, CA 94111

Locations of Offices:
San Francisco, Denver, New York, Washington, DC

Total Number of Professionals (U.S. and worldwide):
250

Company Description

Describe your firm by type of consulting work performed and by types of clients served. What changes are planned in the next few years in terms of services, clients, or locations of offices?

San Francisco Consulting Group (a division of KPMG) is a management consulting firm that focuses exclusively on the converging communications industries. Founded in 1976 to meet the needs of the rapidly changing telecommunications industry, SFCG/KPMG was the first management consulting firm dedicated solely to this fast-growing, highly competitive industry. SFCG/KPMG has completed thousands of engagements with clients throughout the telecommunications and other communications industries, in both the United States and abroad.

SFCG/KPMG's commitment to client service is reflected in its long-term associations with client organizations in all sectors of the global communications industry: Bell operating companies and independent local exchange carriers; national and regional long-distance carriers; wireless service providers; worldwide public telephone operators (PTOs) and new competitive carriers; competitive access providers (CAPs) and competitive local exchange carriers (CLECs); cable television companies; Internet service providers (ISPs); power utilities; telecommunications equipment manufacturers; computer hardware manufacturers; software and systems integration businesses; and financial services firms that are evaluating investments in communications ventures.

The foundation of SFCG/KPMG's practice is its multidisciplinary approach, which supports clients in the development and execution of economically sound strate-

gies. This approach, which features teams composed of consultants with varied backgrounds and years of experience in competitive consulting, is combined with the rigorous use of the most effective analytical methods and tools. SFCG/KPMG brings to each client engagement the firm's total integrated resources, with experience and expertise carefully matched to every situation.

SFCG/KPMG's goal is to provide a working environment that attracts, stimulates, retains, and rewards the best quality of consultant.

Who are your competitors, and how does your approach to consulting differ from theirs?

SFCG/KPMG's competitors are general management consulting firms.

SFCG/KPMG provides superior consulting through the integration of highly technical knowledge with an understanding of business, management, and strategic principles.

Our approach relies on building in-depth knowledge of this very complex, dynamic business. Our clients are not interested in "off-the-shelf" solutions and rely heavily on SFCG/KPMG's ability to do original work.

Summarize your growth in terms of revenues (both domestic and international) and professional staff over the past year; over the past five years.

SFCG/KPMG is a growing firm experiencing high demand for its services in a very dynamic industry. In the past two years, SFCG/KPMG's staff size has doubled and revenues have increased by approximately 50 percent. It is our goal to continue to take advantage of the attractive opportunities for growth offered us, while still producing high-quality consulting in a closely knit, team-oriented environment.

Consultant's Job Description

Describe the career path and corresponding responsibilities for an MBA at your firm.

MBAs enter the firm at the level of consultant and can expect to be exposed to a variety of engagement assignments and client environments. The consultant is encouraged to use this experience to broaden problem-solving skills, technical knowledge, and project management abilities. At the same time, the consultant will be developing client relationships and a network of contacts in both client and nonclient organizations. The professional growth that results from these activities will lead to the assumption of greater project and team management responsibilities and promotion to senior consultant, manager, director, and vice president.

Project managers are usually selected from the senior consultant level or above, though consultants may be given leadership assignments based on the skills needed and the opportunities available.

Rapidity of advancement in the SFCG/KPMG environment depends considerably on the individual. Advancement is based on performance, initiative, experience, the ability to develop and acquire new skills, and the ability to deliver high-quality results.

How big is a typical case team? How many cases does a consultant work on simultaneously?

Size of engagement teams varies considerably with the engagement, usually ranging from three to eight people. It is not unusual for a consultant to be working on two or three engagements at a time.

Discuss the lifestyle aspects of a career with your firm; i.e., average hours per week, amount of travel, flexibility to change offices.

The professional demands on a consultant are high. Consultants work the hours necessary to meet the needs of our clients. This might vary from as few as 45 to as many as 60 or more hours per week, depending on the urgency of the engagement or the nearness to client deadlines.

Consultants should expect to travel 50 percent of the time, again depending on the type of engagement and needs of the client. Rarely are consultants required to relocate on a semipermanent basis.

What is your firm's turnover rate for professionals? What careers do your ex-consultants typically pursue after leaving?

SFCG/KPMG's turnover rate is comparable to or lower than that of other major consulting firms. Consultants generally leave voluntarily for attractive opportunities elsewhere.

The Recruiting Process

Describe your recruiting process and the criteria by which you select candidates.

SFCG/KPMG looks for outstanding intellectual capability, the ability to work effectively with clients, and the capacity to attack problems from a general management perspective. Most selected candidates have a record of strong achievement in both business school and prior work experience.

From which schools do you actively recruit? Do you consider applicants from other schools?

SFCG/KPMG does not actively recruit on campus.

How many full-time consultants do you expect to hire in the coming year?

SFCG/KPMG is a growing firm that experiences a strong demand for qualified consultants. We have no specific hiring target for next year, but we expect to hire at least five to eight qualified consultants.

How many summer interns do you expect to hire? If you have a formal summer program, please describe it. Please be sure to indicate whether the program is in place for all offices or just some.

SFCG/KPMG has no formal summer intern program.

Human Resources Practices

What benefits does your company provide for maternity, paternity, or adoption leave?

SFCG/KPMG provides a full array of health care benefits with minimum cost to the employee.

Please describe any initial training programs or ongoing professional development programs for young professionals.

SFCG/KPMG prides itself on the in-house training programs available. The close interaction of senior staff with every member of each SFCG/KPMG project team provides continual training and development. In addition, SFCG/KPMG provides off-site training programs covering the telecommunications industry generally, as well as specific topics, such as strategic analysis and client account management.

SFCG/KPMG provides a growth environment both inside and outside the company. It actively promotes each employee's personal growth and has an excellent reputation within the industry.

Does your firm provide for on-site day care? If not, do you provide compensation for day care? Is flextime possible?

Due to the amount of off-site work at customer premises, on-site day care has not been shown to be feasible; how-ever, this area, like all other human resources practices, is under ongoing review.

Scient Corporation

500 Technology Square
Cambridge, MA 02139
(617) 768-2007
Fax: (617) 768-2499
Web site: www.scient.com

MBA Recruiting Contact(s):
Elizabeth Gabbay

Locations of Offices:
San Francisco (headquarters), Silicon Valley, Los Angeles, Austin, Dallas, Chicago, New York, New Jersey, Boston, Singapore, Hong Kong, London, Munich

Total Number of Professionals (U.S. and worldwide):
900

Company Description

Describe your firm by type of consulting work performed and by types of clients served. What changes are planned in the next few years in terms of services, clients, or locations of offices?

Scient builds e-businesses from the ground up. We believe successful e-businesses result from enmeshing a balanced triumvirate of skill sets: strategy, customer experience, and technology. Roughly 30% of our business comes from start-ups, with the remainder from Global Fortune 2000 players. Scient also has an accelerator program to work with pre-VC funded companies. We plan to continue to rapidly expand our domestic and global coverage.

Describe your organizational structure. Is the firm geographically structured or based around practices? If you have practices, please list them.

We go to market through global industry-specific business units: eMarkets (start-ups), Financial Services, Telcom, Media & Entertainment, Enterprise, Retail, and Health & Wellness. Across these verticals, span four innovation centers: Consulting, Customer Experience, Technology, and Asset-Based Services. This allows colleagues to be staffed in a variety of engagements. Scient vehemently adheres to a 'One P&L' structure across geographies and business units. Aside from mitigating interoffice squabbling over accounts and resources, we

view this structure as constituting a driving force in our culture, as we are all one, large team working toward a common goal.

Who are your competitors, and how does your approach to consulting differ from theirs?

We compete with a variety of sectors including management consulting practices, systems integrators, and design shops. Our basic difference is that we were born and bred to do one thing—build e-businesses—using an approach that integrates strategy, customer experience, and technology from day one onward. This seamless process benefits our clients by dramatically shortening our time to market, from strategy to launch. In this context, our organic growth model has engendered a one-culture, one-approach firm, sidestepping the angst of integrating different entities and their particular methodologies.

Summarize your growth in terms of revenues (both domestic and international) and professional staff over the past year; over the past five years.

Scient was started in January of 1998. Revenues for the fiscal year ending March 31, 2000 were $155.7 million, an increase in excess of 650% over revenues of $20.7 million for Scient's first fiscal year. Our run rate presently exceeds $300 million for our next fiscal year. Total headcount grew to 1,180 colleagues, up from 874 at the end of the third fiscal quarter. Professional services headcount grew to 828 colleagues, up from 609 at the end of the third fiscal quarter.

Approximately how many professionals do you have at each level, i.e., how wide is your pyramid?

Our "pyramid" probably resembles something more akin to a cone. Though we have a slightly larger number of junior colleagues (in the Consulting Innovation Center), we dedicate our resources +/- 100% to our engagements. Presently, we have roughly 125 colleagues in the Consulting Innovation Center.

Consultant's Job Description

Describe the career path and corresponding responsibilities for an MBA at your firm.

MBAs typically join as leader-level, e-business consultants whose primary responsibilities are the oversight and coordination of Conceive deliverables. From here they have many options. They can become a strategist, project manager, or join a business unit as an engagement manager. Core Services positions are available as well. We do not have a set review performance schedule; if you are a rockstar, you will be promoted very quickly.

As an MBA advances through the firm, how much is he or she required to specialize by level?

Typical MBA advancement requires specialization in terms of relative degrees of knowledge and mastery of the strategy creation and implementation process, with particular focus on the incorporation of technology and customer experience drivers.

How big is a typical case team? How many cases does a consultant work on simultaneously?

Our case teams vary depending on the stage of the engagement. Our team typically starts with 7–10 colleagues but as the scope of our work becomes more tangible, and particularly during the engineer stage of our approach, the team can grow easily to 20–25 people. With rare exception, all of our colleagues are 100% dedicated to a particular project.

Discuss the lifestyle aspects of a career with your firm; i.e., average hours per week, amount of travel, flexibility to change offices.

Culture is key to Scient and though we expect our colleagues to be willing to travel 50%, our medium- to long-term goal is to staff projects from their local offices; it is hard to grow and nurture culture without people! Office switching is not a major hurdle and is actually encouraged when opening new offices. Though they are only required to record 40 hours/week, we find that on average, our colleagues put in roughly 50–55 hours/week on average. These numbers can and do vary depending on the stage of the project and proximity to meeting deliverables. A final note: when colleagues do travel, there is a high probability that they will work out of another Scient office rather than on the client's site.

What is your firm's turnover rate for professionals? What careers do your ex-consultants typically pursue after leaving?

To date, our attrition companywide has fallen consistently below 10%. To our knowledge, fewer than five people who have left have joined a competing firm; everyone else has joined a start-up.

The Recruiting Process

Describe your recruiting process and the criteria by which you select candidates.

Our recruits typically go through two rounds, one on campus and one off. Interviews include role fit and values assessments, which are given equal weight in the consideration process. E-business experience is looked on favorably, as are the abilities to quickly and rationally dismember and rebuild business/competitive landscapes using e-business models.

From which schools do you actively recruit? Do you consider applicants from other schools?

We recruit from Wharton, Harvard, MIT, Kellogg, Stanford, and NYU. Applications from other programs are warmly encouraged.

How many full-time consultants do you expect to hire in the coming year?

We expect to hire thirty.

How many summer interns do you expect to hire? If you have a formal summer program, please describe it. Please be sure to indicate whether the program is in place for all offices or just some.

Our summer intern program is gaining momentum this summer and will be in full swing by 2001. We have hired four interns for this summer out of our San Francisco and New York offices. Other offices will be on-line in 2001, when we plan on tripling the number of interns.

Human Resources Practices

Describe your firm's performance appraisal system for consultants. Are there explicit criteria against which an MBA is evaluated before being promoted? How many times a year is there a performance appraisal and hence an opportunity for promotion? Is there an upward evaluation process too?

Promotion meetings happen on a monthly basis at which time a review board considers sponsor's recommendations. Performance is appraised on three levels: contributions to clients, colleagues, and Scient. Specific criteria exist for each role and level, and expectations are set at the onset of each project and promotion.

What benefits does your company provide for maternity, paternity, or adoption leave?

We provide all legal benefits for these scenarios.

Please describe any initial training programs or ongoing professional development programs for young professionals.

Upon joining Scient, **all** colleagues enjoy a truly legendary week in San Francisco called SPARK, which lays the groundwork for rapid inclusion into our processes and resources. Extensive further training in a multitude of domains is available and encouraged.

Describe your firm's outplacement services.

No demand for such services exists at this time.

Does your firm provide for on-site day care? If not, do you provide compensation for day care? Is flextime possible?

We have a flexible spending account for dependent care, which is taken from pretax income.

Sibson & Company

504 Carnegie Center
Princeton, NJ 08543-5211
(609) 520-2706
Fax: (609) 520-2803

MBA Recruiting Contact(s):
Helaine Isaacs, Director, Professional Recruitment

Locations of Offices:
Boston; Princeton; New York; Chicago; Los Angeles;
Raleigh, NC; San Francisco; Toronto; Johannesburg;
Sydney; London

Total Number of Professionals (U.S. and worldwide):
173 domestic, 47 international

Ownership Structure of the Firm:
Limited liability corporation

Company Description

*Describe your firm by type of consulting work performed
and by types of clients served. What changes are planned
in the next few years in terms of services, clients, or locations of offices?*

Sibson & Company, a wholly owned subsidiary of
Nextera Enterprises, is a leading global management consulting firm. Our mission is to help our clients improve
their business results by more effectively implementing
their business strategies and making change happen
within their organization.

To carry out this mission, we help clients identify and resolve the real issues that drive measurable and sustainable
business results, by improving the return on their human
capital and by capturing the full revenue and profit potential of their products and services.

With no packaged products to offer, Sibson's consultants
develop fact-based, long-term solutions after carefully
evaluating each client's specific business challenges and
issues. We believe a conceptually sound program will fail
if it is not tailored to the company's culture and to the
needs of its customers, employees, and investors.

Our size and talent base are critical to our success. We are
small enough to offer a high degree of autonomy and creativity to our consultants, and large enough to solve the

most difficult, integrated problems of leading companies.
Throughout the firm's 40-year history, its philosophy has
been "lead with expertise, experience, and determination
to make the best companies become even better."

This impact orientation has made us one of the top management consulting firms in North America. We serve
more than 40 percent of the Fortune 100 and have earned
a reputation for providing outstanding client service, with
clients implementing our recommendations more than 86
percent of the time. We also carefully monitor client satisfaction, with 98 percent of our clients reporting a
"satisfied" or "very satisfied" rating.

Our growing list of clients includes both large and small
companies representing a diverse cross-section of industries. Some of our more prominent clients include Levi
Strauss & Company, Walt Disney Company, PepsiCo,
Citibank, Chevron, and AT&T. In recent years, the size
and complexity of our assignments have increased, and
we expect that to continue.

Currently, the firm has domestic offices in Princeton,
New York, Boston, Chicago, Raleigh, N.C., Los Angeles,
and San Francisco. International offices include Toronto,
London, Sydney, and Johannesburg. There are no plans to
expand domestically beyond our seven offices. However,
we may continue to expand internationally through acquisitions and partnerships.

*Describe your organizational structure. Is the firm geo-
graphically structured or based around practices? If you
have practices, please list them.*

In its early years, Sibson & Company established itself as
a compensation boutique, with an emphasis on executive
and general compensation. But as the firm grew, its areas
of expertise also increased.

Sibson & Company has recently aligned its practice offerings with two lines of business: Human Capital, and
Sales and Marketing.

The Human Capital business takes an innovative approach to improving the return on human capital by aligning employees' actions and behaviors with the organization's strategy to enhance efficiency, effectiveness, and
financial performance.

In Sales and Marketing, the goal is to maximize the output of a firm's sales force and channel resources through
improvements in operating and management processes,
practices, and programs. Consultants help organizations
and people build understanding, capability, and flexibility

to execute ever more sophisticated and rapidly changing going-to-market strategies.

Although Sibson serves clients in most industries, the firm builds practice areas to serve the specialized needs of clients. At present they include Financial Services and Health Care. The role of the industry group is to tailor Sibson's work to the specific business issues faced within the respective industry. In this way, the industry groups will be responsible for delivering the full offering of Sibson to their clients.

By design there is overlap in our firm's practices areas. The overlap encourages communication among practice/industry group leaders and collaboration between practices on client work and specific initiatives.

Consultants may align themselves with one or two practices, but they are free to work on any client engagements where they have the necessary skills.

Who are your competitors, and how does your approach to consulting differ from theirs?

Our competitors include organizational effectiveness consultants, strategy firms, and human resources consulting firms.

Sibson & Company is often engaged by companies that are making changes in business or organization strategy—that is, a new direction has been defined, and assistance is needed to mobilize the company. With a focus on people, Sibson has organized itself around the needs and work challenges of three employee groups: senior management, sales force, and work force. However, the strength of our firm is our integrated consulting approach, which acknowledges the need for aligning key management systems to ensure that all employees are organized and deployed to achieve organizational objectives. That approach is bolstered by consultants whose prior corporate or consulting experience has helped them solve complex business problems.

Summarize your growth in terms of revenues (both domestic and international) and professional staff over the past year; over the past five years.

Revenues increased 21 percent in 1999, and the annualized increase in revenues for five years was 19 percent. The professional staff increased approximately 25 percent in 1999, and 94 percent over the past five years.

Approximately how many professionals do you have at each level, i.e., how wide is your pyramid?

Our organization is more of a stovepipe than a pyramid, with a similar number of professionals at each of our four levels. We currently have approximately 220 consultants at Sibson.

Consultant's Job Description

Describe the career path and corresponding responsibilities for an MBA at your firm.

Our firm operates in a largely self-managed environment, where accountability for career progression resides with each consultant. Consultants, for instance, contribute to a project based on their capabilities and prior experience. Depending on the project, new MBA hires may function as the project manager or the primary analytical team member. As part of a project team, consultants develop appropriate business solutions based on a full understanding of a client's business strategy and the key aspects that drive performance. This involves interacting with clients by conducting research through data collection, interviews and focus groups, quantitative and qualitative analysis, and then conveying findings in a compelling manner with reports and client presentations. Consultants also are expected to prioritize their own work to assure timely completion, use initiative to develop project plans, be proactive contributors to the problem-solving process, and network with other team members for assistance.

Once consultants are hired at Sibson, they develop across identified competencies and advance at their own pace, depending on their own abilities. They are encouraged to take on high levels of responsibility early in their career and have immediate and extensive exposure to senior management within both Sibson and at our clients.

As an MBA advances through the firm, how much is he or she required to specialize by level?

When consultants first join Sibson, they are encouraged to gain exposure to all of our practice areas. However, they are free to pursue projects that are of particular interest to them and may choose to specialize at any time in their career. As consultants advance to the senior consultant or principal level, they tend to specialize so they can develop expertise and add value to client's projects. Consultants also can become core members of more than one practice.

How big is a typical case team? How many cases does a consultant work on simultaneously?

Although project teams vary in size, a three-person project team comprised of a client manager, project manager, and associate consultant is common. Some clients, however, require larger teams, which typically work on projects for longer periods.

Most consultants work on three to five projects simultaneously, which has several benefits: project variety, more client exposure, and learning from expert team members. Project duration varies from two months to one year or more. In many cases, consultants establish long-term relationships with a client and work on various projects within different parts of the company.

Sibson also staffs a particular project with the most appropriate people in the firm, which means teams may include consultants across several offices.

Discuss the lifestyle aspects of a career with your firm; i.e., average hours per week, amount of travel, flexibility to change offices.

Although we promote a relaxed environment, such as casual attire in the office, the workload is demanding. Client need, and not firm preference, drive the number of hours worked and work site location. Consultants' billable goals are in the range of 32 to 36 hours per week, with peak weeks as high as 50 to 60 billable hours. Consultants travel to clients for various reasons—to discuss proposals, attend client meetings, conduct interviews or focus groups, work with design teams, or present their findings. However, unlike many other firms, much of the work is performed in our offices. On average, consultants can expect to travel 50 percent of the time.

We have accommodated requests to change offices for personal reasons when appropriate.

What is your firm's turnover rate for professionals? What careers do your ex-consultants typically pursue after leaving?

Turnover is not a major issue at Sibson. But for those who leave the firm, they often go to nonconsulting opportunities, e.g., start-up companies or their own independent ventures.

The Recruiting Process

Describe your recruiting process and the criteria by which you select candidates.

Our recruiting process typically includes an initial interview, followed by two additional rounds of interviews, which focus on a candidate's conceptual problem-solving and analytical abilities and business acumen, as well as

assessing specific competencies that we believe consultants need to succeed at Sibson. Candidates are encouraged to state their preference for office location.

Hiring consultants who are the best fit with our firm is critical to our success. We seek individuals who possess excellent analytical and problem-solving skills, strong listening and communication capabilities, and a broad business orientation and understanding. Consultants also must be team players—willing to support colleagues in meeting client needs and able to partner with client executives to achieve results.

From which schools do you actively recruit? Do you consider applicants from other schools?

Sibson has a national recruiting strategy and actively recruits and posts correspondence opportunities at several top business schools. The firm also tends to attract individuals who are pursuing an independent job search.

How many full-time consultants do you expect to hire in the coming year?

In the coming year, approximately 25 associates or consultants will join the firm directly from campus, and we anticipate hiring an additional 30 consultants or senior consultants from the marketplace.

How many summer interns do you expect to hire? If you have a formal summer program, please describe it. Please be sure to indicate whether the program is in place for all offices or just some.

A formal summer intern program does not exist. However, individual offices do hire summer interns on a case-by-case basis. If students are interested in pursuing a summer internship, they should submit their resume to the Director of Professional Recruitment.

Human Resources Practices

Describe your firm's performance appraisal system for consultants. Are there explicit criteria against which an MBA is evaluated before being promoted? How many times a year is there a performance appraisal and hence an opportunity for promotion? Is there an upward evaluation process too?

One of the things that Sibson does well for our clients is design performance management systems. We also make sure that we apply the same expertise to our own firm. When you join Sibson, you will be assigned a Unit Coach who will guide your orientation and assist in your growth and development. In addition to ongoing feedback on individual projects, we have a thorough performance development process after each six-month operating period that focuses on specific competencies that have been identified as critical for success as a consultant. The descriptions of the competencies include specific examples of behaviors at each level, so you have a clear idea of the criteria you are being assessed against as you advance through the firm. There is an emphasis on feedback and coaching from your project team members. With the emphasis we place on feedback, we do have an upward evaluation process as well.

What benefits does your company provide for maternity, paternity, or adoption leave?

Sibson offers short-term disability for those on maternity leave and provides paid time off for four weeks to three months, depending on length of service. Consultants are eligible to take up to 12 weeks unpaid leave upon adoption of a child and up to three paid days for paternity leave.

Please describe any initial training programs or ongoing professional development programs for young professionals.

Sibson believes people grow and learn most effectively through project work and coaching from colleagues. We also offer a week-long orientation that conveys the firm's business approach to our client's problems, and provides an orientation to our practice areas and the types of projects you will be working on.

We offer several training workshops throughout the year. The content of the workshops is based on an ongoing assessment of the needs of the consulting staff and is related to the competencies required for advancement.

Sibson offers ongoing performance feedback, ongoing project performance assessments, and semiannual performance/compensation reviews.

Describe your firm's outplacement services.

Because turnover has been relatively low at Sibson, there has been no need to provide formal outplacement services. However, the firm will help individuals in any way it can if they seek opportunities outside of Sibson.

Does your firm provide for on-site day care? If not, do you provide compensation for day care? Is flextime possible?

Sibson does not have on-site day care. However, we do provide a dependent care reimbursement account that allows tax-free dollars to be used toward the cost of day care. We make every effort to be as flexible as possible, given the demanding nature of our business. When possible, consultants may work from home and their hours can be flexible. In addition, we have several consultants who have chosen to work on a part-time basis.

Swander Pace & Company

345 California Street, Suite 2500
San Francisco, CA 94104
(415) 296-9200 or (800) 969-9575
Fax: (415) 397-2836
Web site: www.swanderpace.com

MBA Recruiting Contact(s):
Lisa Graybill, Recruiting Coordinator

Location of Office:
San Francisco

Total Number of Professionals (U.S. and worldwide):
46

Company Description

Describe your firm by type of consulting work performed and by types of clients served. What changes are planned in the next few years in terms of services, clients, or locations of offices?

Swander Pace & Company is a San Francisco–based strategy consulting firm serving the food, beverage, and consumer packaged goods industries. In this focused area of expertise, we apply a wide range of capabilities to help our clients capitalize on both challenges and growth opportunities.

Our mission is to help clients create profitable growth. Our services therefore include growth strategies, mergers and acquisitions, and what we call growth enablers. Growth enablers are projects that support strategy development, such as competitive and market assessments, brand strategy, and sales force optimization. Although our work generally includes implementation, we see our role as coaching, rather than supplanting, the line managers responsible for implementation.

Our clients are typically the CEOs of Fortune 500 consumer packaged goods or retailing businesses. In addition, 13% of the firm's business serves companies with less than $250 million in sales.

Our firm and capabilities will continue to evolve as we add and enhance skill sets that help us serve our core client base more effectively.

Describe your organizational structure. Is the firm geographically structured or based around practices? If you have practices, please list them.

Our San Francisco office serves all of our clients. We are strategy consultants within our food/consumer packaged goods practice.

Who are your competitors, and how does your approach to consulting differ from theirs?

We compete with both large generalist firms and small consumer products boutiques. While our approaches to problem solving are similar to the large generalist firms, we bring far more industry-specific knowledge to our clients because of our focus. Even our most junior consultants have more knowledge of the market environment and the unique business tools of a consumer packaged goods business than many of the experienced project leaders of our larger competitors.

We also compete with small consumer products boutiques operated by ex-industry people. Most of the boutiques focus on specific, tactical issues (e.g., market research, sales force management) rather than offering an integrated, strategic approach. Our approach tends to include more analytic rigor and more emphasis on implementation than that of our smaller competitors.

Summarize your firm's growth in terms of revenues and professional staff over the past year; over the past five years.

Our professional revenues have grown in excess of 20% over the last five years. Additionally, we have grown our professional staff from 27 to 46 over the last five years through the selective addition of high-caliber individuals.

Approximately how many professionals do you have at each level, i.e., how wide is your pyramid?

We operate our firm based on a model of one partner or director per one point five principals, two consultants, and two associate consultants. Swander Pace & Company targets a higher director-to-consultant ratio than industry norms because our directors want to consult as well as sell. This structure provides our teams with stronger leadership in project management and reduces the likelihood of an out-of-control "study from hell."

Our firm relies equally on consultants with MBAs (consultants) and consultants with BAs (associate consultants). This creates a greater need for leadership from MBA-level employees early in their careers.

Consultant's Job Description

Describe the career path and corresponding responsibilities for an MBA at your firm.

Our target career path is similar to the large generalist firms: three to five years as a consultant and three to five years as a principal before election as a director. We also offer a nondirector track for principals who want to remain with the firm but do not want to take on the added responsibilities of a director. We are not an "up or out" firm. As a result, we are far more flexible in matching our career paths to the development needs and interests of our consultants.

Because of our industry focus, our consultants quickly become experts on the industry environment and the key issues facing our clients. As a result, our consultants have the credibility with our clients to take leadership roles early in their careers. It is common for consultants to lead a meeting with senior management after their first year with the firm.

As an MBA advances through the firm, how much is he or she required to specialize by level?

All employees become functional generalists within the food, beverage, and consumer packaged goods industry. Individuals are also encouraged to pursue their own particular interests that fall under our industry umbrella.

How big is a typical case team? How many cases does a consultant work on simultaneously?

A typical case team includes a director, two to four full-time consultants (principals, consultants, and/or associate consultants), and several client team members. Consultants typically work on one project at a time, although experienced consultants will occasionally work on more than one case team simultaneously.

Discuss the lifestyle aspects of a career with your firm; i.e., average hours per week, amount of travel, flexibility to change offices.

Even though Swander Pace & Company has developed a reputation as a lifestyle firm, consulting is a demanding profession in any firm. Last year, the consultants averaged 45 to 50 hours per week with about six to eight days of travel per month. Individuals infrequently work on the weekends.

Although travel requirements are driven by client needs, we do not typically camp out at our clients' offices. Few projects require as much as three nights out of town per week throughout the entire course of the project.

Swander Pace & Company offers three weeks of vacation (four weeks after two years of employment) and two months' paid leave of absence after four years of employment.

What is your firm's turnover rate for professionals? What careers do your ex-consultants typically pursue?

Over the last three years, Swander Pace & Company has lost only eight consultants and/or principals. Because of our small size, that equates to a cumulative turnover of approximately 20% over the three-year period. Our ex-consultants have typically pursued careers in marketing, business development, or strategic planning.

The Recruiting Process

Describe your recruiting process and the criteria by which you select candidates.

Our recruiting process targets MBAs with a clear interest in strategy consulting in food and consumer packaged goods who would enjoy work in a growing San Francisco–based firm. MBAs with many different backgrounds have been successful in our firm, so our main criteria are interest in consumer packaged goods and excellent problem-solving, strategic thinking, and communication skills.

Since our practice is of interest to only a limited set of candidates, we recruit on campus on a limited basis. We encourage interested candidates to contact us directly. We typically arrange to meet individuals on one of our trips to their area. Candidates also frequently arrange for an interview when visiting the West Coast. After the first round, candidates may be flown to our office in San Francisco for a full day of interviews.

From which schools do you actively recruit? Do you consider applicants from other schools?

We have hired MBAs from Stanford, Harvard, Northwestern, the University of Chicago, Tuck, UCLA, Michigan, Wharton, and Yale. We will also consider candidates from other schools or from industry.

How many full-time consultants do you expect to hire in the coming year?

At least four.

How many summer interns do you expect to hire? If you have a formal summer program, please describe it.

We do not plan to offer a summer intern program this year; however, interested candidates are encouraged to apply for full-time positions in the fall.

Human Resources Practices

Describe your firm's performance appraisal system for consultants. Are there explicit criteria against which an MBA is evaluated before being promoted? How many times a year is there a performance appraisal and hence an opportunity for promotion? Is there an upward evaluation process too?

Consultants are evaluated immediately following the close of each project assignment where they have been an active team member. Additionally, overall performance evaluations are held twice a year (March and October) for all consultants. There is a professional development and mentoring process in place; project and semiannual performance evaluations are a source of input for that process. Consultant input is actively sought in performance evaluations of project managers.

What benefits does your company provide for maternity, paternity, or adoption leave?

Swander Pace & Company offers maternity, paternity, and adoption leave.

Please describe any initial training programs or ongoing professional development programs for young professionals.

Swander Pace & Company provides an orientation program for new employees. As part of our professional development program, individuals are encouraged to participate on an ongoing basis in industry-related seminars and conferences and to attend specific skill-building workshops on topics such as presentation and writing. In addition, Swander Pace & Company holds two firmwide offsites per year that support team building as well as firm development efforts.

Describe your firm's outplacement services.

Swander Pace & Company does not have any formal outplacement services.

Does your firm provide for on-site day care? If not, do you provide compensation for day care? Is flextime possible?

Swander Pace & Company does not provide on-site day care or compensation for day care. However, there is a flexible benefits program in place into which individuals may put up to $5,000 per year in pretax dollars toward dependent care. Since consultants have widely varying time commitments, flextime will be considered only on an individual basis.

Towers Perrin

335 Madison Avenue
New York, NY 10017-4605
Web site: www.towersperrin.com

MBA Recruiting Contact(s):
Jane Kressler
Manager of Resource Planning
100 Summit Lake Drive
Valhalla, NY 10595
(914) 745-4633

Locations of Offices:
Over 78 offices in 23 countries

Total Number of Professionals (U.S. and worldwide):
More than 8,000

Company Description

Describe your firm by type of consulting work performed and by types of clients served. What changes are planned in the next few years in terms of services, clients, or locations of offices?

Towers Perrin is a global management consulting firm that helps organizations execute their business strategies through cost-effective approaches to managing people, performance, and risk. We offer services to clients in two broad segments:

- Towers Perrin, working to improve business performance through people; and

- Tillinghast-Towers Perrin and Towers Perrin Reinsurance, which provide management consulting to financial services companies, working to improve business performance through quantitative analysis, insight, and execution. Tillinghast-Towers Perrin also consults to the health sector, primarily health insurers and health plans.

One of the largest and oldest organizations in its field, Towers Perrin traces its roots back through several predecessor firms to 1871. It was incorporated as Towers, Perrin, Forster & Crosby in 1934. Currently, Towers Perrin has more than 8,000 employees around the world, and it is owned by more than 650 shareholders, all of whom are active employees.

The firm has offices throughout North America, across Europe, Latin America, Australia, and the Far East. Our presence in so many key business centers gives us firsthand insight into social and economic conditions and the legal and regulatory environment around the world.

Towers Perrin serves leading organizations in 46 countries. Among these are three-quarters of the world's 500 largest companies and 75% of the Fortune 1000 largest U.S. companies.

Towers Perrin delivers a comprehensive and integrated set of human resource and organization consulting services built around a core belief: that people create results for organizations. We focus on two interrelated areas to create the kind of behavioral model that gets measurable results for our clients. One is building employees' commitment to the business and to one another, and engaging their "hearts and minds" to deliver a superior level of sustained performance. The other is managing all investments in people to produce optimal results for the organization, its shareholders, its employees, and other key stakeholders.

Our core competencies are:

Organization Effectiveness and Process Redesign

We improve organization structure and work processes to align the business and its people with marketplace initiatives. We help clients in a broad range of areas including workforce planning, labor market analysis, competitive benchmarking, strategic staffing, workflow analysis and design, and reengineering. Our focus is on both strategy and implementation, creating well-designed processes and programs that are aligned with business needs and can be implemented in practical, day-to-day terms.

Human Resource Strategy and Management

We develop a comprehensive strategy to build an organization's people capabilities and implement a broad array of integrated human resource programs that align with business strategy and workforce and skill needs. We help design and implement recruiting, retention, development, and performance management programs, as well as work with the human resource function to adopt new technologies and more effectively carry out an organization's people strategy.

Mergers, Acquisitions and Restructuring

We assess the human and cultural implications of a pending merger, acquisition, or other restructuring, and develop strategies and programs to minimize conflict and ensure smooth integration.

Change Management

We help organizations manage and master change, whether in a particular process or program or across the entire entity—to sustain energy, unlock employee's discretionary efforts, and build an internal capability for keeping up with the pace of change. We help companies determine what needs to change, build a business case for change, and develop a detailed change implementation plan based on the four elements required to make change "stick": leadership, communication, involvement, and measurement.

Total Rewards

compensation
benefits
learning and development
work environment

We identify the factors that drive business performance and establish relevant financial and operational measures to manage performance and link rewards to value creation.

Organization Communication

We help to connect people and organizations by creating an environment where people have the knowledge and information they need to do the right things at the right time in the right way, with energy and commitment. We help companies develop their unique "voice"—their employee brand—and ensure that their messages are consistent internally and externally. We produce vehicles to channel that voice, increasingly by harnessing the power of Web technology and creating a multidirectional flow of information.

Organizational Measurement

We identify what drives high performance in an organization and understand how employees, managers, and other organizational stakeholders influence performance. We research employee and management perceptions to pinpoint areas of concern or obstacles to improved performance, and distill that research into a set of insights to influence decision-making and ensure the company is taking the right actions to achieve its desired goals and results.

Human Resources Outsourcing

We help clients assess and implement administration solutions for their employee benefit and other human resource programs. We also provide a comprehensive array of outsourced administration services that fully exploit the power of the I*Net on behalf of both our clients and their employees. By leveraging our people and our technology, we can relieve employers of the burdens of administration, delivering higher-quality, more cost-effective services than they can typically provide for themselves, and allow them to turn their attention to more strategic matters.

The firm maintains impressive research and database capabilities, accessible worldwide, to assist in client assignments. Its professional research staff studies and analyzes economic trends, business and competitive developments, and human resources practices in the world's developed and developing industrialized countries.

Towers Perrin consultants recognize the importance to many of our clients of being articulate in the language and unique issues of their industries. Therefore, in addition to our functional expertise, we maintain expertise in a number of key industries including insurance, financial institutions, chemicals, energy, pharmaceuticals, and telecommunications.

Tillinghast-Towers Perrin and Towers Perrin Reinsurance provide management consulting services to the financial services industry. Clients look to Tillinghast for advice in areas that require quantitative analysis, market knowledge, and financial acumen. Tillinghast also consults to the health sector, primarily health insurers and health plans. Tillinghast consultants provide insights, strategies, and solutions that arise from a deep understanding of predictive models, risk, and how economic value is created. Towers Perrin Reinsurance consultants provide assistance in placing all types of reinsurance and in implementing nontraditional risk transfer vehicles.

Tillinghast and Towers Perrin Reinsurance offer the following services to their clients:

- Market Analysis and Positioning. We help financial services clients who are seeking to enter new markets, both locally and internationally. We also assist clients who wish to reposition themselves in their existing markets by refining their product or service offerings.

- Mergers, Acquisitions, and Restructuring. A successful merger, acquisition, or restructuring requires meticulous planning and execution. Our M&A and restructuring experience for the financial services industry uniquely positions us to help clients in the areas of M&A strategy, evaluation of targets, economic value and price assessment, financial and strategic due diligence, and corporate restructuring. Our M&A capabilities are complemented by those of Towers Perrin human resource consultants, who often work with our clients to help integrate people and processes into the newly created organization.

- Shareholder Value Management. We help clients analyze profitability and value creation, pinpoint the key drivers of performance, and use that information to make value driven decisions and manage the value of growth.

- Customer Value Management. We help companies learn more about current and potential customers and work with them to develop strategies for profitable growth.

- Distribution Strategy and Effectiveness. We make sure products and services reach customers efficiently and in a manner they prefer. This ability has become an essential success factor for financial services companies. We work closely with companies to improve distribution effectiveness and to develop new distribution strategies.

- Financial and Business Risk Management. Financial services companies contend with a variety of risks in their day-to-day business, ranging from asset and liability risk to business and catastrophe risk. We help clients quantify, assess, and respond to operational and financial risks. We take an integrated approach that spans risk identification, measurement, control, financing, and monitoring.

- Organizational Effectiveness. We work with companies to help them improve their organizational effectiveness and we help them respond quickly and flexibly to changes in the environment. We frequently form teams with Towers Perrin human resource consultants to deliver a complete service to our clients in areas such as benchmarking, change management, performance management, people performance, and rewards.

- For health insurers and health plans, Tillinghast consults in the areas of finance and operations, clinical issues, and strategy.

- Reinsurance Broking. We provide reinsurance intermediary services and consulting expertise that focus on the creative blending of traditional and nontraditional risk transfer vehicles.

Who are your competitors, and how does your approach to consulting differ from theirs?

Towers Perrin and Tillinghast-Towers Perrin competitors include general management consulting firms, the consulting operations of the major accounting firms, human resources organization consultancies, and financial services consultancies.

We believe our approach to client service is distinguished by the following attributes:

- We are completely independent. We are owned and run by active employees of the firm. We believe this affords us the freedom and objectivity to deliver the best work to clients.

- We strive to recruit and retain the best talent. And we encourage our staff to expand their intellectual boundaries. It's the best way we know to meet our clients' changing needs and to ensure our own growth.

- We measure our success by our clients' success. After all, we are in business for one reason only—to help our clients improve their business. If we haven't done that, we haven't succeeded.

- We consistently invest in building and sharing knowledge on the latest trends and developments in our clients' markets, worldwide.

- We believe that a collaborative partnership delivers measurable results. We work with our clients, usually in teams, and we listen, ask questions, and synthesize information to develop custom solutions to their business problems. As a result, we make intellectual and practical connections between the work we do for a client and that client's overarching business goals.

Consultant's Job Description

Describe the career path and corresponding responsibilities for an MBA at your firm.

MBAs may begin their Towers Perrin or Tillinghast-Towers Perrin careers in any of the numerous service areas listed above.

New MBAs are expected to work with clients in our various business areas. Some people work full-time with one client for six months, while others may work with 10 different clients in a single week during the same six months.

Consultants spend their first three years gaining experience in a wide range of client industries and across our core service areas. Day-to-day activities include facilitating client teams, developing analytical approaches to projects, conducting analyses, and presenting results to clients. After completing his or her work as a generalist, we expect a consultant to choose at least one area of concentration in a business practice area.

We try to give our people the freedom to develop their own career. Frequently, people develop a specialty and set their sights on being the best in a particular area. If you are one of the world's most knowledgeable people in a given area, no matter how narrow, demand for your skill is usually tremendous. On the other hand, if someone combines consulting skills with managerial skills, there are many opportunities for further growth and development. It's a given for us that any manager of our consulting units has proved himself or herself as a consultant. But we recognize that not every consultant has to be a manager or makes a good one.

Unlike many of our competitors, we do not hire with the expectation that only a few consultants will survive to senior levels. Rather, we establish a cooperative environment that enables the large majority of our new consultants to succeed in their careers.

This arrangement offers the best of both worlds: a flexible, entrepreneurial culture coupled with the scale and scope of a global consulting firm. Ours is a flat organization that operates as a meritocracy. Consultants develop direct working relationships with principals and participate in marketing, business development, intellectual capital development, and recruiting efforts from the beginning of their careers—making an impact on the firm early on. This operating philosophy extends to client engagements as well. Consultants often find themselves leading client teams or managing parts of projects in their first year on the job. The early assumption of significant responsibilities is fundamental to the culture in our firm.

A career with Towers Perrin or Tillinghast-Towers Perrin offers everything you should expect from a career in management consulting. We will speed your learning and development immeasurably by exposing you to a wide range of industries and projects. We will work hard to address your personal and professional needs with respect to the kind of projects you are assigned, your role on those projects, and the type and duration of travel. Each consultant works with his or her development advisor to identify personal and professional goals and produce yearly plans that guide the achievement of those goals. Learning takes place on the job, with coaching from se-

nior colleagues, and is augmented by formal training offered through Towers Perrin's and Tillinghast-Towers Perrin's firmwide training and development resources.

How big is a typical case team? How many cases does a consultant work on simultaneously?

In general, there is no "typical" engagement. The size and composition of a case team varies according to the needs of the client; our project teams range in size from two consultants to more than 30. Each person plays a key role, and almost all will get some client exposure.

In the first year, a consultant usually has significant exposure to at least a dozen, and perhaps two dozen, client situations. But in general, consultants will work on two to four cases, increasing as their skills develop.

Each project is managed by a principal who, in turn, relies on the skills of managing consultants, consultants, and associates. On a client consultant team, the team leader guides the efforts of consultants and as many as 10 to 15 client managers. And, because of our firm's breadth and depth, we access the specialized skills of Towers Perrin professionals in other parts of the firm as part of our implementation efforts.

Discuss the lifestyle aspects of a career with your firm; i.e., average hours per week, amount of travel, flexibility to change offices.

Our consultants work the hours necessary to meet the needs of the client and the assignment. There is no average workweek, although the time commitment is usually substantial. Travel averages are also difficult to assess. Overall, however, travel away from the office ranges from 30% to 100%. Our offices work together, and we have accommodated location changes for personal reasons when appropriate.

The Recruiting Process

Describe your recruiting process and the criteria by which you select candidates.

"Building Relationships—Producing Results." This simple phrase sums up the qualities that make Towers Perrin and Tillinghast-Towers Perrin a first-rate consulting firm, as well as an excellent place to work. We believe it also expresses the kind of firm we are and the kind of consultants who work for us. Our success, as that of any company, depends on having the right people in the right places. We make a serious and systematic effort to determine whether a candidate has the combination of skills and qualities necessary for a successful career at Towers Perrin or at Tillinghast-Towers Perrin.

The preferred candidate should have an excellent academic record, enjoy the challenge of complex work, outstanding analytical, quantitative, and problem-solving skills, a passion for client service, and two to three years of relevant work experience. We are particularly interested in individuals who thrive on managing multiple, deadline-driven assignments in a team environment, while maintaining a can-do entrepreneurial spirit. Other important qualities are good business judgment, a creative flair, and outstanding communication skills. In addition, a candidate needs to have self-confidence, intelligence, independence, a constant drive to learn, and the ability to work with other people.

We are looking for candidates who realize the importance of relationships in business. He or she must be able to work effectively with a client team, in order to create the right communication and involvement strategy, and to measure the results. The ability to work in-depth with people is a key element in becoming a successful consultant.

Tillinghast-Towers Perrin primarily recruits MBAs for their financial services practices and Towers Perrin predominately recruits MBAs for their Stategy and Organization; People Performance and Rewards; and Change Management, Communication, and Measurement practices.

Qualifications vary slightly for the particular business practice where a candidate is interested in working. For example, candidates who are interested in working for Tillinghast-Towers Perrin should have three to five years work experience in the financial services industry, in the health insurance industry, or in a managed care environment. Individuals who are interested in the People Performance and Rewards business practice should preferably have compensation, financial, performance measurement, tax, or legal experience. In another example, we prefer that candidates who find the Change Management, Communication, and Measurement practice appealing have experience or background in Industrial/Organizational Psychology, Human Resources, Communication, Business Administration, or other relevant fields.

How many summer interns do you expect to hire? If you have a formal summer program, please describe it. Please be sure to indicate whether the program is in place for all offices or just some.

Summer internships are available for MBA students in most Towers Perrin and Tillinghast-Towers Perrin U.S. locations.

Summer interns work as consultants, performing assignments in a variety of functional areas within a specific industry and line of business. Interns are expected to be contributing team members and work with clients immediately. The intern is involved in all aspects of an assignment, within the limitations of a brief summer experience. At the conclusion of the summer, the intern should have a good understanding of consulting at Towers Perrin or Tillinghast-Towers Perrin and all that it entails.

Human Resources Practices

What benefits does your company provide for maternity, paternity, or adoption leave?

Towers Perrin provides a competitive and flexible benefits package to meet the needs of our employees.

Please describe any initial training programs or ongoing professional development programs for young professionals.

Towers Perrin's commitment to learning and development is a critical component of the "total rewards" available to our employees globally. Learning and development is recognized as an ongoing process throughout a professional's tenure with the firm. Competencies are developed through client assignments, the sharing of knowledge among practitioners, attendance at external courses and programs, and through formal learning and development programs offered by the Towers Perrin Institute.

Describe your firm's outplacement services.

Towers Perrin does not offer a formal program of career transition services; however, outplacement assistance is provided in exceptional circumstances.

Does your firm provide for on-site day care? If not, do you provide compensation for day care? Is flextime possible?

Towers Perrin provides a Flexible Spending Account for employees so they can pay for their day care expenses with pretax dollars. When appropriate, employees can work on a mutually acceptable flextime schedule.

Value Partners

Via Leopardi, 32
20123 Milan, Italy
Web site: www.valuepartners.com

MBA Recruiting Contact(s):
Olga Di Cesare, Recruiting Coordinator
E-mail: recruitment@valuepartners.com

Locations of Offices:
Main Offices: Milan, Rome, São Paulo,
Bueños Aires

Total Number of Professionals (U.S. and worldwide):
90

Company Description

Describe your firm by type of consulting work performed and by types of client served. What changes are planned in the next few years in terms of services, clients, or locations of offices?

Value Partners is a management consulting firm created to help managers and entrepreneurs solve complex problems and search for new opportunities.

Value Partners assists several large companies and groups that are leaders in their industries: energy, high tech, components, consumer goods, media, telecom, and financial services. We are seeing a rapid growth in assignments with fast-growing businesses and Internet start-ups.

Value creation is our professional objective, which is achieved through a partnership with our clients. We work on strategic projects that impact the overall performance of the client company. Our engagements focus on areas such as: core business development; globalization; cost reduction; turnaround and/or change management. Value Partners' activities include portfolio strategy (acquisitions, divestitures, joint ventures, etc.); e-business strategy; business unit strategy; value-based management; restructuring/turnaround management; as well as function-specific issues in such areas as R&D, production, distribution, etc.

Our improvement objectives are ambitious but attainable, designed to provide measurable economic results in the short- to medium-term. Our experience in assisting companies to overcome severe economic and financial crises, to quickly capture new market opportunities, or to tackle deregulation and/or globalization has enabled us to create strong, permanent relationships with our clients, built on a trust that derives from mutual satisfaction.

Describe your organizational structure. Is the firm geographically structured or based around practices? If you have practices, please list them.

Founded in 1993 by a group of fifteen senior consultants with international experiences, Value Partners now employs around 90 professionals based in its main offices in Milan, Rome, São Paulo, and Bueños Aires, while serving clients worldwide. We are also a member of an international network, which includes OC&C Strategy Consultants, McKenna Group, VP Web, and other specialized firms.

A significant portion of our client base is active in multiple geographic markets, and as a result our culture has a very strong international perspective. Value Partners teams have worked in many countries outside those of our main offices, including Australia, Hungary, Mexico, Turkey, the U.S.A., and throughout the EU.

As a result of our international focus, the professionals we recruit have a strong international profile. Besides Italian and Brazilian nationals, we currently have consultants from Germany, Hungary, Israel, Mexico, Portugal, Russia, UK, and the U.S.A.

Who are your competitors, and how does your approach to consulting differ from theirs?

Value Partners' natural competitors are the major international management consulting firms. Our rapid development and achievements are built on three fundamental qualities: entrepreneurial drive, managerial knowledge and experience, and intellectual capability. We follow a very pragmatic approach in assisting companies to improve their strategy, organization, and operations. We become partners to our clients, thus sharing with them the responsibility for obtaining real, lasting improvements.

Summarize your growth in terms of revenues (both domestic and international) and professional staff over the past year; over the past five years.

Our annual growth rate has averaged 30 percent over the past five years and is increasingly focused on growth outside of Italy (our traditional market of reference).

Approximately how many professionals do you have at each level, i.e., how wide is your pyramid?

Business Analysts, Associates, and Other Professionals	60
Engagement Managers and Senior Engagement Managers	16
Principals	11
Directors	3

Consultant's Job Description

Describe the career path and corresponding responsibilities for an MBA at your firm. As an MBA advances through the firm, how much is he or she required to specialize by level?

A typical career path in Value Partners leads to the election to principal within 7 to 8 years.

Career steps	Years in position
Business Analyst	1–3
Associate (entry level for an MBA)	2–3
Engagement Manager	2
Senior Engagement Manager Principal	2

Value Partners expects everyone to contribute his/her own initiative and entrepreneurial spirit to the successful development of clients and key competencies. A post-MBA associate is hired as a generalist and is not encouraged to specialize in one particular industry at the outset of his or her career.

Although individual performance targets are stringent, the work environment at Value Partners is non-hierarchical and supportive, as is typical of a truly entrepreneurial company. We expect our professionals to be driven to succeed, while making sure we give them the tools to fully exploit their capabilities.

How big is a typical case team? How many cases does a consultant work on simultaneously?

Although every engagement is different, teams often consist of three to five consultants. A newly hired associate works on one project at a time, with some overlap possible at the beginning and/or end of each project.

Assignments generally last two to three months and include a significant amount of teamwork (both within

Value Partners and with client executives) and in most cases Value Partners teams work on client premises.

Discuss the lifestyle aspects of a career with your firm; i.e., average hours per week, amount of travel, flexibility to change offices.

Value Partners strongly believes in striking an equitable balance between professional dedication/achievement and maintaining a rewarding personal life as well. Value Partners strongly emphasizes the importance of working on-site with clients and, if a client is out of town, a substantial amount of travel may be involved.

Value Partners offers the opportunity for a temporary or extended geographic transfer. In a temporary or study transfer an individual is transferred for a specific purpose (such as client assignment), while an extended (two to three year) interoffice transfer (usually in the third, fourth, or fifth year of an individual's career) can be arranged in accord with the development of the individual and the practice.

What is your firm's turnover rate for professionals? What careers do your ex-consultants typically pursue after leaving?

Value Partners' turnover rate is low compared with that of the consulting industry as a whole. Our alumni have gone on to careers in many industries, as well as starting Internet businesses.

The Recruiting Process

Describe your recruiting process and the criteria by which you select candidates.

The Value Partners recruiting process begins with resume screening and is followed by two or three rounds of interviews either on- or off-campus. Both case and noncase interviews are utilized in the selection process.

The ideal Value Partners candidate should demonstrate the following characteristics:

• Strong analytical skills

• Intellectual curiosity

• Commitment to hard work and professional excellence

• Self confidence

• Willingness to take initiative

- Real desire to participate in a cooperative professional environment

- Clear orientation to practical results

- An international background

- Ability to solve problems

- Ability to build relationships

- Ability to get things done

- Strong language skills

From which schools do you actively recruit? Do you consider applicants from other schools?

Although we encourage all strong applicants to contact us, we actively recruit in the United States at the top business schools (HBS, Columbia, MIT, Wharton, Darden, etc.) and in Europe at INSEAD, London Business School, and the SDA Bocconi and MIP (Italy).

How many full-time consultants do you expect to hire in the coming year?

In 2000–2001 we expect to hire 30 full-time consultants.

How many summer interns do you expect to hire? If you have a formal summer program, please describe it. Please be sure to indicate whether the program is in place for all offices or just some.

Value Partners actively recruits for summer interns for all of our offices. The length and structure of internships is designed on a case-by-case basis, ensuring the most rewarding experience for the intern, and the greatest involvement in project work with clients.

Human Resources Practices

Describe your firm's performance appraisal system for consultants. Are there explicit criteria against which an MBA is evaluated before being promoted? How many times a year is there a performance appraisal and hence an opportunity for promotion? Is there an upward evaluation process too?

Value Partners measures the performance of its consultants along the following criteria:

- Problem-solving skills

- Teamwork

- Client interaction

- Communication skills

- Information/resource management

- Office leadership

Appraisal at Value Partners is both formal and informal. An associate is formally appraised, usually by the engagement manager, at the closing of each project and twice a year in structured meetings with a principal who is assigned to him or her as a development leader. These meetings are designed to discuss the performance appraisal and allow for feedback, with the goal of helping guide the professional growth of the associate. Promotions, which are decided on a case-by-case basis, are based on the consultant's individual performance, tenure, and overall impact in the firm.

Informally, Value Partners promotes a culture of open communication at all levels that encourages all consultants to seek the advice and comments of their colleagues on an ongoing basis.

Please describe any initial training programs or ongoing professional development programs for young professionals.

We consider this to be a very important part of our company culture. Although the nature of consulting work provides ongoing on-the-job training, new consultants receive extensive formal training (e.g., in basic analytical skills, communications, financial and cost accounting) when they enter Value Partners. Throughout his/her career a consultant also receives at least 15 days per year of structured training and is given the opportunity for personalized training as well (e.g., to attend industry specific seminars, etc.). Training is carried out in cooperation with other members of our international network.

Does your firm provide for on-site day care? If not, do you provide compensation for day care? Is flextime possible?

In specific cases where professionals (either men or women) have particular personal or family needs, Value Partners can offer flexible solutions and innovative working schedules or temporary internal assignments. Although all commitments to our clients must provide first-rate professional work, the firm allows its consultants with special needs to temporarily reduce the level of their professional involvement in order to meet their personal time constraints.

ZEFER

711 Atlantic Avenue
Boston, MA 02111
(617) 451-8000
Fax: (617) 451-8001
Web site: www.zefer.com

MBA Recruiting Contact(s):
Shannon Moffitt
711 Atlantic Ave, 6th floor
Boston, MA 02111
(617) 210-1089
E-mail: smoffitt@zefer.com

Locations of Offices:
Boston, MA; Chicago, IL; London, UK; New York, NY; Pittsburgh, PA; San Francisco, CA

Total Number of Professionals (U.S. and worldwide):
481 as of December 31, 1999

Company Description

Describe your firm by type of consulting work performed and by types of clients served. What changes are planned in the next few years in terms of services, clients, or locations of offices?

ZEFER is a leading Internet consulting and services firm that works with forward-looking senior executives at major corporations and dot-com startups to create and implement winning strategies for the digital economy.

Describe your organizational structure. Is the firm geographically structured or based around practices? If you have practices, please list them.

We have an organizational matrix structure based on geography and industry/service practices.

We are building our expertise in growing selected key industries. We have targeted Financial Services, Health Care and Pharmaceuticals, Technology, Consumer Packaged Goods and Retail, and Media and Entertainment.

Our other practices include:

• Customer Relationship Management

• Security

• Supply Chain

We use the geographic structure to create community and association between professionals. Our practice areas are designed to ensure we provide leading edge thinking to the clients we serve. We deliver this by creating solutions around business strategy, experience design, and technology.

Who are your competitors, and how does your approach to consulting differ from theirs?

Our primary competitors are other "pure play" Internet consulting firms as well as the leading management consulting firms, but we have several important distinctions.

First, ZEFER believes that in the fast-changing Internet economy, only the most adaptable businesses will thrive. We work with our clients to create Internet strategies and solutions that can continually evolve in response to changing market conditions.

Second, we believe that all e-business decisions must be made in the context of an overall business strategy. We are committed to setting this strategic context up front with our clients before developing a solution. And our business strategy competency is deeper than that of any of our pure-play competitors. More than 20% of our consultants are in the business strategy competency.

Third, our unique methodology is fully unified. Project teams blend people from our four competencies—business strategy, experience design, technology, and project management. People from these competencies participate on the team from kickoff to launch, ensuring that the solutions we create are visionary yet practical.

Fourth, we bring strategic thinking to all of our competencies. Our technologists, for instance, don't merely implement the solutions created by the team, but lend strategic insights from the start of the project, ensuring that we create solutions that are not only technically feasible, but also visionary.

And fifth, we are uniquely able to bring "dot-com thinking" to the Fortune 1000, sharing the insights we gain from some of the most innovative players on the competitive landscape.

Summarize your growth in terms of revenues (both domestic and international) and professional staff over the past year; over the past five years.

Since its founding in 1998, ZEFER has experienced strong market demand and extremely rapid growth. As of

March 2000, we have offices in Boston, Chicago, London, New York, Pittsburgh, and San Francisco.

Approximately how many professionals do you have at each level, i.e., how wide is your pyramid?

We have a model of one partner-level individual per eleven team members.

Consultant's Job Description

Describe the career path and corresponding responsibilities for an MBA at your firm.

Consultants who join us after recently completing their MBA have two career paths. The first is to become a partner in our consulting group. As a partner, the primary responsibility remains client service. There is also a career track for office management and P&L responsibility.

We are also seeking a select group of dot-com focused strategists bringing exceptional expertise or knowledge of Internet trends and dot-com business models to ZEFER.

As ZEFER is a relatively young company, a career at ZEFER is still very dynamic. There are no set tracks and processes for advancement at this time.

As an MBA advances through the firm, how much is he or she required to specialize by level?

ZEFER has both industry vertical and horizontal services. At the highest level of the firm, ZEFER would like each individual to be associated with one of these client-facing groups.

How big is a typical case team? How many cases does a consultant work on simultaneously?

Team members are dedicated to one case at a time. A project team typically starts out between 5 and 8 consultants during initial strategy studies and then grows to 15 to 50 people as we enter the implementation phases.

Discuss the lifestyle aspects of a career with your firm; i.e., average hours per week, amount of travel, flexibility to change offices.

ZEFER is a very young and dynamic workplace. A typical week will average 50 to 60 hours. Travel is common but typically limited to 30% or less of a person's week. Most work is performed out of the team member's office.

It is quite easy to change offices at this time. The firm tries to provide individuals with as much control over their lives and schedules as possible.

The Recruiting Process

Describe your recruiting process and the criteria by which you select candidates.

We select candidates based on their attitude and skills. From an attitude perspective, we look for people who are able to work in fast-paced, client centric, teamwork-based environments. From a skill set perspective, we look for strong analytics, independent thinking, creative problem solving, and strong communication skills.

From which schools do you actively recruit? Do you consider applicants from other schools?

We actively recruit from Harvard, MIT, Carnegie Mellon University, Columbia, UC-Berkeley, Stanford, Duke, and New York University

We consider applicants from all schools.

ZS Associates

1800 Sherman Avenue
Suite 700
Evanston, IL 60201
(847) 492-3600
Fax: (847) 492-3409
Website: www.zsassociates.com

MBA Recruiting Contact(s):
US Offices:
Sally Johnston, Recruiting Coordinator
E-mail: sally.johnston@zsassociates.com
John S. Logan, Recruiting Coordinator
E-mail: john.logan@zsassociates.com

Europe Offices:
Eva Nilsson, Recruiting Coordinator
E-mail: eva.nilsson@zsassociates.com

Please submit all write-in applications to:
careers@zsassociates.com

Locations of Offices:
Evanston, IL; Princeton, NJ; Menlo Park, CA;
Frankfurt, GER; London, UK; Paris, FRA

Company Description

Describe your firm by type of consulting work performed and by types of clients served. What changes are planned in the next few years in terms of services, clients, or locations of offices?

ZS Associates is a global management consulting firm providing world-class expertise in sales force management and marketing issues. We have concentrated our resources and energies in helping our clients achieve lasting competitive advantage in sales and marketing. Since our founding in 1983, we have maintained our entrepreneurial spirit by delivering powerful and innovative approaches to our clients' issues.

While we serve a variety of firms within different industries, the majority of our work is with large multinational pharmaceutical and healthcare companies. Our roots originate from Northwestern University's Kellogg Graduate School of Management, where our Managing Directors, Andris Zoltners and Prabha Sinha, conducted research on optimal sales force sizing and resource allocation.

ZS has carved out an attractive niche in the consulting industry based on a unique combination of competencies: our implementation-oriented methodologies, our analysis skills, our focus on sales and marketing issues, and our expertise in selected industries. The services we perform for our clients range from long-term strategy studies for senior management to the development of customized micro-marketing systems that enable front-line sales personnel to achieve a lasting competitive advantage. Most of our assignments are for clients with whom we have long-standing relationships, and more than 30% of our work is done outside the United States. About 80% of our clients are in the pharmaceutical and healthcare industries.

Additionally, we are investing heavily in developing new practice areas, industry competencies, and service offerings. One new practice area includes helping our clients address ongoing changes in the healthcare environment. Another growing practice uses market research to analyze the effectiveness of business decisions. In addition to healthcare, we are working with clients in industries such as telecommunication, consumer products, durable goods, and publishing.

Finally, our practice is expanding geographically. Our six existing offices, four of which have opened during the last five years, service clients in more than 60 countries. We are actively expanding geographically, by focusing on projects and clients in Latin America, Canada, and Japan, and have strategic plans for additional offices over the next several years.

Describe your organizational structure. Is the firm geographically structured or based around practices? If you have practices, please list them.

ZS is best described as a "flexible" organization. While we do have six different offices, many projects have team memberships that span two or more offices. The reason ZS has multiple offices is driven by two key elements of our organization. First, much of our work is done within our offices, so we want them somewhat proximate to clients to minimize travel. The other driver is office size: we feel multiple smaller offices, rather than one very large one, best support our informal collaborative work style.

In terms of practice areas, ZS does identify key practice areas based on issues clients ask us to address in projects. Our practice areas include strategy, geographic deployment, compensation, forecasting, analytic data warehousing, market research and marketing support, analytic support systems, and sales force effectiveness.

211

Who are your competitors, and how does your approach to consulting differ from theirs?

Our combination of issue focus, select industry expertise, and tested measurement processes for understanding how markets behave gives ZS its competitive advantage in the consulting marketplace. We work with marketing and sales executives to develop action plans by combining insights from statistical analysis of historical data with managerial judgment. In addition, we set ourselves apart with comprehensive implementation processes and methods. Our excellent implementation track record has resulted in an enviable level of repeat business and excellent growth opportunities for new consultants. Many new clients learn about our services through recommendations from other clients.

ZS's largest competition often comes from our client organizations. Our consulting style incorporates clients in each project team so the expertise and learning gets carried into the client organization. ZS's focus on continuous improvement and innovation feeds constant changes to our consulting services.

Summarize your growth in terms of revenues (both domestic and international) and professional staff over the past year; over the past five years.

Since its founding in 1983, ZS has grown consistently in terms of size, revenues, practice areas, and industry expertise. During the past two years, we have experienced unprecedented growth on all these dimensions. Since 1989, our revenues have grown at a 20% compounded annual rate. Today, nearly 35% of our revenues come from international assignments.

Approximately how many professionals do you have at each level; i.e., how wide is your pyramid?

ZS has four professional levels: principal, manager, consultant, and associate. Our flat organizational structure, comprising principals (5%), managers (20%), consultants (30%) and associates (45%), encourages interaction at all levels of the firm. Principals actively participate in project management, resulting in unparalleled accessibility to senior members of the firm.

Consultant's Job Description

Describe the career path and corresponding responsibilities for an MBA at your firm.

MBAs at ZS progress from consultant to manager to principal. Our moderate size allows our consultants to strengthen their analytic and project management skills and establish a solid knowledge base in sales force and marketing issues, as they interact directly with client management personnel. Our consultants take on higher levels of responsibility more quickly than at most consulting firms, while they develop creative and actionable solutions to clients' needs. The consultant is responsible for directing projects, for managing a close, ongoing relationship with each client, for motivating and coaching others, and for participating in thought-leadership and innovation. As consultants exhibit core competencies, they play an increasing role in mentoring new professionals and developing new business opportunities.

As an MBA advances through the firm, how much is he or she required to specialize by level?

Consultants, managers, and principals at ZS participate in a wide variety of projects covering multiple practice areas and several industries. Individuals are encouraged to help expand the business by exploring new service opportunities with nontraditional clients. Specialization is not a requirement for advancement; however, some associates do focus on a particular practice area or industry with time.

How big is a typical case team? How many cases does a consultant work on simultaneously?

Our project teams are usually comprised of three to four people drawn from different levels of the firm, usually under the direction of a principal. The small team environment requires everyone to assume substantial responsibility throughout the project. This responsibility and close working relationship with ZS's senior members contributes significantly to professional development. Consultants are generally assigned to more than one project at a time. This provides them with significant project variety, content expertise, and client exposure. Projects usually are two to four months in duration.

Discuss the lifestyle aspects of a career with your firm; i.e., average hours per week, amount of travel, flexibility to change offices.

A high degree of energy and flexibility is required to be successful in any consulting environment. While the average workweek for consultants at ZS is about 50 hours, the number of hours worked per week and the amount of travel vary over the course of a project, depending on the nature of the work. Unlike many consulting firms, much of the project work is done in our offices rather than at the client site. This reduces overall travel requirements for new consultants to an average of three to five days per month, which contributes to realistic work-life balance. The work environment has been described as both intense and casual. While our people are highly committed to producing the highest quality of work for our clients, our interactions with each other are informal.

Transfers between offices are arranged individually based on performance and skills and office capacity needs. ZS actively encourages transfers between offices, as this fosters a strong one-firm culture and a sharing of our expertise as well.

What is your firm's turnover rate for professionals? What careers do your ex-consultants typically pursue after leaving?

In 1999, our turnover rate for professional staff was 21%. Note that this number includes a large number of promoted associates returning to school in pursuit of MBAs or other graduate degrees.

The turnover rate at ZS is in line with that of the consulting profession. Our alumni have gone on to positions of significant responsibility in line management, business development, and marketing in a variety of industries. The two most common post-ZS destinations are careers within our client organizations and returning for additional education.

The Recruiting Process

Describe your recruiting process and the criteria by which you select candidates.

Our consultant recruiting process entails three stages, all of which are held on or near our target school campuses. In the initial rounds, candidates participate in two rounds of case and behavioral interviews, meeting two to four ZS interviewers. Candidates progressing to the final round of interviewing participate in evaluative and informative interviews and make a presentation. Write-in candidates from other sources may begin with telephone or in-office interview rounds.

We look for people with a high energy level, outstanding problem-solving and analytical abilities, organizational and communication skills, a commitment to developing superior solutions, a keen sense of creativity, and integrity. We also seek individuals with career intentions—we look for candidates to help us grow our business and become leaders within the organization.

From which schools do you actively recruit? Do you consider applicants from other schools?

ZS actively recruits from the top business schools in North America. Our recruiting plans include the following MBA programs: Chicago, Columbia, Darden, Ivey, Kellogg, Michigan, Rotman, and Wharton. In Europe, our targeted schools include Bocconi, IESE, INSEAD, and London Business School.

ZS welcomes write-in applicants from other top business schools.

How many full-time consultants do you expect to hire in the coming year?

We plan to hire approximately 25 new consultants this year for our three U.S. offices, including growing practices focusing on Latin America, Canada, and Japan. Additionally, we will also be looking for approximately 10 outstanding individuals to work in our European offices.

How many summer interns do you expect to hire? If you have a formal summer program, please describe it. Please be sure to indicate whether the program is in place for all offices or just some.

Current expectations are to offer internship opportunities in all of our U.S. offices based on the number of qualified candidates identified in our internship recruiting process. Our Summer Associate internship is structured as a mentoring program. Summer Associates work closely with a ZS principal or manager on several projects and assume the same kinds of responsibilities as our new consultants. Summer Associates are hired from all of our U.S. "target" schools.

Human Resources Practices

Describe your firm's performance appraisal system for consultants. Are there explicit criteria against which an MBA is evaluated before being promoted? How many times a year is there a performance appraisal and hence an opportunity for promotion? Is there an upward evaluation process too?

Feedback is ongoing at ZS. Project reviews are conducted at the conclusion of each engagement. Formal performance appraisals are conducted once a year. Upward evaluations are included in this process. During a consultant's first year with the firm, he or she receives two formal reviews: one after six months and one at the end of twelve months. Consultants are first eligible for consideration for promotion after two years.

What benefits does your company provide for maternity, paternity, or adoption leave?

Full-time employees are entitled to up to sixteen weeks of family leave, six weeks of which are paid. In addition, ZS's benefits package of medical, dental, and a vision plan extends to domestic partners.

Please describe any initial training programs or ongoing professional development programs for young professionals.

New consultants participate in a two-week orientation program, which covers topics ranging from career path at ZS and consulting process, to ZS practice areas, decision frameworks, and industry overviews. Our New Employee Orientation offers new hires a unique opportunity to meet nearly all of the ZS principals. Additionally, hires from each office are brought together for this training, so new employees meet colleagues from all locations and have the opportunity to build ties within the hiring class.

Consultants also participate in ongoing training activities aimed at improving communication and consulting skills as well as ZS expertise. The most important learning, however, comes from on-the-job experiences within project teams and in client situations.

Describe your firm's outplacement services.

Outplacement arrangements are developed on an individual basis at ZS. In addition to providing professional services, we help individuals leaving the firm through counseling, networking, and referrals.

Does your firm provide for on-site day care? If not, do you provide compensation for daycare? Is flextime possible?

ZS offers a flexible benefits program that enables associates to pay for dependent care costs on a pretax basis. Flexible work arrangements have been offered in the past and are developed on an individual basis.

Management Consulting Career Resources

Mallory Stark
Career Resources Librarian
Baker Library, Harvard Business School

Some MBAs will want to expand their job search to companies not included in this book. The following bibliography provides additional sources—directories, industry guides, periodicals, and Internet sites—that will be useful to a job search. Directories and industry guides offer lists of consultants and consulting firms, as well as company rankings, industry trends, statistics, and other information. The periodicals cited are keys to understanding recent activities and developments in the consulting field. The Internet sites provide a variety of information helpful in finding consulting jobs and tracking the consulting industry.

Associations & Organizations

Academy of Management
Managerial Consultation Division
[http://www.uwf.edu/~mcd/]
This Web site has relevant information about the Managerial Consultation Division of the Academy of Management including membership requirements, constitution and bylaws, conference schedules, awards and the division newsletter, current officers, and task groups.

Association of Management Consulting Firms
[http://www.amcf.org/]
For 60 years, AMCF has been the international association of firms engaged in the practice of consulting to management. Their Web site contains information about membership, an annotated list of research publications, and a schedule of conferences and professional development programs. The site offers a free referral service for identifying potential consultants for hiring. Firms can be screened by industry and specialty. There is also a section of advertised positions.

Federation of European Management Consulting Associations (FEACO)
[http://www.feaco.org]
The Federation of European Management Consulting Associations (FEACO) provides opportunities for members to further their contacts in, and knowledge of, consulting markets in Europe. The Web site has a directory of members organized by country, as well as industry and association news, and listings of events in Europe.

Institute of Management Consultants (U.S.)
[http://www.imcusa.org/]
Founded in 1968, the Institute of Management Consultants (IMC) represents management consultants with members in the U.S. and overseas. The Web site includes a searchable directory of members plus information on joining the IMC, a description of the certification process, an interactive forum, notification of IMC activities, and current and back issues of *IMC Times*.

Management Consultancies Association
[http://www.mca.org.uk/home.html/]
The Management Consultancies Association was formed in 1956 and is the association for leading management consulting firms in the United Kingdom. The Web site provides an online directory of members, relevant news about the profession and the association, information regarding careers in management consulting, and a searchable database of firms with open positions.

Management Consultant Network International
[http://www.mcninet.com/]
The Management Consultant Network International (MCNI) is a global network of management consultants and management consulting resources. The Web site includes a searchable directory of individual consultants called *GlobalLook* (described below), the *Journal of Management Consulting,* announcements of conferences, and information on research and publications.

Directories and Industry Guides

The Consultant Directory
Charlottesville, VA: Money Market Directories. Annual.
Profiles firms offering general consulting services to clients within the financial community. Many listings contain biographical profiles of key executives. It includes indexes by service, geography, and client type.

Consulting and Consulting Organizations Directory
Detroit: Gale Research. Annual.
This two-volume directory provides information on more than 22,000 consulting firms and independent consultants in the United States and Canada. Indexes provide addi-

tional access by location, consulting activity, personal name, and firm name. Entries include company name, address, phone and fax numbers, e-mail and Web addresses when available, founding date, staff size, annual revenue, names and titles of officers and executives, types of services offered, recent publications and/or videos, workshops and seminars, and branch offices.

Consultants Sourcebook
Fitzwilliam, NH: Kennedy Information. Annual.
A buyer's guide of vendors offering products and services needed by consultants, including marketing, office support, research, and publications.

D & B Consultants Directory
Parsippany, N.J.: Dun's Marketing Services. Annual.
This annual directory lists more than 30,000 consulting firms arranged alphabetically with separate lists by geography and consulting activity. The main entries include company name, address, and phone number, annual revenues, staff size, consulting activities, geographic areas served, industries served, key personnel, and branch offices.

Directory of Management Consultants
Fitzwilliam, N.H.: Kennedy Publications. Biennial.
More than 1,800 management consulting firms are listed in this biennial directory. Each entry includes company name, address, phone and fax numbers, e-mail and Web addresses, founding date, staff size, revenue, contact name(s), a brief description, and lists of industries and geographic areas served and services provided. Entries are arranged alphabetically, with separate indexes by industry, service, geography, and names of key principals. The directory also includes selected articles about management consulting from the publishers of *Consultants News*.

Directory of Management Consultants in the U.K.
London: Alan Armstrong. Annual.
Profiles of almost 3,000 British firms are included in this source. Entries include name, address, phone number, officers, founding date, staff size, a description of the company's activities, areas of specialization, branch offices, and industries served. Firms are indexed by geography, specialization, and other categories. The directory also includes salary survey information.

Directory of Member Associations of the Federation of European Management Consulting Associations (FEACO)
[http://www.mca.org.uk/html/default_feaco.html]
Directory of members organized by country.

Directory of Members (Association of Management Consulting Firms)
New York: ACME. The Association of Management Consulting Firms. Annual. Partial information on the Web.
[http://www.amcf.org/memberfirms.html]
ACME's annual directory gives detailed profiles of member firms from around the world. Each profile includes name, address, phone and fax numbers, a general description, lists of offices and subsidiaries, and a review of the firm's areas of practice. The directory also includes indexes by specialty and industry.

Directory of Members—Institute of Management Consultants
New York: IMC.
[http://www.imcusa.org/imc.html/]
IMC's directory lists individual members rather than firms. Each entry includes the consultant's name, firm, address, phone number, and a brief description of the type of services offered. Cross-references by location, industry, and specialty are also provided. The Web site contains a database of the IMC directory.

Directory of Members and Service (Turnaround Management Association)
Cary, N.C.: The Association.
This directory of turnaround management professionals including consultants also offers an overview of the turnaround profession. Entries are arranged by individual rather than firm, and include firm, address, phone number, educational and professional background, years in practice, specialties, geographic area served, revenue breakdown, and other details. Members are indexed by various categories.

The Fast Track: the Insider's Guide to Winning Jobs in Management Consulting, Investment Banking, and Securities Trading
Mariam Naficy. NY: Broadway Books, 1997.
Written by Mariam Naficy, who worked as an analyst at Goldman, Sachs & Co. and as a consultant at Gemini Management Consulting, where she recruited new employees, this book focuses on all stages of the recruiting process for the competitive fields of management consulting and investment banking. For management consulting, it includes examples of job descriptions for consultants, interviews with key players in the field, valuable information on resume preparation and case interviewing, and profiles of leading management consulting firms. It also includes advice on choosing the right job, with tips on evaluating an offer and salary negotiation.

GlobalLook
Management Consulting Network International.
[http://www.mcni.com/search.html]
GlobalLook is a searchable directory of individual management consultants maintained by Management Consultant Network International, Inc. (MCNI) (see above). Profiles of consultants range from a 30-word practice summary to a 600-word profile and biography. The database is searchable by keyword.

Industry Insider: So, You Want to Be a Management Consultant
San Francisco: Wet Feet Press.
[http://www.wetfeet.com/asp/home.asp]
Part of the Industry Insider series produced by Wet Feet Press, *So, You Want to Be a Management Consultant* is designed to provide current and comprehensive information from the job seeker's perspective on the realities of working in the field of management consulting. Information is derived "from a variety of private and public sources, including company recruiting literature, articles from the business press, interviews with company staff, and our own subjective analysis." Topics covered include an industry overview, a discussion of self-assessment, and profiles of leading companies in the industry. The guide also has sections on the recruiting process, a description of typical projects assigned to consultants, an explanation of the case interview method, and long-term career development issues to think about when considering a job in this industry. Wet Feet Press also publishes the Company Insider series that includes profiles on leading management consulting firms.

Operating Ratios for Management Consulting Firms: A Resource for Benchmarking
United States Edition. New York: Association of Management Consulting Firms. Annual.

Operating Ratios for Management Consulting Firms: A Resource for Benchmarking
European Edition. New York: Association of Management Consulting Firms. Annual.
These annual reports contain industry statistics, including performance ratios, profitability, staffing, compensation, and revenues.

Vault Reports Guide to Management Consulting
New York: Vault Reports.
[http://www.vaultreports.com/index.cfm]
Similar to the Wet Feet Press guide, the *Vault Reports Industry Guide to Management Consulting* provides a revealing look at what it is like to work in this field. It includes valuable information on the corporate culture and life style of a management consultant with issues ranging from dress codes and physical work environment to training programs and performance feedback. There is also a lengthy section on case interviewing and getting hired. Detailed profiles of 29 leading firms are included. The report is a product of primary research conducted by the company including surveys of over 100,000 employees concerning their job experiences, one-on-one interviews with employees, and information from inside contacts at each company profiled.

Periodicals

Boston Consulting Group. Perspectives
Boston, MA: Boston Consulting Group. Irregular.
These are brief booklets, each addressing a different topic, such as total brand management and breaking compromises.

Consulting Magazine
Fitzwilliam, NH: Kennedy Information. Bimonthly.
[http://www.consultingcentral.com/]
Geared toward management consultants, articles cover innovative ideas, business strategies, client performance, career options, and guidance.

Consultants News
Fitzwilliam, N.H.: Kennedy Publications. Monthly.
[http://www.consultingcentral.com/news/newsletters.html]
Consultants News is a monthly newsletter with news, commentary, analysis, and other information about the field of management consulting. The June issue includes the "50 Largest U.S. Management Consultant Firms" ranked by revenue. The Web site provides only a sampling of information from the newsletter with information on subscribing.

IMC Management Consulting Times
New York: Institute of Management Consultants. Monthly.
[http://www.imcusa.org/imcTimes.html]
This newsletter for practitioners contains information on timely management consulting topics, news, meetings, and events.

Journal of Management Consulting.
Burlingame, California: Journal of Management Consulting. Semiannually.
[http://www.jmcforum.com/]
Published twice a year since 1981, the journal covers all aspects of the profession. Articles are divided into the following sections: Issues and Trends, Consulting Process,

Practice Management, Recommended Reading, Best Practices, Technology Applications, Professional Ethics, and Our Readers Report. In 2001, the journal will be published quarterly.

Management Consultancy
London: VNU Business Publications. Monthly.
Monthly trade journal for management consultants covering industry news, analysis of key issues in the profession, plus monthly industry surveys.

Management Consultant International
Dublin: Lafferty. 10/yr.
Newsletter providing worldwide news and trends in the management consulting industry.

The McKinsey Quarterly
New York: McKinsey & Co. Quarterly.
[http://mckinseyquarterly.com/home.htm]
Published four times a year by McKinsey & Co, articles cover a range of industries from information technology to food and agriculture. The text of articles published from 1993 to the present is available on the company's Web site and accessible by industry category or chronological issue.

General Career Planning

The sites and CD-ROMs described below are specifically geared to management consulting.

ConsultingCentral
[http://www.consultingcentral.com/]
This site has information about publications from Kennedy Information on the management consulting industry. It has descriptions and subscription information on *Consultants News* and *Directory of Management Consultants*. It also has a link to career information with an overview of the industry and the *Consultants News* ranking of the top 50 firms.

ConsultingScene
[http://www.voxcap.com/anon/c7/cover.dhtml]
This resource is produced by Tim Opler, who teaches at the Fisher School of Business at Ohio State University and works for a Wall Street firm. This newsletter provides information about the field of consulting, including skills and educational requirements of typical consulting jobs, key job areas, current positions, print resources, other Internet resources, and salary information (when available). Job announcements are also posted.

Management Consulting: Exploring the Field, Finding the Right Job and Landing It
Boston: Harvard Business School Publishing.
Co-developed by Convergence Multimedia and Harvard Business School Publishing, this multimedia resource provides video footage of a variety of job applicants, consultants, former consultants, and clients discussing this field, what they do, and what they look for when hiring new consultants. It provides descriptions of over 50 firms with contact information. The CD-ROM also includes an interactive example of a case interview.

Yahoo-Management Consulting Companies
[http://dir.yahoo.com/Business_and_Economy/ Companies/Corporate_Services/Consulting/ Management_Consulting/]
This section of the Yahoo hierarchy of Internet resources includes links to hundreds of management consulting company sites. There are also several subcategories of management consultants, including Business Development, Change Management, Leadership Development, Operational Analysis, Organizational Development, Process Improvement and Re-Engineering, Project Management, Small Business, and Team Building.

Case Interviewing and Resume Preparation

Ace Your Case
San Francisco: Wet Feet Press.
This report analyzes and describes all aspects of the consulting case interview. It provides an overview of the consulting case interview with a description of what to expect and "seven steps to surviving the case." It also analyzes the five categories of the consulting case giving examples of sample case questions. Other useful information includes an explanation of the recruiter's evaluation. Wet Feet also publishes more practice case questions in *15 Questions: More Practice to Help You Ace Your Case*.

The Buy & Fly Case
[http://www.mckinsey.com/career/case/intro.html/]
McKinsey & Company's Web site offers two interactive cases—*Solving the Systems Dilemma* and *Buy and Fly in Brazil*.

Boston Consulting Group's Sample Case Interviews
[http://www.bcg.com/careers/interview_splash.asp]
This Web site offers simulated and interactive case examples. There are also five sample business problems that can be used as practice cases.

Case Interviewing Workshop
[http://www.stern.nyu.edu/~cfombrun/caseint.html/]
This site, based on a case interviewing workshop at New York University's Stern School of Business, offers tips on the interview process, including what interviewers are looking for, how to package yourself, and different types of cases (i.e., calculation cases, problem cases, and probing cases) with examples of each.

Killer Consulting Resumes
San Francisco: Wet Feet Press.
This guide addresses all areas related to resume preparation for those interested in a career in management consulting. It answers questions ranging from how recruiters in this industry use resumes, to the specifics of formatting. It gives seven different situational examples including MBA with nontraditional business background, Ph.D. with nonbusiness background, and basic undergraduate. The guide gives a critique of each of the seven examples.

Job Posting Sites

There has been a virtual explosion of career related Internet sites in the past year. Listed below are examples of some of these sites. The jobs posted on these sites may include but are not limited to positions in management consulting.

CareerBuilder [http://careerbuilder.com/]

CareerCentral [http://www.careercentral.com/index.asp]

CareerPath [http://careerpath.com/]

CareerMosaic [http://www.careermosaic.com/]

MBAjob [http://www.mbajob.com/]

Monster Board [http://www.monster.com/]

Online Career Center [http://www.occ.com/]

Mailing List

This is a mailing list of companies profiled in this book. Entries are arranged alphabetically and contain company name, address, telephone number, and MBA recruiting contact. This book profiles sixty firms with a wide range of professional focuses and corporate cultures. Readers are encouraged to evaluate each firm individually before writing a letter of application. Before sending letters to the firms on this list, always call to verify the address and the name of the recruiting contact.

Michael Henderson
Human Resources
Abt Associates Inc.
55 Wheeler Street
Cambridge, MA 02138-1168
(617) 349-2402
Fax: (617) 492-5219

Michelle Benoit
Director of Human Resources
Alliance Consulting Group, Inc.
745 Boylston Street
Boston, MA 02116
(617) 424-1111
Fax: (617) 424-1112
Web site: www.alliancecg.com

Allan Jones
Manager, College Recruiting
American Management Systems, Inc.
4050 Legato Road
Fairfax, VA 22033
(703) 267-5000
Web site: amsinc.com
E-mail: ams_recruiting@amsinc.com

Tom DeMello
Arthur D. Little, Inc.
Acorn Park
Cambridge, MA 02140
(617) 498-5000
Fax: (617) 498-7140
Web site: www.arthurdlittle.com

Campus Recruiting
A.T. Kearney, Inc.
222 West Adams Street
Chicago, IL 60606
(312) 223-6030
Web site: www.atkearney.com
E-mail: campusrecruiting@atkearney.com

Courtney Kirkland
MBA Recruiting Coordinator
Bain & Company, Inc.
Two Copley Place
Boston, MA 02116
(617) 572-2000
Web site: www.bain.com

Kristina Herbert
Booz•Allen & Hamilton
22 Battery March Street
2nd Floor
Boston, MA 02109
Web site: www.bah.com

Chantel Lindsay
Recruiting Coordinator
The Boston Consulting Group, Inc.
Exchange Place, 31st Floor
Boston, MA 02109
(617) 973-1006
Fax: (617) 973-1339

Melissa Owens
Recruiting Coordinator
Braun Consulting, Business Strategy Group
2 Atlantic Avenue
Boston, MA 02110
(617) 367-7600
Fax: (617) 367-8780
Web site: www.braunconsult.com

Howard Shetter
The Cambridge Group
30 Rockefeller Plaza, 40th Floor
New York, NY 10112
(212) 218-7250
Fax: (212) 218-7251
Web site: www.thecambridgegroup.com
For the New York office
E-mail: recruiting_ny@thecambridgegroup.com
For Chicago office,
E-mail: recruiting_chicago@thecambridgegroup.com

Joanna Kamins
Recruitment Coordinator
**Cambridge Strategic Management Group
(CSMG)**
One Memorial Drive
Cambridge, MA 02142-1311
(617) 864-0022
Fax: (617) 876-7087
Web site: www.csmgusa.com

Jenni Pozar
CFI Group, Inc.
625 Avis Drive
Ann Arbor, MI 48108
(734) 930-9090
Fax: (734) 930-0911
E-mail: HR@mail.cfigroup.com

Amy Connolly
Recruitment Manager
**Charles River Associates
Incorporated**
200 Clarendon Street, T-33
Boston, MA 02116-5092
(617) 425-3000
Fax: (617) 425-3132

Associate Recruiting Director
Cornerstone Research
1000 El Camino Real
Menlo Park, CA 94205
(650) 853-1660
Web site: www.cornerstone.com

Yasunori Nakagami
Vice President & Director
Corporate Directions, Inc.
Hirakawa-cho Kaizaka Bldg.
1-6-8 Hirakawa-cho
Chiyoda-ku, Tokyo 102
Japan
(03) 3221-0211
Fax: (03) 3221-6335
Web site: www.cdi-japan.co.jp

Janet Shields
Recruiting Specialist
Heather Gotlesman
Recruiting Specialist-Business Strategy
CSC Consulting
200 Clark Avenue
32nd Floor
New York, NY 10166
(212) 251-6230

Diane Owens
Recruiting Manager
CSC Healthcare Payor/Provider Consulting
1325 Avenue of the Americas, 6th Floor
New York, NY 10019
(212) 401-6000
Web site: www.csc.com/industries/healthcare

Recruiting Coordinator
Dean & Company
8065 Leesburg Pike, Suite 500
Vienna, VA 22182-2738
(703) 506-3900
Fax: (703) 506-3905
Web site: www.dean.com

Tina Ege
Deloitte Consulting
John Hancock Tower
200 Clarendon Street
Boston, MA 02116
(617) 850-2600
Fax: (617) 850-2001
Web site: www.dc.com
E-mail: tege@dttus.com

Jennifer Tarlow
Director of Human Resources
Delta Consulting Group
1177 Avenue of the Americas
New York, NY 10036
(212) 403-7500
Fax: (212) 221-5882
Web site: www.deltacg.com
E-mail: Careers@deltacg.com

Jill Marie Rupple
Director of Recruiting
Christa Setterlund
Campus Recruiting Manager
Diamond Technology Partners Incorporated
875 N. Michigan Avenue
Suite 3000
Chicago, IL 60611
(312) 255-5000
Fax: (312) 255-6000
Web site: www.diamtech.com
E-mail: setterlund@diamtech.com

Peggy Novello
Digitas LLC
800 Boylston Street
Boston, MA 02199
(617) 867-1000
Web site: www.digitas.com
E-mail: pnovello@digitas.com

Tom Jarman
Edgar, Dunn & Company
847 Sansome Street
San Francisco, CA 94111
(415) 397-5858
Fax: (415) 397-0142
Web site: www.edgardunn.com
E-mail: tjarman@edgardunn.com

Ernst & Young LLP
Web site: www.ey.com
MBA Recruiting Offices(s):
Atlanta (Charlotte):
600 Peachtree St.
Atlanta, GA 30308

Chicago (Minneapolis, Milwaukee):
233 South Wacker Drive
Chicago, IL 60606

Cleveland (Detroit, Pittsburgh, Cincinnati, Indianapolis, Columbus):
1300 Huntington Building
925 Euclid Avenue
Cleveland, OH 44115

Dallas (Ft. Worth, Irving):
104 Decker Court
Irving, TX 75201

Houston Area:
1221 McKinney St., Suite 2400
Houston, TX 77010

Los Angeles (Irvine, Phoenix):
Pacific Corporate Towers
200 North Sepulveda Blvd.
El Segundo, CA 90245

New York (Boston):
750 Seventh Avenue
New York, NY 10019

Philadelphia (Fairfax, D.C., Baltimore):
Two Commerce Square, Suite 4000
2001 Market Street
Philadelphia, PA 19103

St. Louis (Kansas City, Denver):
701 Market St., Suite 1400/Gateway 1
St. Louis, MO 63101

San Francisco (Seattle):
555 California St., Suite 1700
San Francisco, CA 94104

Nancy K. Vanitvelt
The Farrell Group
21311 Hawthorne Boulevard, Suite 230
Torrance, CA 90503
(310) 316-4420

Sandra L. Westervelt
Director of Recruiting
First Annapolis Consulting, Inc.
900 Elkridge Landing Road
Suite 400
Linthicum, MD 21090
(410) 855-8500
Fax: (410) 865-8899
Web site: www.1st-annapolis.com

Human Resources
First Manhattan Consulting Group
90 Park Avenue, 18th Floor
New York, NY 10016
(212) 557-0500
Fax: (212) 557-0163
Web site: www.fmcg.com/career

Diane Provini
Recruiting Manager, North America
Gemini Consulting
1114 Avenue of the Americas
35th Floor
New York, NY 10036
Web site: www.gemcon.com

Lisa Caravello
Director, Human Resources
Greenwich Associates
8 Greenwich Office Park
Greenwich, CT 06831-5195
(203) 629-1200
Fax: (203) 629-1229
Web site: www.greenwich.com

Marian N. Crandall, Principal
Director of Recruiting
Hamilton•HMC
1355 Peachtree Street, NE, Suite 900
Atlanta, GA 30309
(404) 892-3436
Fax: (404) 253-0388
Web sites: www.hamiltonhmc.com;
www.kurtsalmon.com

Marcia O'Connor
National Recruiting Manager
Hay Group, Inc.
100 Penn Square East
Philadelphia, PA 19107
(215) 861-2000
Web site: www.haygroup.com

Recruiting Coordinator
Health Advances, Inc.
40 Grove Street
Wellesley, MA 02482
(781) 235-6626
Web site: www.healthadvances.com
E-mail: rec@healthadvances.com

Gino Morelli
I•F Consulting, Inc.
101 Federal Street
19th Floor
Boston, MA 02110
(617) 342-7053
Fax: (617) 342-7370
E-mail: i-fchannels@i-f.com

Valerie Paric
Integral, Inc.
104 Mount Auburn Street, Floor 3R
Cambridge, MA 02138-5019
(617) 349-0600
Fax: (617) 864-3862
Web site: www.integral-inc.com
E-mail: recruiting@integral-inc.com

Bob Barry, President
John Barry & Associates
3020 Newport Boulevard
Newport Beach, CA 92663
(949) 675-3551

Sean Huurman
(214) 754-2000
Mary E. Sullivan
Director of Human Resources
(201) 307-7000
KPMG, LLC
Consulting Practice
Three Chestnut Ridge Road
Montvale, NJ 07645
Web site: www.kpmgconsulting.com

Marian N. Crandall, Principal
Director of Recruiting
Kurt Salmon Associates
1355 Peachtree Street, NE, Suite 900
Atlanta, GA 30309
(404) 892-0321
Fax: (404) 253-0388
Web site: www.kurtsalmon.com

Catherine Dupuis
Recruiting Coordinator (United States and Australia)
Sheila North
Recruiting Coordinator (London and all European offices)
L.E.K. Consulting LLC
28 State Street, 16th Floor
Boston, MA 02109
Web site: www.lek.com

Denise Le Van
Senior MBA Recruiting Coordinator
Marakon Associates
300 Atlantic Street
Stamford, CT 06901
(800) 695-4428
Fax: (203) 961-1460
Web site: www.marakon.com

Francine Even
Director of Administration
Mars & Co
Mars Plaza
124 Mason Street
Greenwich, CT 06830
(203) 629-9292
Web site: www.marsandco.com

Leslie Holley
Recruiting Administrator
McKinsey & Company, Inc.
75 Park Plaza, 3rd Floor
Boston, MA 02116
(617) 753-2001
Fax: (617) 753-2099
Web site: www.mckinsey.com

Dana Grube (North America)
Mercer Management Consulting, Inc.
1166 Avenue of the Americas
New York, NY 10036
(202) 778-7560
Web site: www.mercermc.com

Cathy Baker
(Worldwide Recruiting)
Mercer Management Consulting, Inc.
2300 N Street NW, Suite 800
Washington, DC 20037
(202) 778-7181

Rachel Dardinski
Monitor Group
2 Canal Park
Cambridge, MA 02141
(617) 252-2523

Terri Tippets and Sydney Higa (Menlo Park and
Houston)
Kim McDonald (Boston and New York)
Caroline Craig (London)
Navigant Consulting/Strategic Decisions Group
2440 Sand Hill Road
Menlo Park, CA 94025-6900
(650) 854-9000

David Rigali
Director Nextera Recruiting
Nextera Enterprises, Inc.
One Cranberry Hill
Lexington, MA 02421
(781) 862-3200
Fax: (781) 674-1300
Web site: www.nextera.com

Ronna Hermann
Global Head of Recruiting
Oliver, Wyman & Company, LLC
666 Fifth Avenue, 16th Floor
New York, NY 10103
(212) 541-8100
Fax: (212) 541-8957

Eileen McBride
Recruiting Coordinator
The Parthenon Group
200 State Street
Boston, MA 02109
(617) 478-2550
Fax: (617) 478-2555
Web site: www.parthenon.com

Consulting Recruiting Coordinator
PHB Hagler Bailly, Inc.
1776 Eye Street, NW
Suite 500
Washington, DC 20006
Fax: (202) 785-4052

Kathleen Ferris
Recruiting Coordinator, Eastern Region
E-mail: kferris@prtm.com
Jane Jacobson
Recruiting Coordinator, Western Region, Asia
E-mail: jjacobson@prtm.com
Pittiglio Rabin Todd & McGrath
1050 Winter Street
Waltham, MA 02451-1297
(781) 647-2800

1503 Grant Rd., Suite 200
Mountain View, CA 94040
(650) 967-2900

25 The Quadrant
Abingdon Science Park
Abingdon, Oxford OX14 3YS
England
+44(0)1235-555500
Web site: www.prtm.com

Karen Kantor
Recruiting Manager
PricewaterhouseCoopers Management Consulting Services
11 Madison Avenue, 18th Floor
New York, NY 10010
Web site: www.pwcglobal.com
(212) 591-4866
E-mail: karen.kantor@us.pwcglobal.com

Sue Golden
Recruiting Coordinator
Quantum Associates, Inc.
43 Water Street
Beverly, MA 01915
(978) 232-3450
Fax: (978) 232-3499

Tara Barry
Director of U.S. Recruiting
Roland Berger & Partners
350 Park Avenue
27th Floor
New York, NY 10022
(212) 651-9660

San Francisco Consulting Group
Suite 1700
3 Embarcadero
San Francisco, CA 94111

Elizabeth Gabbay
Scient Corporation
500 Technology Square
Cambridge, MA 02139
(617) 768-2007
Fax: (617) 768-2499
Web site: www.scient.com

Helaine Isaacs, Director
Professional Recruitment
Sibson & Company
504 Carnegie Center
Princeton, NJ 08543-5211
(609) 520-2706
Fax: (609) 520-2803

Lisa Graybill
Recruiting Coordinator
Swander Pace & Company
345 California Street, Suite 2500
San Francisco, CA 94104
(415) 296-9200 or (800) 969-9575
Fax: (415) 397-2836
Web site: www.swanderpace.com

Towers Perrin
335 Madison Avenue
New York, NY 10017-4605
Web site: www.towersperrin.com

Jane Kressler
Manager of Resource Planning
Towers Perrin
100 Summit Lake Drive
Valhalla, NY 10595
(914) 745-4633

Olga Di Cesare
Recruiting Coordinator
Value Partners
Via Leopardi, 32
20123 Milan, Italy
Web site: www.valuepartners.com
E-mail: recruitment@valuepartners.com

Shannon Mofitt
ZEFER
711 Atlantic Avenue, 6ᵗʰ Floor
Boston, MA 02111
(617) 210-1089
Fax: (617) 451-8001
Web site: www.zefer.com
E-mail: smofitt@zefer.com

ZS Associates
1800 Sherman Avenue
Suite 700
Evanston, IL 60201
(847) 492-3600
Fax: (847) 492-3409
Website: www.zsassociates.com
Email: careers@zsassociates.com

US Offices:
Sally Johnston
Recruiting Coordinator
E-mail: sally.johnston@zsassociates.com
John S. Logan
Recruiting Coordinator
E-mail: john.logan@zsassociates.com

Europe Offices:
Eva Nilsson
Recruiting Coordinator
E-mail: eva.nilsson@zsassociates.com

Tools for Leadership . . .

Tools for Scholarship . . .

 # Harvard Business Review

For over 75 years, one publication has been defined as indispensable for those who aspire to succeed in business . . . the same publication that was voted the most influential magazine in the United States in a 1992 survey of over 1,700 opinion leaders. The *Harvard Business Review.*

HBR is synonymous with excellence in business education. Subscribers are exposed to groundbreaking work and new management strategies in articles authored by leading executives in companies from around the world. It's not a view from the ivory tower . . . it's a view from the boardroom, the corner office, the production line. From the real world of business.

Every issue of *HBR* has articles that show you how real-life managers are motivating and leading people; how executives in business today are developing the financial tools to allow their companies to grow; how managers are using new technologies to approach marketing in ways that were impossible just a few years ago; how organizations are coping with the ever changing business environment of a global economy.

Harvard Business Review is the magazine your competitors will be reading in a few years. Shouldn't you start reading it now?

SPECIAL OFFER FOR STUDENTS OF BUSINESS

Over 200,000 executives in companies around the world pay over $95 a year for access to the invaluable information found in every bimonthly issue of *HBR*. As a student you are entitled to a very special price of $48 for a one-year, six-issue subscription.

To subscribe at this special rate, please send your name and address, along with a copy of your valid student I.D. from an accredited college or university, to:

HARVARD BUSINESS REVIEW
Subscription Services
P. O. Box 52623
Boulder, CO 80322-2623

Payment must accompany the order. Please enclose a check, or your VISA, MasterCard, or American Express card number and expiration date, with your order. This offer is valid for subscriptions addressed within the United States only.